THE SEA AND THE ICE

By LOUIS J. HALLE

THE SEA

AND THE ICE

A Naturalist in Antarctica

With a Foreword by Frank H. T. Rhodes

Illustrated with photographs, maps, and diagrams

Cornell University Press
Ithaca, New York

Maps and diagrams by Graf-Tech

Cornell Paperbacks edition first published 1989 by Cornell University Press.

Printed in the United States of America

Library of Congress Cataloging-in-Publication Data

Halle, Louis Joseph, 1910–
    The sea and the ice : a naturalist in Antarctica / by Louis J. Halle.—Cornell paperbacks ed.
        p.   cm.
    Bibliography: p.
    Includes index
    ISBN 0-8014-9575-X (alk. paper)
    1. Natural history—Antarctic regions.   2. Birds—Antarctic regions.   I. Title.
QH199.5.H34   1989   508.98'9—dc 19   88-43303

The paper in this book is acid-free and meets the guidelines for permanence and durability of the Committee on Production Guidelines for Book Longevity of the Council on Library Resources.

Foreword to the Paperback Edition

by Frank H. T. Rhodes

ANTARCTICA IS UNIQUE. No other place prepares the visitor for the experience of this remote land. It is earth's last bastion: the coldest, highest, driest, most isolated, and most inhospitable continent, a continent that must be understood at several levels. This book explores those levels.

On the surface, *The Sea and the Ice* is an account of a brief visit to the Antarctic continent in the austral summer of 1970–1971. The voyage out from Wellington, New Zealand, on the icebreaker *Staten Island*, the brief stop at Campbell Island, the entry into the pack ice, visits to Ross Island, the Pole, the dry valleys of Victoria Land, and Byrd Station: all this is tidily told, though without the vivid detail and descriptions of scenic grandeur that one finds in the accounts of Cook, Ross, Scott, Wilson, Amundsen, Shackleton, Pye, and others.

At another level, this is a book of natural history. Emperor and Adélie Penguins, Killer Whales, Weddell Seals, the Royal Albatross, and Wilson's Storm Petrel are all described in this account —as are the complex food web, the essential role of krill, the southern ocean, and the katabatic winds that carry the continent's cold far out to sea. Even the Great Skua receives honorable mention, its heroic solitary flights to the heart of the ice sheet at least partially redeeming its reputation as a garrulous, predatory marauder. This is natural history at its best—lively, informative, creative—linking cause and effect, species and environment, morphology and habitat.

One particularly successful aspect of the book is its power to convey to the reader information about a species in general while giving a feeling for its individual members. It is, for example, a measure of Halle's artistry that he can introduce us to questions of the mechanics of the flight of the albatross and the homologous structure of the avian wing with a simple description:

> "A lone albatross without a nest, perhaps a young bachelor, was standing in the grass near the top of the ridge, so we put the question to it. Crompton held it by the bill while I unfolded one of its wings and walked it out to its full length. Then the secret was out."

No lifeless pedagogy, this is the joy of discovery—and we are caught up in it.

The book speaks at a third level: its author is a forceful advocate for responsible global stewardship. There is a quiet intensity, a controlled passion in his advocacy. He describes whaling over the past century as "a history of human cupidity and cynicism so ugly that one hesitates to enter upon it." It is a history of devastatingly triumphant technique, "for the men no longer run any risk and the whales no longer have any chance." That condemnation—written fifteen years ago—is as applicable today as it was then.

The book invites attention at still another level, though not all readers will perceive it. Here and there are glimpses of another view of nature, a complementary view of human experience. The subtitle of the epilogue, *A Report to the Greeks*, reflects it, but Halle gives other, subtler hints of the mystery and wonder of that remote continent, intimations of questions that lie beyond mechanistic answers, of art beyond science. Listen:

> "The Weddell Seal in the wintry darkness under the Ice

Shelf and the Emperor Penguin in the wintry darkness above it are the two outstanding examples of the highest orders life has developed so far, mammal and bird, at the ultimate frontier. Who can say that life, on this sphere lost in space, is not beautiful, heroic, and tragic?"

Such gems are well hidden in the text. In musing on man's place in the universe, Halle concludes that Krutch "was right to say to the Spring Peepers, in his confrontation with them: 'Don't forget, we are all in this together.'" Looking down on the Transantarctic Mountains, Halle writes, "This is as close as I can ever come to the world that preceded Original Sin."

What other recent writer, discussing the nesting of the Light-mantled Sooty Albatross, would conclude with this question and answer:

"What, one may ask, does the work of a Picasso have to do with the work of a blind process like natural selection? The question is pertinent, because this bird on its nest is more plausible as the product of the former than of the latter."

Nowhere is Halle's sensitive and reflective view of life better shown than in his treatment of the men of the heroic age of Antarctic exploration. He compares such Antarctic pioneers as Edward Wilson—doctor, artist, explorer, naturalist—with today's scientists:

"Surely they are good men for their purpose, highly trained in the technical procedures that belong to one or another branch of specialized investigation, or in the operation of machinery. But they are for the most part without general education or the ranging curiosity with which such education endows the mind."

In an age that takes glee in deconstructing its dreams and debasing its heroes, Halle is a voice to be heard. To set foot at the

South Pole is still, for him, to tread hallowed ground, and to write of it requires, not prose, but poetry. What other book of recent times could conclude a chapter on the South Pole with the quotation:

"But yet I know, where'er I go,
That there hath passed away a glory from the earth."

And the intriguing thing is that such writing is done without pretense, without being intrusive. It is a serene view of nature, full of beauty and insight, packed with careful observation.

Inevitably, were *The Sea and the Ice* to be written today, one would change it. Some scientific sections could be usefully updated, others strengthened. Yet it is the subtle blending of information and insight, fact and philosophy that mark Halle's book not simply as a travelogue or a descriptive natural history but as a work of art. As such, it needs no refinement.

Ithaca, New York
November 29, 1988

Preface

➤ IN THE FALL of 1969 the Office of Polar Programs in the National Science Foundation, Washington, D.C., invited me to visit Antarctica under its auspices. No invitation I have ever received has been more welcome. I was able to accept it because the Graduate Institute of International Studies, in the person of its Director, Professor Jacques Freymond, granted me the necessary leave of absence, and because my colleague, Professor Urs Schwarz, agreed to carry on alone the seminar that he and I normally conducted together.

It was Dr. Philip Ritterbush who had proposed that I be invited. Messrs. Philip M. Smith and George Toney of the Office of Polar Programs took a lot of trouble over the arrangements for my trip, and those arrangements could not have been better. In New Zealand Dr. Richard Penney, the representative of USARP (U.S. Antarctic Research Program), made the wheels turn that sped me on to Antarctica. At McMurdo Station the USARP representative for Antarctica, Mr. Donald C. Shepherd, saw to it that I was well taken care of, and Mr. Emmett Herbst spared nothing to make sure that my visit would be successful in enabling me to get to all the sites I had hoped I might visit.

My transportation was provided by the U.S. Naval Support Force Antarctica (Operation Deep Freeze). In the book that follows these remarks, I refer to the memorable hospitality I

enjoyed aboard the U.S.C.G.C. *Staten Island* at the hands of
Captain S. G. Putzke, U.S.C.G.

I already had an Alpa 35-mm camera that I had used for bird
photography. When the manufacturers of this Swiss precision
camera (Pignons, S.A. of Ballaigues) learned of my plans for
photography on the trip, their Technical Director, M. Benjamin
Bourgeois, loaned me two extra cameras and made other helpful
provision for my success. M. Michel Darbellay of Martigny,
himself an experienced photographer of wildlife, was helpful in
testing my equipment under Alpine conditions, in supplementing
it, and in giving me the advice of an old hand.

To all the persons mentioned above I acknowledge a debt of
gratitude. Each made his contribution, in some cases indispensable, to an episode in my life that came to me at the time as if by
miracle, and that I now look back on with a sense of having
experienced the beneficence of Providence.

I am grateful as well to the following persons, who nobly met
my requests for advice or information, often at considerable
trouble to themselves: Dean Amadon of the American Museum of
Natural History; W. R. P. Bourne of The Seabird Group, British
Museum (Natural History); Mr. Bucher of the University of
Bern; Gordon D. Cartwright of the U.S. Mission in Geneva; Guy
G. Guthridge of the National Science Foundation; Geoff Hicks of
Wellington; LeRoy Holcomb; Alex Kennel of the U.S. Depart-
ment of Commerce; F. C. Kinsky of the Dominion Museum,
Wellington; G. L. Kooyman of the University of California, San
Diego; Captain T. McDonald, U.S.C.G.R.; Masayoshi Murayama
of the National Science Museum, Tokyo; Carleton Ray of The
Johns Hopkins University; K. G. Sandved of the National Science
Foundation; P. K. Senko of The Arctic and Antarctic Research
Institute, Leningrad; N. S. Suzuki of the World Meteorological

Organization; G. A. Tunnicliffe of the Canterbury Museum, Christchurch; George E. Watson of the Smithsonian Institution; Richard B. Weininger; Robert C. Wood of The Johns Hopkins University; Mr. and Mrs. Alan Wright of the Department of Internal Affairs, Portobello, New Zealand.

Appendix A, on the Coriolis effect, is the product of extended discussions with Oliver Ashford, who as a meteorologist represents the professional competence in matters of this sort that I lack. If, as is possible, he is not quite easy about the degree of simplification that it represents, it remains true that whatever merit it may have is in large measure due to the benefit I derived from exploiting his patience and good will.

As on so many previous occasions, I am indebted to Mme Philippe Braillard (previously Miss Ulrike Wuttig) for the endless labor of typing and checking — a contribution to this book that, in addition to being second only to my own, is less open to criticism.

•

I had no intention, when I visited Antarctica, of writing a book about the experience, although I could have guessed that I would. When, shortly after my return to the northern hemisphere, Les Line of *Audubon* magazine and Paul Brooks of Houghton Mifflin jointly suggested that I should, nothing more than the prospect of collaboration with them was needed to set me off. And that is how I have just arrived at that wonderful moment when one writes "The End" at the bottom of a page that is the last.

L. J. H.

Les Granges sur Salvan, 9 April 1972

Citations of published works in the text or in footnotes are fully identified in the Publications Cited list at the end of the book.

The scientific names of species referred to in the text by their vernacular names are given in the Index.

Contents

Contents

Illustrations

THE SEA
AND THE ICE

1. The Ring of Ice

◆━ ACCORDING TO THE OLD TALE, the palace where the Sleeping Beauty and all life lay asleep was guarded by an impenetrable ring of thorn bushes. The kings' sons who tried to break their way through it found that "the thorns and bushes laid hold of them as if with hands, and there they stuck fast."

Long after all the other lands of the earth had been invaded by our spreading humanity, the Antarctic continent, sleeping under its cover of ice, was still guarded against intrusion by an impenetrable ring of pack-ice. In the 1770s Captain James Cook tried to break through it, but the ice laid hold of his ship as if with hands and he had to retreat. About 1820, one or more sea captains saw on the southern horizon the pinnacles of a distant land, just as a prince ranging along the ring of thorn bushes might have seen the pinnacles of a distant palace. The breakthrough was not achieved until 1841, when Sir James Ross, in *Erebus* and *Terror*, two double-hulled ships constructed for the purpose, pushed through the ice-floes to emerge in the open water inside.

We may think of the Antarctic continent as a circular shield of ice, some 2,600 miles in diameter, rising toward its center at the South Pole. On the side exposed to the central Pacific there is a gap in the shield, as if a giant had taken a bite out of it. This gap is known today as the Ross Sea, but most of it is permanently covered by the Ross Ice Shelf, which is larger than France.

Having got through the ring, Ross pursued his way south, at last entering the sea that would bear his name and continuing parallel with the line of icebound mountains along its western shore. The sun now wheeled continuously overhead, completing its round every twenty-four hours without even approaching the horizon. In the daylight that had become perpetual the southward sailing company at last saw before them the white peaks of two mountains, which they named Erebus and Terror after their ships. The mountains rose out of what would later prove to be a roughly triangular island, fifty miles in its greatest dimension, since named Ross Island. At its eastern angle, which would be called Cape Crozier after the captain of the *Terror,* the ships came up against the edge of the ice-shelf larger than France, a white cliff fifty to a hundred and fifty feet high that, to the east, as we now know, extended unbroken for more than five hundred miles. Ross was not the last explorer who would range along it, like a tiger before the bars of its cage, trying to find a way through; but its edge would prove to be the farthest south that a ship could sail on the surface of the sea.

•

For hundreds of thousands of years our proliferating species had been spreading over the earth. It had spread over Africa, around the Mediterranean and into Europe, along the shores of the Indian Ocean to Australia. It had spread northward into Siberia, across the narrow waters to North America, and on south over both the American continents. It had thus covered all the lands of the predominantly land hemisphere north of the Equator, and in the oceanic hemisphere south of it had occupied the intrusive land-masses of Africa, South America, and Australia. Although this expansion and proliferation had gone on for a million years, it was not until some five hundred years ago that we men had sufficiently developed the means of finding our way about the open oceans so that we could begin to explore the southern hemisphere as a whole.

Already a millennium earlier, the inhabitants of Hellas had surmised the existence of an icebound Antarctic region; for they knew they inhabited a globe and, believing in an order of nature that favored symmetry, they concluded that, just as the climate became progressively colder toward the globe's North Pole, so it must become progressively colder toward its South Pole. All advances in human knowledge have been based on such assumptions of an order in the realm of being, and in this case the prediction to which the assumption gave rise was to be fulfilled after the lapse of a thousand years.

Bartholomew Diaz and his crew were the first to feel the breath of the Antarctic when, in 1488, they passed the southern end of Africa and sailed into the circumpolar ocean beyond. In the centuries that followed, other mariners adventuring into this ocean were sometimes driven "south along" by "the Storm-blast," like Coleridge's Ancient Mariner, until "there came both mist and snow, / And it grew wondrous cold. . . ." None, however, is on record as having crossed the Antarctic Circle until, in the 1770s, Captain Cook followed the edge of the guardian ice all around the world, trying repeatedly to penetrate it like a dog looking for a hole in a fence.

Even Ross's expedition in 1841, having at last broken through the ring into the open water beyond, could not effect a landing on the Antarctic continent itself. So it was that, long after the other six continents had come under the dominion of mankind, Antarctica had still not sustained the print of a human foot but continued to sleep under its white mantle.

Not until 1895 did the first man step ashore on the Antarctic mainland, and it was not until after the beginning of our own century, which is still within living memory, that its exploration began.

.

North of the ice ring is our familiar world. South of it lies what might be another planet. Vast and splendid as is the scenery of this sequestered continent, human beings can survive on it only as they survive on the moon: temporarily, by ingenious artifice, and on the basis of operations organized in military fashion to keep them alive by the maintenance of supply lines from the north.

Almost a million years ago, much of what is now our familiar world was as Antarctica still is today. Most of North America and Europe was under a covering of ice through which only the mountain-peaks protruded. In South America, the southern Andes lay under the same unbroken ice-sheet as the South Pole. However, with the rise of global temperatures in the millennia that followed, all this ice melted back from the mid-regions of the earth and from the mountain-chains, until Antarctica remained the only continent still glaciated as in the Pleistocene. Those who visit it today are transported back almost a million years to see what much of the world was like at a time when their own species was evolving out of an earlier anthropoid.

The Antarctic is quite different from the Arctic, for it is a continent surrounded by ocean rather than an ocean surrounded by continents. The Arctic has an oceanic climate, and an oceanic climate is moderate by comparison with a continental climate because the relatively invariable temperature of the ocean tends to stabilize the temperature of the adjacent air, thereby mitigating the heat of low latitudes and the cold of high. The ice around the North Pole is a layer of sea-ice floating on salt water above the freezing point, so that the area of the North Pole is not subject to such extremes of temperature as occur farther south, in Siberia and Alaska. The area of the South Pole, by contrast, is not only far inland but at an average altitude of ten thousand feet. The lowest temperatures known anywhere on our planet occur in the center of Antarctica, where $-126.5°$F. has been recorded, and where the mean annual temperature may be $-67°$F. These are not temperatures favorable to the survival of any form of life, although, as we shall see, there are forms of life that survive them.

It was not until the most recent years that the Antarctic ice-sheet was known to have a continent under it, rather than scattered islands and archipelagos only. The question of how much of what underlies it is continent and how much mere chains of islands is, however, based on criteria that do not have the relevance to this strange realm that they have to our familiar world. The fact is that the whole area of what we call the Antarctic continent is under a mass of freshwater ice thousands of feet deep, representing the accumulation of snow over at least twenty thousand years. One could say that, where the bottom of this mass rests on rock below sea-level, it should not be classified as land at all; for if the ice were removed and it remained at the same level it would be submerged beneath the ocean that would flood in upon it. But this is academic, if only because the melting of the mass of ice, which represents between 90 and 95 percent of all the snow and ice in the world, would cause the earth's crust, released from its weight, to spring up, while at the same time the addition of all that fresh ice-water to the world's oceans would raise the sea-level by some two hundred feet. The essential situation is that the South Polar region is covered by freshwater ice

Toward the
Antarctic Peninsula

resting on rock, while the North Polar region is covered by salt-water ice that floats upon the sea. One may think of the Antarctic ice-sheet as itself constituting the continent, five and a half million square miles of solid matter surrounded by ocean.

The continent, roughly the shape of a circular shield, is rimmed with mountain-ranges that contain the ice as in a bowl. But ice flows like water seeking its level, if more slowly, and so the ice massed to such heights in the interior flows slowly out through all the gaps along the rim, either in the form of glaciers or in out-ward moving shelves like the Ross Ice Shelf. The ends of the glaciers and the edges of the shelves are constantly breaking off, calving to give birth to the icebergs that then drift north into the ever warmer climates where they dwindle, fall apart, and finally melt away altogether. The calving ice-shelves produce tabular icebergs, flat-topped and up to a hundred miles across, their edges sheer cliffs, which illuminate the Antarctic waters with their whiteness. Nothing like them is known in the northern hemisphere. They provide roosts for such birds of the ice as Antarctic Petrels and Snow Petrels, but are too lofty for access by the flightless penguins and the seals, which can haul out only on the floes of saltwater ice.

The freshwater ice flowing down to the edge of the continent, where it breaks off and eventually melts, reduces the salinity of the surrounding sea. Since the fresher water is lighter than the saltier, even though colder, it remains on the surface, spreading northward, while from the warmer regions of the earth the heavier salt water spreads south to meet it. Over a wide belt of ocean around Antarctica, then, the colder water from the south overrides the warmer water from the north, until a point is reached, at the outer edge of the belt, where the salinity of the colder water has increased to such an extent that it sinks down at last to flow under the water from the north. However, sinking deeper as it continues northward, it can still be detected in the depths of the ocean beyond the Equator, thus extending its contribution to the oceanic environment even into the northern hemisphere. The line at which it at last sinks beneath the surface, called the Antarctic Convergence and, for the most part, running irregularly between 50°S. and 60°S., is marked by an abrupt change in the surface temperature of the sea. This is also a biological line of demarcation, separating organisms adapted to the warmer and saltier surface from those adapted to the colder and fresher. Persons whose main interest is in this life at the surface, and what depends on it, may properly regard the Antarctic Convergence as the true frontier of the Antarctic, rather than the unmarked Antarctic Circle that they cross at 66°33′S.

Just as the cold water flows north from the edge of Antarctica, so the cold air flows north from the interior. It comes down the slopes of its own weight and spreads out over the ocean to chill much of the southern hemisphere. Consequently, the middle and high latitudes of the southern hemisphere are colder than the oceanic regions of equivalent latitudes in the northern hemisphere.

·

The unconscious but stubborn determination of life to perpetuate itself and extend its range, and the corresponding extremes of its adaptability, are not only among the wonders of the world but also among the fundamental facts of being as we know it. They are nowhere better exemplified than in Antarctica.

The main limit to life on the Antarctic continent is its covering of ice, for nothing is able to live and grow on ice alone. Life must have land or water. Oceanic water supports the greatest quantity and variety of life in the high, cold latitudes at either end of the earth, and the waters that surround the Antarctic continent are perhaps the richest of all, cornucopias of organic being, the watery equivalent of tropical rain forests. Therefore, when I say that the Antarctic continent, of all areas on earth, is by far the most inimical to the survival of life in any form, I do not refer to the life that lives exclusively in the sea, whether microscopic plankton or whales.

If the continent were entirely under ice there would be no life on it at all except such visitors from the sea as seals and seabirds. However, where mountain-peaks and coastal cliffs are too steep to hold snow, the exposed rock provides lodgment for lichens, which have consequently been found as close to the Pole as 266 miles in an environment permanently below freezing, swept by desiccating gales in which almost nothing else could survive. Presumably these patches of bare rock absorb a modicum of heat from the sun during the half of the year in which it remains above the horizon, as well as providing mineral nourishment to the symbiotic combination of fungus and algae to which we give the name lichen. This lichen grows at the outer edge of the margin of subsistence on earth. Beyond is only death.

Minute animal life, however, also occurs at this outer edge, a species of mite having been found 424 miles from the Pole. As the mites survive through the months of Antarctic daylight, so their eggs must survive through the months of Antarctic darkness, under the harshest conditions to be found this side of outer space.

Besides the exposed faces of cliffs and pinnacles there are, on the Antarctic continent, two other habitats capable of supporting land organisms. The most important is constituted by scattered small areas along its coast where the snow melts off completely during the months of the austral summer, from late November to March. It should be borne in mind that on the coast the summer temperature commonly rises above freezing, and under such circumstances sufficient sunshine may melt off a winter's accumulation of snow in places where scouring winds have prevented it from becoming too great. The stony ground in such places, unmodified by any vegetation, absorbs and then radiates the sun's heat. Consequently, where there is enough moisture, patches of algae may grow, and there may be mosses — but, for the most part, there is no vegetative life visible to the naked eye, even in such areas.

With an exception that I shall record further on, there are no land animals on these patches of exposed coast that one can see without a microscope or, at least, a magnifying glass.

The third habitat that might support life is that of the ice-free or "dry" valleys. Here and there in the coastal mountains, especially across McMurdo Sound from Ross Island, there are deep valleys without any covering of snow or ice, summer or winter. The tongues of glaciers lick down the slopes of these valleys, only to stop abruptly halfway; glacier-fed streams run through them, sometimes broadening into ponds that are only partly frozen at the height of summer. Standing in such a valley brings one as near as most of us will ever get to the sensation of visiting the moon. Because the dry valleys are back from the sea, however, they are more lifeless than the exposed strips along the coast, which receive the visits of penguins, skuas, and seals.*

I have referred to the Antarctic continent, here, as the circular shield of ice, rimmed with mountains, that lies within the Antarctic Circle. There is, however, a long and narrow extension of it, the Antarctic Peninsula, that goes well beyond the Antarctic

* For a fuller account of these valleys see Chapter 13.

Circle toward the tip of South America, and that is continuous, under the sea, with the Andean chain. It, and various islands that are still within the Antarctic region, albeit as interruptions of the surrounding ocean, provide environmental conditions in which some grasses and other flowering plants grow, and in which at least one native insect may be found.

•

I have mentioned three circumpolar boundaries by which one may, in one's mind, delimit the Antarctic. The Antarctic Circle is the most abstract of these, an astronomer's boundary, representing the northern limit of the circumpolar area that is simultaneously illuminated by the sun when, having reached its farthest south with reference to the surface of this tilted earth (as this tilted earth makes its annual tour of the sun), it is over the Tropic of Capricorn — of the circumpolar area that is everywhere in darkness when, having reached its farthest north, it is over the Tropic of Cancer. It represents the lowest latitude at which the sun remains above the horizon throughout the twenty-four hours of December 21 (the summer solstice of the southern hemisphere), and below it throughout the twenty-four hours of June 21 (the winter solstice). At the South Pole, itself, day and night are each six months long, including transitional periods of twilight. Between the latitudinal limits of the Pole, on the one hand, and the Circle on the other, the periods of continuous daylight in summer, of continuous dark in winter, progressively lessen northward, and the twenty-four-hour alternations of day and night become increasingly extended and evident during the transitional periods between these two seasons.

The Antarctic Convergence, lying outside the Antarctic Circle, differs from it in its irregularity, its latitude varying with the local geography. It is mundane rather than astronomical, for it marks the boundary between one oceanic environment and another. However, one does not actually see this boundary as one crosses it; one is made aware of it only if, taking the temperature of the surface water at regular intervals or examining the surface organisms, a sudden change occurs.

The most vivid boundary is that formed by the guardian ring of pack-ice behind which the Antarctic continent remained, until so recently, beyond the reach of mankind. One may well wonder why, during the long summer day, this ice should be separated by open water from at least part of the continent it encircles.

Long before the end of winter the continent is enclosed by a margin of sea-ice often several hundred miles wide, which is continuous with the ice that covers the land. At the beginning of summer the outer edge of this margin begins to melt back and the sea-swells from the north break it into floes. Meanwhile, at its inner edge, the lifting and sinking of the tide cracks it all along the shore, breaking its hold on the continent. This inner ice, fragmented, is then carried northward by the currents of the sea and the air until it reaches the edge of the belt where the west wind reigns (about 65°S.). Here the wind, patrolling the frontier, stops its further progress. Against this northward limit, then, it accumulates in the form of the guardian ring that encircles the continent.

Also as the season advances, the glaciers and ice-shelves calve, and the resulting icebergs are carried north. But the west wind cannot stop them at the frontiers of its domain as it does the pack-ice, for it has access to only the small portion of their mass that rises above the surface of the sea, while the oceanic current that carries them northward bears against the rest.* So it is that in

---

* The pack-ice is so shallow, by contrast with the bergs, that it is moved only by the surface water, which is pushed eastward by the west wind rather than flowing northward with the underlying current.

late December, as the icebreaker in which one is travelling approaches Antarctica from the central Pacific, the first ice one comes to is in the form of icebergs — high, cliff-edged, flat-topped islands that shine as if with an inner light, or smaller, irregularly shaped islands, some crowned with the pinnacles of fairyland. These are the outermost sentinels of Antarctica. After continuing southward through their ranks for perhaps twenty-four hours, at last one sees far ahead, like some illumination from beneath the sea, the edge of the pack-ice. The ship comes to it and enters, pushing the floes aside or overriding and breaking them, sometimes making her way through meandering leads. So she continues for a few hours, when suddenly all opens up again. She has broken through the ring to emerge into the world beyond.

2. Wind, Waves,
and the Flight of Birds

➤ NEW ZEALAND lies in the South Pacific just west of the 180th meridian, halfway around the world from Greenwich. At 41°S., 175°E., Wellington, its capital, is opposite Valladolid, Spain. The two cities are antipodes, like the North and South Poles.

In the open ocean between New Zealand and Antarctica occasional desert islands afford nesting sites for seabirds. Campbell Island, at 53°S., is roughly opposite Hamburg. The first icebreaker to go south in this quarter of the globe, after the summer season has begun, takes some three days from Wellington to Campbell, and another three to the edge of the pack-ice, which is at 66°S. A day later, having gone through the pack, she passes within distant sight of Cape Adare on the Antarctic continent, at the entrance to the Ross Sea. From there to her destination at Ross Island is a distance of some 460 miles along the coast, part of the way blocked by ice-floes that have become jammed against it and by the solid ice that still covers half of McMurdo Sound.

The passenger in the icebreaker travels a great-circle distance of 2,487 miles from Wellington to McMurdo Station at the southwest corner of Ross Island. The first 1,700 miles, to the pack-ice, are across a world of wind and waves such as he has known in the open oceans of the northern hemisphere, although the birds he sees are strange. At the edge of the pack-ice, however, he finally enters a world that is no longer familiar, and finds himself surrounded by still other birds. The birds north of the boundary are the product of wind and wave; while these others, which remain always south of it, are the product of a different environment.

•

In the temperate zones of the northern and southern hemispheres alike westerly winds prevail as a consequence of the earth's rotation.* These winds are particularly strong and steady in their uninterrupted course across the Pacific between about 40°S. and 65°S. (Presumably the traditional term for this west-wind belt, the "roaring forties," excludes the fifties and low sixties only because ships did not commonly sail that far south.)

Corresponding to the wind are the waves it raises, which increase in height with their fetch — that is, with the distance they have travelled from their origin. Most of the oceanic birds of the southern seas, north of the pack-ice, are especially adapted to flight in these conditions. They are adapted to having the energy of the wind support them with a minimum effort on their part. Wings outstretched, they ride the air currents that are deflected upward along the slopes of the running waves. The albatrosses and some of their relatives also take advantage of the difference between the speed of the wind just at the surface, where it is retarded by friction against the waves, and its greater speed higher up. Banked on extended wings, they wheel in circles that are tilted toward the surface, accelerating as they coast downwind from the top of the circle; and then, with the consequent momentum, rising up once more into a wind that, slower at the

* The effect of the earth's rotation is known as the "Coriolis effect." Since so many features of our environment are manifestations or consequences of the Coriolis effect, and since it is so fascinating in itself, I have thought it worthwhile to offer an explanation of it in Appendix A.

surface, accelerates under them as they rise, thereby increasing its lifting power to return them to the pitch at which they began. The beauty of their flight is in its demonstration of vector mathematics. Observing them, we are moved by an unconscious awareness of their obedience to the laws of nature. The manner of their flight proclaims the rule of law.

Because momentum is proportional to mass, and the larger a bird's body the greater its mass, the possibility of using the wind and the waves in this fashion depends on size. A butterfly, undertaking to oppose its momentum to the wind, would be blown away. The little storm petrel has to beat its wings and keep down in the trough. It is not surprising, then, that one of the largest of flying birds (largest of all in wing-spread) occurs in the west-wind belt of the southern hemisphere. The Wandering Albatross, with a wingspread of up to 11½ feet, is the product of wind and wave in what is the greatest expanse of ocean on earth. Wind and wave are its father and its mother.

One may speculate that such size was made possible by the absence, from the South Pacific islands, of predatory land mammals. If there had been foxes in Polynesia and the islands farther south, or primitive men, such large birds would hardly have found sites safe for breeding. Unlike the smaller seabirds, they could not have nested in burrows, in crevices among the rocks, or on the narrow ledges of cliffs. It is characteristic of the large avian and mammalian species that inhabit the latitudes above 40°S. (the reader should recall that the higher latitudes of the southern hemisphere are those farther south, although lower on his map) that they show little or no adaptation in physiology or behavior to terrestrial enemies. For most of them there have been no terrestrial enemies to which they have had to adapt. If there had been Polar Bears in the Antarctic, as in the Arctic, there

Wandering Albatross

would surely not be penguins there, and if there had been foxes or men in the islands there would have been no albatrosses.

Greek legend had it that the kingfisher raised its young in nests afloat on the open sea, but in fact there is no bird, however pelagic its habits, that does not have to come to land (or, in the unique case of the Emperor Penguin, onto the sea-ice) to lay its eggs and raise its young. With the great albatrosses this process has not been subject to such stringencies as limit it in other species. The swans are even larger than the albatrosses, but their rate of mortality is so high that they need a correspondingly high rate of reproduction to survive as species. The Mute Swan, for example, lays five to seven eggs once a year. Its young leave the nest a day or so after hatching and are able to fly some four months later. The Wandering Albatross, by contrast, lays one egg every other year, while the single young that hatches from it is not ready to leave the nest until a year after the whole process began. The defenceless nestling can safely sit for the best part of that year on an unhidden nest, unguarded by parents who, for most of this time, are foraging far out in the open sea. The species can then afford to have its young take ten years before it has become sufficiently mature to begin breeding itself, by contrast with the young swan, which is ready to breed at two or three years old; for the hazards of the albatross's environment are so low that every individual has a fair expectation of living to an advanced age, perhaps forty or fifty years, and some may live to between seventy and eighty. It does not have to breed like a rabbit or a salmon to compensate for a high rate of mortality in early life.

There is a sense in which the Wandering Albatrosses knew, long before we men, that the earth was a globe, for in their navigation they return to their nesting sites by continuing in the direction of their departure, making the circuit of the earth. Carried by the west wind like a fish in a stream, an albatross may, in the course of its life, circumnavigate the world again and again. Imagine an eagle that, after it had nested in the Rocky Mountains, flew across North America and the Atlantic, across the British Isles and Europe, across Russia, Mongolia, Manchuria, and the North Pacific, to return to its nest in the Rockies some six months later. If it simply soared on fixed wings, revolving and revolving while the wind carried it eastward, it would match what is undoubtedly a common practice of the albatross. An individual banded off the east coast of Australia on August 25, 1959, was at its breeding grounds on the opposite side of the world, at the island of South Georgia, by February 26, 1962, was off the east coast of Australia again on August 25, 1962, was there again in July 1963, and then was back in South Georgia for the next breeding season.* It could not have beat its way against the west wind, either to go from South Georgia to Australia or from Australia to South Georgia, for that is not the manner of its flight. It went, rather, like the wind around the world, knowing intuitively that going on would bring it back.

An albatross shot at 43°S., 79°W. on December 30, 1847, had a vial about its neck that contained a paper reading: "Dec. 8th, 1847, Ship 'Euphrates,' Edwards, 16 months out, 2300 barrels of oil, 150 of it sperm. I have not seen a whale for 4 months. Lat. 43°S. long. 148°40′W. Thick fog, with rain." The shortest distance between these two points is 3,397 miles, which is therefore the distance the bird would have flown in twenty-two days if it had not deviated from a straight line.

Wandering Albatrosses follow ships for the garbage they discharge and the organic matter brought to the surface by the

* Tickell, 1968, p. 12.

disturbance of their passage. One individual may follow the same ship day after day, through dark and daylight, and so be drawn north of its home latitudes. Or some other agency, if only a psychological idiosyncrasy, may impell it to go beyond its normal range, as is the way with occasional individuals of many species. In the days of sail mariners commonly caught the birds on hooked and baited lines trailed over the stern, then kept them as pets on decks where they lacked room to take off. So an albatross might be carried by ship to any part of the oceanic world and there released. The speed of modern ships, however, has generally ended this practice, so that it can no longer be readily taken as the explanation of an individual's presence far outside the normal range. Presumably, one killed near Sicily, in the middle of this century, and another observed off the Portuguese coast about the same time, had entered the North Atlantic on their own.*

•

Birds that occur within the Arctic Circle tend to be circumpolar because they inhabit a largely unbroken ocean, bounded by the continents to the south. South of the circle, however, the continents separating the Atlantic and Pacific oceans, and the oceans separating the Eurasian and North American continents, tend to prevent the circumpolar spread of any species.

In the southern hemisphere, the fact that there is one circumpolar ocean from the Antarctic Circle all the way to about 35°S. (let the reader imagine a circumpolar ocean in the northern hemisphere that extended down to the latitude of North Africa), interrupted only by the projecting tip of South America, has the consequence, not only that birds of the open sea are commoner in

* Ibid., p. 10.

these latitudes than anywhere else, but also that their ranges tend to be defined by latitudinal rather than longitudinal limits. Each species occurs around the world within certain belts of latitude.

In common usage the word "seabird" may refer to any species associated with salt water. The great majority of such species in the northern hemisphere are coastal, many of them resorting to the land to roost when night comes, or at dawn if they are nocturnal. With few exceptions, all the flying birds that have their customary abode in the open ocean, not coming to land except for breeding, belong to the order Procellariiformes, which dominates the southern hemisphere. All the members of this order are distinguished by a feature exclusive to it, the location of the nostrils in a distinct tube or tubes on top of the bill. Otherwise they represent a variety of forms that can be matched by few other orders.

·

In every bird that one sees in its natural habitat, what one sees is both an individual and a species. But one's observation is more complete if one can also see in it a genus, a family, and an order — and, indeed, one should be able to see in each individual the grandest category of all, that of life on earth. I have therefore thought it well, in preparation for what follows, to give herewith an account in general terms of the great seabird order that dominates the oceanic scene from New Zealand to the Antarctic.

In the range of their size the Procellariiformes have no match, for they include the Wandering Albatross at one extreme and, at the other, storm petrels no larger than swallows. Their order is divided into four families: (1) the Diomedeidae or albatrosses, (2) the miscellaneous Procellariidae, (3) the Hydrobatidae or storm petrels, and (4) the Pelecanoididae or diving petrels.

Diomedeidae, the albatross family, is composed of eleven species in two genera, *Diomedea* and *Phoebetria*. It was Linnaeus, the inventor of the binomial system'for the classification of birds into genera and species, who in the eighteenth century coined the name *Diomedea* in reference to the companions of the Homeric hero Diomedes, who were changed into birds at his death. The Wandering Albatross and its ten congeners are, nominally, the descendents of the men who fought with Diomedes "far on the ringing plains of windy Troy."

Their list is led by the two so-called great albatrosses, the Wandering and the Royal, which are indistinguishable, in their adult plumage, at any distance beyond what would allow the observation of small details. However, the young of the Royal Albatross assume the predominantly white plumage of the adult upon fledging, while those of the Wanderer assume a predominantly dark plumage, which changes to the adult plumage so gradually that the transformation may not be completed for twenty to thirty years. Most of the Wanderers one sees from a ship are in immature or incompletely adult plumage, and therefore distinguishable from the Royals of any age.

The other nine members of the genus *Diomedea*, while still among the largest of seabirds, are markedly smaller than the two great albatrosses. Most of them are white with a dark mantle, like the various species of black-backed gulls. Just as sailors, who do not note fine points of distinction, have never distinguished the great albatrosses as two separate species, referring to them simply as "goneys," so they have tended to group the smaller, dark-mantled albatrosses as "mollymawks." Because it is not always easy, at any great distance, to tell whether a particular bird is the Black-browed, the White-capped, the Yellow-nosed, the Gray-headed, or Buller's Albatross, the collective term has its convenience. A bird seen at a distance is either one of the great albatrosses or a mollymawk.

The two species of *Phoebetria,* the Sooty Albatross and the Light-mantled Sooty Albatross, are not only devoid of white plumage but are distinguished from the other albatrosses by the slender elegance of their bills, bodies, wings, and pointed tails. They have an aerial deftness and delicacy that make one expect to see them, at any moment, pirouette on the wing like ballet dancers.

Most of the thirteen species of the family Diomedeidae, like the great majority of the Procellariiformes generally, are confined in their range to the southern hemisphere, with its predominance of ocean over land. But one species, the Waved Albatross, breeds in the Galápagos Islands off the Pacific coast of South America at the Equator, and three species — the Black-footed, the Short-tailed, and the Laysan Albatross — occur in the North Pacific. Presumably these three are descended from ancestors that, ranging the South Pacific, found their way across the barrier of tropical waters in which there is little to nourish any seabird. (The Waved Albatross in the Galápagos depends on the organic life peculiar to the cold waters of the Humboldt Current.) The Diomedeidae have not yet found their way across the tropics into the North Atlantic, but I set forth here grounds for hope that they may.

The most abundant and widespread of the albatrosses is the Black-browed Albatross. I remember an afternoon when there were never fewer than seventy within view from the icebreaker, although of other species one never saw more than three or four at a time. If, then, an albatross were to spill over into the North Atlantic and proceed to populate it, the statistical chances are that it would be the Black-brow. In fact, this species has al-

Black-browed Albatross

ready occurred in the North Atlantic under circumstances that arouse hope.

The most famous occurrence was that of one first observed in 1860 at the Faroe Islands, between Iceland and Britain, where it was living as part of a breeding colony of Gannets. Every November for thirty-four years thereafter, it migrated with the Gannets to lower North Atlantic latitudes, returning with them to Faroe every February — until in 1894 someone shot it.

From May to August 1967 another Black-browed Albatross lived with another breeding colony of Gannets on Bass Rock in the Firth of Forth, Scotland. And from 1963 to 1967, of eighteen occasions on which an albatross was seen in waters off the coasts of Britain, the identification of this species has been rated certain in eleven and probable in the rest.* It is an odd fact that the Black-brow has been recorded closer to the North Pole than to the South, one having been shot in Spitsbergen, at 80°11′N., in 1878. It would be even more astonishing to find a Black-brow at so high a latitude in the southern hemisphere, for there it would be at least a hundred miles from the nearest open water.

Let the reader make his own guess at how many albatrosses in the North Atlantic go unrecorded for every one reported. It may be that the almost total absence of records from the high latitudes of the central and western North Atlantic reflects simply the absence of observers.

The recorded occurrences of the Black-browed Albatross in the North Atlantic suggest the possibility that it might at any time establish itself there. The bird shot at Faroe in 1894 proved to be a female in breeding condition at what was the breeding season for the northern but not the southern hemisphere. This is to say that its annual cycle had come to conform to the seasons in its new location. And, in the absence of a member of its own species, the bird that summered at Bass Rock repeatedly courted individual Gannets. Who knows but what, if a male and female should occur together in the North Atlantic, they might colonize the area? Then we might find Black-browed Albatrosses commonly following ships in the North Sea, in the English Channel, and in the wider waters that separate the European coastline from the American. It is a good guess that the Great Skua, originally confined to the cooler parts of the southern hemisphere, became established in the North Atlantic in just such fashion, and the Arctic Fulmar as well.

* Waterston, 1968.

•

By contrast with the other three families of the order Procellariiformes, Procellariidae seems, to one who is not a professional
taxonomist, a grab bag for those genera and species that could not
be fitted in elsewhere. Its members fall into subgroups that, in
some cases, themselves appear to be of uncertain definition, and
that are, in fact, differently made up by different authorities.

There are the fulmars, totaling six species that constitute four
genera besides the type genus, *Fulmarus,* to which two species
belong: the Arctic Fulmar of the high northern hemisphere, and
the Antarctic Fulmar. That leaves one species apiece for each of
the remaining four genera: the Giant Petrel, the Cape Pigeon, the
Antarctic Petrel, and the Snow Petrel. Then there are the prions
or whalebirds of the genus *Pachyptila;* the gadfly petrels, chiefly
Pterodroma; and the shearwaters, divided between *Procellaria*
and *Puffinus.*

The two remaining families are that of the storm petrels,
Hydrobatidae, and that of the diving petrels, Pelicanoididae. The
storm petrels are little birds that flutter in the trough of the wave
like swallows, the typical species appearing black with a white
patch on the upper side at the base of the tail.

The diving petrels are hardly any larger, but altogether different. Black and white birds the size of Starlings, they have small
wings that, like flippers, are better adapted to underwater flying
than to flight above the surface, which they manage only by a
whirring not to be sustained for long distances. They have gone
part of the way along the evolutionary road that led the penguins
and the Great Auk of the north to lose their ability to fly through
the air in exchange for speed, agility, and ease underwater. Confined to high latitudes of the southern hemisphere, they are best
known for the example they provide, in conjunction with the
Alcidae or auks that occur only in high northern latitudes, of

convergent evolution. The two families are wholly unrelated, the auks belonging to the same order as the gulls. However, the two, becoming adapted to a similar environment and a similar way of life in the course of their respective evolution, have come to look alike. If they occurred together in the same part of the world it would be virtually impossible to distinguish, by field identification in the open sea, a Magellan Diving Petrel from a Little Auk or Dovekie, although there would be no difficulty in distinguishing the diving petrel from its relative the albatross or the auk from its relative the gull.

The extent of the separation, on the tree of life, between species that are superficially so similar is associated with the fact that the Procellariiformes constitute one of the most primitive avian orders left on earth, while the Charadriiformes, to which gull and auk belong, are relatively advanced. The Procellariiformes branched off some hundred million years ago, fifty million years after the first birds evolved out of reptilian ancestors. The Charadriiformes not only came later but developed further (their branch is longer). Just as a loon is more primitive than a sparrow, so an albatross, a shearwater, a storm petrel, or a diving petrel is more primitive than a gull, a skua, a sandpiper, or an auk.

3. The Icebreaker

➤ THE TWENTY-FIRST OF DECEMBER, 1970, was such a summer's day as normally occurs, I think, only in the Kingdom of Heaven. Wellington is called "the windy city," but when I stepped off the airplane from Christchurch there was merely a breeze to moderate the midday heat of the sun.

Although the icebreaker *Staten Island*, U.S.C.G., was not due to sail until the twenty-third, I took a taxi to the pier where she lay. At the head of the gangway stood a young ensign with a patriarchal beard who introduced himself as Ralph Yates. No, he said, I needn't go to a hotel pending the ship's sailing. I should make myself at home in the junior officers' quarters, which turned out to be a narrow ship's dormitory, amidships and below decks, lined with three tiers of bunks on either side.

A few minutes later three of my fellow passengers and roommates joined the ship — Mike Gibson and Paul Stephenson, both Queen's Scouts, and Ross McArthur of the Boys' Brigade. Having achieved the highest distinction in New Zealand scouting, they were being rewarded by a season at New Zealand's Scott Base in Antarctica, where they would do repairs and odd jobs. In their first interview with the Captain they were gentle but firm in their insistence that, although they were on board as passengers and guests of the U.S. Navy, they meant to work their way. The Captain therefore assigned to each daily watches on the bridge, during which each should be available to run messages and do odd jobs. It is not always that I feel admiration for the species to which I belong, but when I think of those three I do.

We four passengers shortly became six by the addition of two New Zealand scientists: Peter Gill, a geophysicist whom we would leave at Campbell Island, and Geoff Hicks, a planktonologist on his way to Scott. The Captain, coming aboard the morning of sailing, assembled the six of us on deck to welcome us. That done, he asked me to his cabin and there, over coffee, invited me to share his quarters. So it was that, with just a twinge of regret at parting from the others, I came to join him in his lofty isolation.

The population of every naval vessel falls into three classes: the enlisted men, who have their own living quarters and mess; the officers, who eat and congregate in the wardroom; and the Captain, who lives and eats all by himself. Our Captain's cabin, behind and below the bridge, ran the width of the ship's superstructure. Opening off its forward side were two staterooms (one marked CAPTAIN over the door, the other, COMMANDER OF THE FLEET) with a bathroom between. Abaft it was a completely equipped galley. To take care of us we had a Filipino steward and a Filipino cook. One of the Captain's problems, of which I was now to bear my share, was that the morale of his cook, Abi, depended on the ability of the consumer, day after day, in calm or in tempest, to eat international banquets that, while they would have been the admiration of Escoffier, might have fazed even Henry VIII. I say they were "international" because a Chinese feast at noon might be followed by a culinary *fiesta mejicana* in the evening, to be followed the next noon by some gastronomical glory designed around an Indian lamb curry. Abi was always after us, moreover, to command such rare dishes as would challenge his art. I think the Captain was not sorry to have a guest with whom to share the delectable burden.

The reader should picture the Captain and me facing each other athwartships at a table, in the middle of the cabin, to which our armchairs are lashed. The ship may be rolling 30 degrees each way, according to the swinging needle of the instrument for measuring roll on the forward wall. (Of course the needle does not actually swing but remains stationary while the ship herself

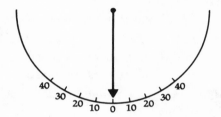

leans over from one side to the other.) Abi's colleague comes in from the galley like a tightrope walker, teetering dangerously and recovering himself, taking one long step backward and then two dancing steps forward, but all the time holding aloft and safe a heaped dish that he places in the outstretched hands of the Captain, who lowers it gently to the table, where he keeps it in place with one hand. Another dish is delivered in similar fashion to me — and here we are, conversing and eating, the Captain at one moment above me and looking down . . . then, as the ship recovers and rolls the other way, looking up at me from below.

An icebreaker is round-bottomed, so that (I was warned in advance) she will roll even when fast to the dock in a flat calm. The rule was that, when the rolling reached 30 degrees, course was altered — for beyond that no one aboard could spare any attention from the task of keeping himself in place against the floor or the wall, if not the ceiling. But I have known the *Staten Island,* while the Captain and I were banqueting, to roll 35 degrees before she could be brought to a new angle with the waves.

I am a man of manifold weaknesses, unfit for much, but I thank God that the motion of ship or roller coaster has always filled me with a childlike joy and a sense of well-being. If the Captain or I were sometimes unable to do full justice to Abi's cooking, it was not because of the ship's admirable habit of lying over first on one side and then the other.

Sleeping was another matter, and here a reform is called for. A ship's bunks run lengthwise of the ship because, I am told, if one were to slide forward and back with each roll all one's skin would be rubbed off by morning. As it is, propped on one's elbows or using one leg against the outer edge of the bunk to brace oneself against the wall, one has to make a muscular effort at each roll to keep *in situ;* and this necessarily precludes sleep when the ship is rolling handsomely. The problem did not exist before bunks replaced hammocks at sea, for hammocks swing freely against the roll (or, rather, like the needle of the roll-meter remain still while the ship rolls around them), and I can testify from long experience in the American tropics that a properly designed hammock, properly used, is as comfortable as any bed ever designed for a princess. The objection to hammocks in ships is, apparently, that they require more room than bunks. In the place occupied by two hammocks, one above the other, three bunks can be stacked, and bunks do not require room to swing. Now, however, with the automation of ships, the size of crews is being drastically reduced, and the problem of living space correspondingly eased. I warn the U.S. Navy that if it shows the least hesitation in adopting the proposal I make herewith, that hammocks be brought back in place of bunks, I shall not scruple to allow its adoption by the Russian or Chinese navy.

•

Having enjoyed conversation with Captain S. G. Putzke at three meals a day throughout our trip, I speak with conviction when I say that I found him a prince among men. He had come up through the ranks, was fifty years old, and now faced the imminent prospect of compulsory retirement after thirty years' service. Whomever he was talking with, he was soft-voiced and modest in speech; but when he spoke on ship's business to the men under him he spoke, albeit gently, with a brevity that carried authority. He had in full measure a quality characteristic of the best military professionals: an unostentatious dedication to whatever the job to be done was, no matter what the circumstances in which it had to be done.

Sharing the Captain's quarters with him, I improved my education by seeing how a ship is run. I also had a demonstration of what personal responsibility means. The captain of a ship has no set work, for it is all parcelled out among his officers, who stand their watches and carry on, respectively, all the functions involved in running a ship. The Captain of the *Staten Island,* in addition to sitting in his swivel chair on the bridge, might spend part of the day napping on the cabin sofa, although he might also be up two or three times during the night, for no decision on change of course or speed might be made without him. He had a telephone at his bedside that rang not infrequently. It was evident, however, that, sleeping or waking, he was always alert, as if listening for a momentarily expected signal of some event that would require quick action on his part. He seemed to have invisible antennae extending to every part of the ship, constantly telling him something, perhaps about the throb of the engines or a change in the wind. Once, when the barometer kept falling until it was below 29, lines of worry came into his face. Then I had the impression that, even asleep on his sofa, he remained like a cat ready to spring.

The unique responsibility of the captain, to whom everyone else looks, is what, more than any formality, sets him apart — whether in the *Staten Island* or in the White House.

Captain Putzke was constantly alert, as well, to another kind of responsibility: that which encompassed the well-being of every man in his ship. He was moved by a native humanitarianism that had the quality of a vocation. I never asked him about any officer or member of the crew but what he told me something of his personal background and any special problems he had. Under other circumstances he might have become one of those rare ministers whose lives are dedicated, by vocation, to helping their parishioners in their private griefs and troubles. He told me he had asked the Coast Guard to assign its hard cases to his ship; and he had a special place in his heart for the inscription on the Statue of Liberty:

> Give me your tired, your poor,
> Your huddled masses yearning to breathe free,
> The wretched refuse of your teeming shore,
> Send these, the homeless, tempest-tossed, to me. . . .

He had, as I say, come up through the ranks, and he was a liberal rather than an authoritarian officer. It was by the deliberate pursuit of a liberal policy that he, for his part, dealt with what was, at the beginning of the 1970s, the greatest problem of the American military services.

The *Staten Island* hardly had what could be called a professional or a professionally competent crew. Almost every man I talked with was candid in saying that he had enlisted for four years only as an alternative to being drafted into the Army with the prospect of being sent to fight in Vietnam. Some of the younger officers had entered the Coast Guard Academy for the same reason, intending to return to civilian life as soon as possible. There could be no doubt that, once the war in Vietnam was over, the problem of recruitment would be formidable. In a society of unprecedented affluence, with a wide variety of well-paid civilian jobs available, with military organization widely decried by the young as unnecessary and evil, few were those to whom a military career seemed attractive.

What was most remarkable about the crew of the *Staten Island* was a level of education that would have been unimaginable in a ship's crew of old. Perhaps over half had gone to college, and many thought of going to graduate school after their service. Such men cannot be dealt with effectively by the old ways of command. Their morale cannot be sustained by make-work tasks that have no other purpose, like coiling, uncoiling, and recoiling ropes. They are not readily trained to unthinking obedience. Under these circumstances Captain Putzke's policy was to avoid, within reason, insistence on traditional military forms, even at some price in punctilio. I doubt, however, that punctilio would have been greater under another policy. To the degree that it was lost, its loss was inherent in the situation.°

° This is as good a place as any to explain that, while all U.S. icebreakers now belong to the Coast Guard, in the Antarctic they operate as part of the Navy in its Operation Deep Freeze, under which it carries on all construction and all the logistic support of the U.S. scientific research that is conducted under the auspices of the United States Antarctic Research Program (better known as USARP) of the National Science Foundation, a government agency.

•

Icebreaker *Staten Island* in McMurdo Sound

It is 12:30 on December 23. A gap is widening between the *Staten Island* and the pier at which she has been lying. Now, as she gains way, her bow comes around to the south and she heads toward the outlet of the harbor, bound for the open sea and the ice. (On the pier behind her she leaves a girl sobbing, while on the well deck forward a young sailor looks self-conscious, as if he didn't know how he should look — just as young sailors have undoubtedly looked, in such circumstances, ever since the Carthaginian grain vessels sailed out of Massalia, leaving behind them who knows what new life to be born.)

The *Staten Island* was one of the oldest icebreakers in U.S. service, having been delivered to the Soviet Union under the lend-lease agreement, and having served the Russians for seven years thereafter in the far north as the *Severny Veter* (the "North Wind"). Since her return to the United States she had operated chiefly in the Pacific and American Arctic, where she had showed her mettle in certain episodes for which she had been awarded citations. Unostentatious as she was, she was still not quite the nobody in the world of shipping that one might have thought from looking at her.

When I first saw her at Wellington, alongside a pier that was too long for her, I found her stubbier than I had expected. Although she had just come through tropic seas from her home port of Seattle, her paint was still fresh. As white as the snow and the ice of the polar regions she had been built to assault, she wore a broad ribbon of red that ran diagonally down and back from her foredeck to the waterline, and on it the Coast Guard insignia. Her service and number, 278, were painted in large black letters on her flank. She differed most notably from ordinary ships in that the bottom of her prow, from perhaps three feet above the waterline, had been cut back at a sharp angle. On the slope thus formed an icebreaker rides up and over the top of the floating ice until, by her weight, she breaks down through it, splitting it apart to leave an open passage behind.

The half of her superstructure abaft the beam was occupied first by a hangar for two helicopters and then by the deck for their launching and landing. Helicopters are indispensable to modern icebreakers. They explore ahead, radioing back information on leads to follow through the ice; they perform rescues; and they carry passengers between ships, or between ship and shore. There are always two of them because in the polar wastelands, where the unforeseen is what must be foreseen, it is generally as imprudent for one to go out alone as for an alpinist to undertake a dangerous climb alone.

To conclude this description: the *Staten Island* was 269 feet long. (Compare this to the length of harbor tugs, from 70 to 150 feet, and the length of World War II destroyers, from 340 to 400 feet.) She displaced 6,515 tons (compared to the destroyers' standard displacement of 1,500 to 2,200 tons), for she was 63 feet in the beam and carried two exceptionally powerful engines, such as an icebreaker needs to drive her twin screws when she is trying to force a way through ice that brings her, time and again, to a full stop, requiring her to back off and charge again.

•

We are still in Polynesia, far from the ice. New Zealand might be California without its population, and therefore unspoiled, alone in the ocean a thousand miles from the nearest important land-mass. Its two halves, North Island and South Island, are sepa-rated by Cook Strait. Wellington, the capital, is on the north side of the strait, built around a circular bay with a narrow outlet to the south. It is radiant with sunlight, its residential sections ter-raced on the steep green slopes that enclose the bay.

A breeze in the bay, as we move out across it, raises wavelets that break into foam-flowers. From the moment of leaving the pier we have ship-followers of two species. One is the Southern Black-backed Gull, which, as seen on the wing, differs in no visible way from the Lesser Black-backed Gull of the northern hemisphere (which, in turn, intergrades with the common Her-ring Gull to form a group of populations with mantles that vary, in the adults, from black to medium gray). This remote species of the southern hemisphere corresponds exactly, in its mantle, to the black extreme represented by the Arctic and Scandinavian populations of the Lesser Black-back. Only as a matter of book learning do I know now that the company of gulls hanging over

Giant Petrel

the stern or scattered down our bubbling wake are not the familiar Lesser Black-backs of the North European coasts.

In any case, the gull family is associated primarily with the northern hemisphere, and what I am seeing here, at the start of my first venture upon the waters of the southern hemisphere, is merely the strayed representative of a group that belongs to my home hemisphere.

The case is different with the one other species in our tail. It is the first I have ever seen that belongs exclusively to the oceans around the Antarctic continent, and only twenty-four hours have passed since I first saw it. What any observer of anything anywhere is most likely to see is what he has been taught to expect; but, although I had been reading up on southern-hemisphere seabirds for forty years, intensively during the last year, there had been nothing to tell me what I might expect to see in Wellington

Harbour, aside from the gulls. Walking along the waterfront at midday on the twenty-second, I noticed far away, through my binoculars, that among the gulls following a ship were some all-dark, narrow-winged birds with wedge-shaped tails. They were scaling on motionless wings, rising high and sweeping down again, generally uptilted on one wing. Stupidly, because I could think of nothing else, I took them to be some species of New Zealand shearwater — but I was puzzled by the fact that they seemed immensely larger than the gulls, as no shearwater could be. It was only later, when one came sweeping close by me along the shore, that by its gigantic size and its disproportionately great bill I knew it for the Giant Petrel.

Although the only land I had associated, in my mind, with this pelagic species had been the desert islands of the sub-Antarctic where it nests, it is ubiquitous, generally in its brown variety but sometimes (since it is dimorphic) in a white or intermediate variety. It is one of the common harbor birds of Wellington.

I say that all of us see, generally, only what we are taught to see; but the persistent observer can train himself over the years, if he will, to see, instead, what is there. The Giant Petrel, which is the size of the lesser albatrosses or mollymawks, has the reputation of an ugly duckling — a reputation justified by two characteristics. One is its plumage, mottled and stained and looking as if patched. The other is the curious disproportion between its great bill and little head, as if it had gone into a store and bought a bill that didn't fit. (The albatrosses have equally large bills in proportion to their size, but they fit.) The bill comes down almost over the eyes. In the literature, then, it is customary to contrast the Giant Petrel unfavorably with the albatrosses, which may be fair enough in terms of its color, its lack of pattern, its head and bill. However, even the greatest of all observers and students of seabirds, Robert Cushman Murphy, goes to some length in decrying its lack of grace on the wing by contrast with the albatrosses.* I can only speculate that this is what comes of preconception. With Dr. Murphy's description in mind, I was to live in the company of the Giant Petrel now, as in that of the albatrosses, until we reached the Antarctic; but I am bound to report that I could see no less grace in its flight. Tipped up on one wing or the other, the great bird comes scaling down until the lower wing-tip seems about to furrow the wave, rising up again in a long circular sweep — and so, rising and falling in circles, like music, occasionally punctuating its flight by a beat or two of its wings, it continues all day. Its flight does not differ from that of the albatrosses.

We are proceeding down the bay with our escort of gulls and Giant Petrels. At the narrow mouth we drop the pilot. That done, and now gaining way again, suddenly we emerge into the wave-spangled plain of the open Pacific. In every direction, now, I see the birds I had known, until this moment, only in the books I had read and the pictures I had studied.

* Murphy, 1936, pp. 593–594. (All citations of Murphy hereafter are 1936 unless otherwise indicated.)

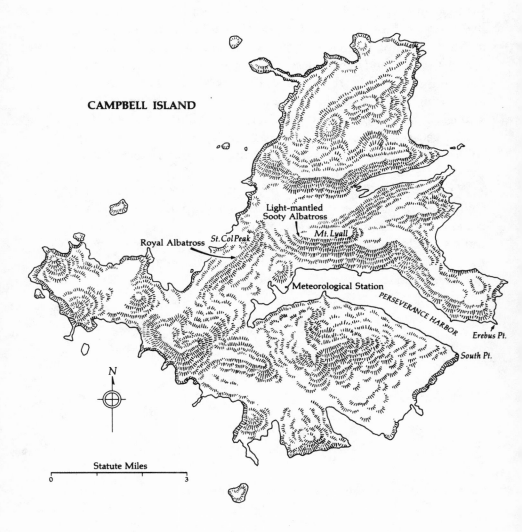

CAMPBELL ISLAND

Light-mantled
Sooty Albatross

Mt. Lyall

Royal Albatross   *St. Col Peak*

Meteorological Station

PERSEVERANCE HARBOR

Erebus Pt.

South Pt.

N

Statute Miles

0   3

4. An Island in the Sea

◆— AT THE LATITUDE of Wellington (41°S.) the west wind is interrupted in its course around the world by only three remaining slivers of land: the tail of South America; Tasmania, off the southernmost point of Australia; and New Zealand itself. The first afternoon out, and all the next day until evening, we remained in the lee of South Island. That second evening we cleared it. Now there was uninterrupted ocean all around the world — except for the tip of South America, 16,582 miles away as the west wind blows. There is no human habitation south of this latitude (47°S.) except some mining communities, some shepherds, and a remnant of Indians at the bottom tip of South America. The morning after the following day, which had been Christmas, we cleared this tip. Now, at 54°S., there was nothing but ocean the world around. It was as if we had sailed off a rim.

I had been informed by correspondence, during the year of preparation for this trip, that it would be impossible for me to visit the scattered islands, east and south of New Zealand, where the seabirds nest. All are uninhabited, except for a six-man meteorological station at Campbell Island (the island farthest south), and there are no regular means of transportation to any of them. After my arrival in New Zealand, however, I learned that the *Staten Island* would be stopping at Campbell to leave mail and a geophysicist at the station. She would then go on to the ice and through it, through the Ross Sea and along the mountainous coast of Victoria Land to McMurdo at the edge of the Ross Ice Shelf.

I have begun with a general account of the voyage, which I mean to report in somewhat less general terms now, to conclude at last with a particular account of seabirds and ice birds, of seals and dolphins and whales.

•

We emerged from Wellington Harbour at midday, December 23, into the sun-spangled ocean, and all afternoon ran south along the east coast of South Island, which receded as it bent away to the southwestward — until, at last, all that was left, in every direction, was unending sea and sky. The wind was moderate from the west and we rode up and down over a long swell. (These lovely swells, so different from the Atlantic chop, are characteristic of the Pacific, where they have thousands upon thousands of miles in which to build up.) In all directions were birds great and small, the greatest being the albatrosses, and always an escort circling us or following in our wake. The sky was clear until evening, when clouds began to gather around the horizon.

At noon on the twenty-fourth our position was 45°15′S., 172°E. All day we had an overtaking wind and a following sea — and that evening, as I have said, we cleared South Island. Throughout the morning there was fog out of which the silhouettes of seabirds loomed or into which they faded. In the early afternoon the sun irradiated the fog, finally dissipating it to preside over clear horizons. But that evening a high overcast formed.

All this day of the twenty-fourth there were fewer seabirds in our wake than the previous day, or than there were to be in the days to follow — perhaps because it is awkward for a planing bird to remain in the wake of a ship that is being overtaken by the wind. A great bird can hang obliquely in a crosswind, facing partly in the direction of its own movement, changing its angle, allowing itself to be carried forward no faster than it wishes. There would be something wrong, however, in gliding obliquely backward after a ship, and such birds as escorted us today tended to circle us, generally at some distance.

The next day was Christmas. Having gone off the rim of man's world, however, we were beyond the jurisdiction of Father Christmas. Out of the lee of the land now (except for the tip of South America 16,582 miles to the west), we were caught by the west wind and an accompanying swell in which the ship rolled with a lovely slow rhythm, over on one side and then over on the other, all day long. It was drizzling during the first half of the morning, but the sun shone for the rest of the day, hidden only occasionally by masses of cloud in passage. At noon our position was 49°45′S., 170°30′E.

The Captain and I were out to Christmas dinner at midday, having accepted the invitation of the officers to be their guests in the wardroom — the Captain sitting at the right of the Executive Officer, Commander Schenck, who presided, I at his left. We fared well. Before going out to dinner, the Captain, the ship's doctor, and I had had an eggnog in the Captain's cabin. ("Christmas, my dear!" said Bob Cratchit to his wife — in another land, in another time, and in another context. But this is, after all, one seamless world, if only our comprehension were wide enough to embrace it as such.)

So we observed the ancient Nordic festival which, in the dark forests along the shores of the North Sea and the Baltic, marked the winter solstice, the beginning of the sun's return to the north.

Again the ship had her swarm of followers, all day without interval or diminution, including the albatrosses that had, for the most part, disdained to follow us in yesterday's following wind. Today they crossed and recrossed the undulating wake we made over the sea-swell, or hung in the crosswind above our travelling stern, suiting their pace to ours by slight adjustments of wing and tail.

The next morning at 4:15, sky and sea gray, we were approaching Campbell Island.

•

Campbell is simply the worn and irregular cap of a mountain that projects through the sea. It is some ten miles in its two longest dimensions, north-south and east-west, and its highest peak rises to 1,876 feet. Its most remarkable feature is a long, narrow, rectangular bay that, running in from the east, goes three quarters of the way to cutting the island in two. This is Perseverance Harbour, named after the brig *Perseverance* in which Frederick Hazelburgh, in 1810, discovered the island. It is some four and a half miles long, but not much more than half a mile wide.

What we saw first, as we approached the island from the north in the grayness of a damp and cloudy morning, was the shape of cliffs that we came under as we rounded Erebus Point at dead slow and entered the mouth of Perseverance Harbour. We proceeded up its length between steep hills on either side. A reception committee, consisting most conspicuously of Royal Albatrosses and Light-mantled Sooty Albatrosses, waited on overhead. Southern Black-backed Gulls and Great Skuas fell into place behind us, forming a procession at the head of which we continued our slow and majestic way up the harbor. Other birds, Antarctic Terns and Campbell Island Shags, passed us, going up or down, but took no note of what a fine sight we must have made. Finally, off the low white huts of the meteorological station on the north shore, we dropped anchor. It was 5:00 A.M. I went below and had breakfast while the helicopters were got ready.

The Captain assigned Mike Gibson to share my shore leave so as to help me carry photographic equipment. At 5:30 the helicopter landed the two of us and Peter Gill (the geophysicist who was to remain here) at the station, where six bearded young meteorologists waited to welcome us and the mail we carried.

Campbell Island is near the southern tip of the underwater New Zealand Plateau, which does for a continental shelf around New Zealand. Other of the widely scattered desert islands based on the plateau, which rise out of the sea as accidental points of land, are the Chatham Islands, the Bounty Islands, the Antipodes, and the Auckland Islands. The great seabirds of the world-girdling ocean, which take to land only for nesting, fill these islands with their nesting numbers in season — and the season is now. On Campbell (as I know from my reading) there are breeding colonies of Yellow-eyed Penguins, of Rockhopper Penguins, of various albatrosses. An assortment of petrels, an endemic shag, a flightless duck, a pipit, and I don't know how many other species also nest on it. It may well be imagined that I was grateful to the Captain when he generously allowed Mike and me five hours on shore.

Within sixty seconds of landing we had found an ornithological guide in the person of Mark Crompton, a meteorologist whose avocation it was to observe and make records of the respective breeding colonies of the Royal and Light-mantled Sooty Albatrosses. Within another sixty seconds he had got the permission of the station's chief to decamp with us, and our plans were laid instantly.

What would we have done in five hours if a thoughtful Providence had not provided a Mark Crompton for our guidance? The penguin colonies, he said, were too far to reach in the time available, but that time would just do to visit the Royal Albatrosses, to visit the Light-mantled Sooties, and to take in Elephant Seals on the way. Immediately, Mike and I were outfitted with high rubber boots ("Wellingtons" in the language of the Commonwealth), since the soil of the island was sucking black peat into which one sank ankle-deep.

•

Although a desert island, Campbell is not in its pristine condition. For some years sheep grazed here under the eyes of a few shepherds brought from New Zealand. This enterprise had at last been abandoned, but the sheep, left to be fruitful and to run wild, had gone far toward destroying the original vegetative cover. An expedition had been sent to Campbell some time before to extirpate them, in order to preserve what remained and restore what might be restored, and although it transpired that not quite all the sheep had been caught or killed (a few in a remote corner of the island had been overlooked) there would be no problem, we were told, in completing the job. No doubt meteorologists, like the rest of us, relish mutton.

The other destructive agency is rats — unintentionally carried by ships to every land and islet in the world, I daresay, except those in the high polar latitudes. So virtually all the ground-nesting seabirds in the world have been afflicted, for man's sins, with a never-to-be-exterminated enemy that, by stealth and under cover, makes off with eggs and young.

There are no trees on Campbell, but woody plants no taller than a man grow so thick in the gulleys that one cannot break through them. The herbaceous vegetation makes great hummocks on the peat. An enormous cushion plant is common. (I think one could sink up to one's knees in it.) A cushion Androsace (as I took it to be) was spangled with yellow jewels. A number of plants had large showy flowers, the most common being one with yellow floral spikes. Finally, I saw what, in the Alps, would have been a Vanilla Orchid (*Nigritella*), but could not stop to examine it. Our time was passing and we had greater quarry.

Just above the head of an inlet, amid tussocks of grass, was a wallow in which several female or young Elephant Seals lay, as black and shining as the mud that coated them. They lifted their heads when we walked up to them, and a couple of them trumpeted at us. This was their private mud bath, where they got rid of the cleanness acquired in the open sea, and they eyed us askance as we took photographs of them in it. One finally made off, laboring down the slope toward the inlet, but slid into a muddy hollow with steep sides, tried to heave itself up and out again, failed, and gave up. I had the impression that its thoughts, as it looked up at us with its big dark eyes, were as dark as the peat water in which it lay.

Under a fine drizzle, now, we climbed the steep slope of St. Col Ridge, through the tussocks of grass, until we came to the first of the Royal Albatross nests that dotted the slope at intervals of, perhaps, four hundred to six hundred feet. When at last the three of us stood beside the great black and white fowl on its grass nest it merely clapped its bill several times in acknowledgment of our presence. But it closed its bill on Crompton's arm, albeit in halfhearted fashion, when he pushed his hand under it and heaved it up to draw its single white egg out and put it back again.

Seen on its nest at one's feet, a Royal Albatross, although not as large as a swan, is of the same order of magnitude. Its shape, however, is altogether different. The swan has a body of smooth curves diminishing toward the tail. The body of the albatross is a square box, relatively short, and higher in back than in front. Its neck, although not long, is not missing. Its head is distinctly larger than a swan's head, as it must be to support such a massive bill. Most beautiful is the color and texture of the plumage. The head, out of which the dark eye looks, and the forepart of the body have an even whiter whiteness than the whiteness of swans. The plumage of head and neck, in texture and color alike, could be ermine. The slaty mottling of the upper wing coverts blends aft into slate-black feathers finely edged with white.

One thing puzzled me as I looked at the high, boxlike body. In all long-winged birds, when at rest, the wing-tips project behind, generally crossing each other above the tail, and the joint of the wing is sometimes conspicuous by being carried far forward on either side of the breast — as in terns. Here, however, was the bird that, except for the almost identical Wandering Albatross, had perhaps the longest wings of any living species — but where were they? Short as the body was, no wing-tips projected, and the joints were hidden under the fluffed-out contour feathers. There were, however, a couple of humps on the back, two thirds of the way toward the tail, such as I had seen on no other birds, and which accounted for the fact that the body became higher aft.

A lone albatross without a nest, perhaps a young bachelor, was standing in the grass near the top of the ridge, so we put the question to it. Crompton held it by the bill while I unfolded one of its wings and walked it out to its full length. Then the secret was out.

The extended wing of other species — for example, gulls — has

Nesting Royal Albatross on Campbell Island

only two noticeable segments, an inner and an outer, meeting at a joint in the middle. The difference in wing length between short-winged and long-winged birds is, for the most part, a difference in the length of the inner segment. In fact, these two segments are homologs of the human forearm and hand respectively, the joint between them being homologous to the human wrist.

Where, then, is the upper arm?

On most birds this innermost of three segments is so short and close against the body that it does not show at all as a distinct part of the wing, which appears to have only the two segments and the one articulation between them. The case is different with the great albatrosses, which owe some of their extraordinary length of wing to the length of this inner segment. Where the wing appears to fold only once on most birds, it may be seen to fold at two joints on the great albatrosses, at the elbow as well as at the wrist. The folded wing, from its articulation with the body at the shoulder, extends backward along the body to the hump I have already referred to, which is the elbow; from there it extends forward again to the wrist; and from the wrist back again along the flank. Where virtually the entire wing of any other bird lies in only two folds, that of a great albatross lies in three, so that its entire length is accommodated against its short body without the tip projecting behind or the wrist protruding in front.

I have set down this explanation in detail because I have seen no account in the literature of a great albatross's wing or of the way it folds.

All the nests of the Royal Albatrosses were on the lee or southeast slope of St. Col Ridge, so that when one of the birds wanted to take to the air (which they can do only into the wind and, unless the wind is strong, by launching themselves from a height), it had first to walk laboriously up through the hummocks to the ridge, where it could take off facing the western ocean and the wind that came around the world from the west.*

Leaving the Royal Albatrosses and turning right to descend the

* Some weeks later I had occasion to visit a remarkable nesting colony of Royal Albatrosses on the Otago Peninsula in New Zealand. However, rather than interrupt my narrative of the southward voyage here, I give my account of it in Appendix B, to which the interested reader may wish to refer.

Nesting Light-mantled Sooty Albatross and chick

slope of the hill obliquely, we marched down into a draw and on up the other side of it toward the peak of Mt. Lyall (1,355 feet). The slope got steep toward the top, where some volcanic scree led to a series of short stepped cliffs. On one of the first steps, merely a narrow ledge clothed in grass and fern, was a fantastic bird on a grass nest built up into a truncated cone. This was the Light-mantled Sooty Albatross. It was slighter, slenderer, and more somber than the Royal Albatross, a bird of shades and shadings rather than black and white. The dark bill was comparatively thin and elegant. The forepart of the head was almost black, shading behind and down the neck to what became a most delicate light gray on the back and underparts. The wings folded against its flanks were a medium gray, and all deepened into sooty dark toward the tail. Most references to nature as an artist are mere cant, but there are occasions when one is suddenly struck by the truth of the statement, by the fact that it is so in a profound sense. Surely this fantastic bird is the product of something more than the mere utility that is the basis of natural selection.

What, one may ask, does the work of a Picasso have to do with the work of a blind process like natural selection? The question is pertinent, because this bird on its nest is more plausible as the product of the former than of the latter. (There are philosophical implications here, if we would only apply our minds to them.)

The last and most striking touch of the artist is a small half-ring of pure white against the black head, simply outlining the posterior half of the dark eye. It is the only white on the bird, and the only abrupt mark in a design of pastel shadings. The artist, when he got to this point, saw that without it the bird would appear incomplete, as if it had no eye. The eye had to be made to stand out, and it was beautifully done.

This elegant bird greeted us, as we climbed up to its pedestal, like the royalty we had just left, by bill-clapping. Because its more delicate bill made less noise, however, the clapping had to be supplemented by grunts. Like the Royal Albatross, it closed its bill on Crompton's arm when he put his hand under its body to draw out and check on the egg.

We turned, now, having seen what we had set out to see, and made our way back to where the helicopter waited for Mike and me. The five hours were just up as we took off our Wellingtons.

Soon the *Staten Island* was moving out of Perseverance Harbour and rounding South Point, with its cliffs, to make south under gray skies and a wild west wind. Shortly after that she was being flung about like a cork on the ocean. When men and objects began to break loose and hurtle about inside her, we changed course eastward to run more nearly with the wind and the sea. For all our easting, however, we were still moving south along.

> The ship drove fast, loud roared the blast,
> And southward aye we fled.

5. Wanderers All

On December 27 a rough sea under a heavy west wind compelled us to run south-southeast until midday, when our position was 56°40′S., 173°E. In the afternoon a northward shift in the wind enabled us to correct course to south by east. The weather was overcast and there was the thinnest of fogs. Sometime during the evening we crossed the Antarctic Convergence, that line beyond which the surface of the sea is composed of the colder, fresher water that flows north from the melting ice.

The morning of the twenty-eighth was again overcast, the wind heavy from the northwest, and by midday the barometer had fallen below 29. Then it began to rise again, and the wind came around some 180° to blow from the southeast. So it was that the day after we had come to our first Antarctic surface water we came to our first Antarctic air; for this was the katabatic wind that flows down off the continent and, curving westward, becomes the prevailing east wind of these high latitudes. It brought the Antarctic cold with it. All day the temperature dropped until it was below freezing, and for a good part of the afternoon a light snow fell. By evening, however, the sea had become relatively calm and the sun of the Antarctic summer had emerged to shine over it — as it still was shining at ten o'clock, when I went below.

It was on this same day, the twenty-eighth, that we came to the

Cape Pigeon

first outposts of the Antarctic. The watch had sighted an iceberg between two and three that morning. I saw our second on the horizon ahead at eleven, rising above the sea like "an arm clothed in white samite, mystic, wonderful." By nine in the evening we were sailing among ice islands to right and left, the progeny of the Ross Ice Shelf. Their tops were flat; their sides were cliffs perhaps a hundred feet high, sometimes hollowed into shining caves within which the waves foamed. There were also smaller bergs worn by the sea into fantastic shapes. These bergs, great and small, had come north to meet us and give notice that we were approaching a new world.

The next day we entered that world.

The Cape Pigeon

There are two marine environments, which I shall call the sea and the ice, and between them a boundary almost as sharp as a shore-line. Corresponding to the two environments, there are birds of the sea and birds of the ice, seals of the sea and seals of the ice. From Wellington to the frontier was all one avifauna, from there on a different avifauna. Consequently, having now arrived at the remote end of the sea, I pause to give an account of its bird-life before entering the world beyond.

All the birds to be seen away from land, in our course from New Zealand to the Antarctic, belonged to the only order made up exclusively of fliers that roam the open seas, the Procellari-iformes. Those I saw when we came out of Wellington Harbour were new to me, except for the gulls and Giant Petrels that I had met for the first time only so recently. It seemed as if all the birds I had been reading about for forty years were there, including Wandering Albatrosses, smaller species of albatross, and . . . . But I must take them one at a time in this narrative, as I had, at

last, to take them one at a time from the helicopter deck of the
Staten Island.

I would not have believed beforehand that under such circumstances the Wandering Albatross would not have been the first for
my attention. Elsewhere I have told how my interest in birds was
originally aroused by William Beebe's account of it in his *Arc-
turus Adventure*. I was, at the time, an undergraduate who
should have been studying for examinations. By revulsion from
the dimness of my academic vision, however, I had turned in
imagination to the seabirds of the southern hemisphere, and first
of all to *Diomedea exulans*, greatest of all. For several years
thereafter I did what I was supposed to be doing with my left
hand, while devouring all the literature on the albatross and the
other oceanic wanderers that I could obtain. This interest had
never died. For forty years, as occasion allowed, I had read about
the birds of the sea — and always the great albatross had led the
list. As we emerged from Wellington Harbour into the open
Pacific, however, my first great albatrosses were off in the distance, while ranging close in to the ship were birds I had also
read about for years without seeing, and which now held my
attention.

I have already published observations on the form and flight of
the Arctic Fulmar (pronounced *ful'mer*), which is one of the few
Procellariiform species that breeds in the high latitudes of the
North Atlantic. About the size of a Ring-billed or a Common
Gull, with basically the same gray and white coloration, it is built
for swift flight in the gales of the open sea, rather than, like a gull,
for drifting and soaring over coastal waters. Its big head continuous with its body, its tail short and broad, it is a flying cylinder.
The straight and narrow wings stick out from its body like laths
on which it alternates intervals of gliding with intervals of rapid

beating. The birds that were now crisscrossing our wake in fast flight, coming repeatedly under our counter, were, in their form and manner of flight, small fulmars.

Because the Cape Pigeon (also known as Pintado Petrel) is so abundant over all the south temperate and sub-Antarctic seas, and such an addicted ship-follower, it has always been the best known of seabirds to the mariners in southern oceans — which explains its possession of an affectionate if unscientific vernacular name. It is so distinctively a fulmar in its outward form that I would not have been surprised if the taxonomists had included it in the genus *Fulmarus*, rather than giving it a genus, *Daption*, all to itself. It is usual to group the two species of *Fulmarus* (the Arctic and the Antarctic Fulmar) with the Cape Pigeon, the Giant Petrel, the Antarctic Petrel, the Snow Petrel, and the prions as constituting a group referred to as the fulmarine petrels — or, simply, the fulmars. If the species of *Fulmarus* represent the type, then in terms of outward form and manner of flight I can see the association unmistakably only in the case of the Cape Pigeon, which I would immediately identify as a fulmar even if I had never before heard of it. I can see it hardly at all in the case of the Giant Petrel, which is why I have not been quite able to adopt, here, its alternative vernacular name, Giant Fulmar. But I could easily have called the Cape Pigeon "the Little Fulmar" or "the Pied Fulmar," for it is a little pied fulmar that follows ships.

In their shape and flight the birds now swarming around our stern and crisscrossing our wake were perfect little fulmars: the same thick cylindrical bodies that, in the absence of necks, made one piece with the round heads; the same tails, broad at the base and short; the same lathlike wings; the same rapid, stiff wing-beats. They differed entirely, however, in the striking pattern of their plumage, which made a sharp contrast of black and white. The whole upper surface of the Cape Pigeon's extended wings is black, with two white patches on each, one close to the body and one farther out. The head is black, as is the upper part of the back, which becomes mottled with white aft. The tail is white with a broad black terminal band. The black of the head continues down the throat to a sharp separation from the white underparts. The undersides of the wings are white bordered with black, and when the bird is seen from below against a bright sky the two white patches on the upper side of each wing show on the underside as translucent windows.

The plumage I have just described varies, some birds having more white, depending on geographical provenance, degree of wear, and perhaps the age of the individual bird.

Resting on the surface, as in flight, the Cape Pigeon is a small fulmar, its short body wedge-shaped, broadest in the bow. One swimming with folded wings surprised me by a quick surface dive, disappearing completely like a grebe, but only for a second or two. (Birds that have their feet far aft, as the fulmars do, can dive from the surface the more easily, but have difficulty walking on land.)

The Cape Pigeons that followed us occasionally demonstrated the manner in which the albatrosses and all except the smallest petrels take off from the water, by hydroplaning. Facing into the wind, the bird extends its wings and, lifting its body out of the water by the action of its feet, runs along the surface until it has gained flying speed and can bring its feet up to rest under its tail. (Gulls, when they use their feet at all for takeoff, work them together in a series of hops.) Like the Arctic Fulmar, in a calm sea it sometimes adopts hydroplaning as a mode of progression in itself, running over the water with stiffly extended wings but not taking off. Also like the other Procellariiformes, it has the trick of holding its wings above its back when it alights on the water for only a moment or two. Procellariiform birds, for the most part, do not fold away their wings unless they mean to settle down for a spell.

The Cape Pigeons were with us most of the time every day until we got well into the pack-ice, when I saw no more — until one surprised me by showing up in the Ross Sea off the coast of Queen Victoria Land, at about 72°S. While they tend to avoid the pack-ice, they nest at a number of points along the Antarctic coast between about 50°E. and the Ross Sea at 170°E. (Enderby Land and Wilkes Land).

The Great Albatrosses

I mentioned in Chapter 2 that the albatrosses are divided into the eleven species of the genus *Diomedea* and the two of *Phoebetria* (the sooty albatrosses). The species of *Diomedea* that occur in the southern hemisphere fall, in turn, into two groups. There are the two great albatrosses, the Wandering and the Royal, indistinguishable from each other in the adult plumage (unless seen close up), and the mollymawks, which are smaller but still of great size.

All that first afternoon and evening out of Wellington we were followed by Wandering Albatrosses, generally four or five, which could be distinguished from Royals by the fact that none wore quite the full adult plumage (which it takes them half a lifetime to acquire). The next day, when we had an overtaking wind, three passed separately during the morning but paid no attention to us. In the evening a young one in the brown plumage stationed itself in our wake and was still following us at nightfall, about eleven o'clock. All the next day, Christmas, there were several great albatrosses following us, mostly young Wanderers, but the proportion in the adult plumage increased during the afternoon until they were in the majority. Presumably the Wanderers were being joined by Royal Albatrosses, and this was the more likely because we were in the latitudes of the Royal breeding colonies in the Chatham Islands and on the Otago Peninsula of South Island. All the great albatrosses I saw from the ship the next day, when we made Campbell Island, were in the adult plumage, and presumably most of them were Royals. None, however, undertook to follow us. The next day I saw no great albatrosses at all; and the day after, when we came among the first icebergs, I saw a total of three Wanderers: a brown young in the morning, a near adult in the early afternoon, and another near adult among the bergs in the evening. None took notice of us, and they were the last I saw. The range of the Wandering Albatross, although it extends farther south than that of the Royal, stops at the ice.

In legend and literature the Wandering Albatross is known almost exclusively as a follower of ships. It will be seen from the above account, however, that many of those I saw paid no attention to our ship. Those that did follow, moreover, never came right up to her like the Black-browed Albatrosses, the Giant Petrels, and the Cape Pigeons. Since none of the great albatrosses in the full adult plumage followed us at all, it follows that we were never followed by a Royal. If the great albatrosses did come in as close to ships as the Black-browed Albatrosses, for example, hanging over the stern rail, there would be no difficulty in distinguishing the fine details (the construction and coloration of the bill) that make it possible to tell the one species from the other. Indeed, at a hundred feet there should be no difficulty for any observer armed with binoculars. As the authorities agree that it is virtually never possible to make the distinction from shipboard, I conclude that, in fact, these birds normally remain some distance behind the ships they follow. A plausible explanation would be that, in the competition to be first at the food dumped overboard or stirred up by a vessel's passage, the smaller birds, being more agile, would have the advantage. On the other hand, the great albatrosses would have no trouble in driving them away from the big dumps that they had reached first.

I should add that the size of the great albatrosses makes possible an adequate general view even of a bird that approaches no closer than a couple of hundred feet and that may, for the most part, remain three hundred feet or more behind.

In my account of the Royal Albatrosses nesting at Campbell Island I mentioned that the innermost of the three parts into which a bird's wing is divided, corresponding to the upper arm in man, is longer in the great albatrosses than in other birds. This was quite apparent in the flying birds, being a principal factor in their distinctive appearance, especially at such moments as their wings happened to be slightly drawn in rather than fully outstretched.

For the most part, the uniquely long, narrow wings of the great albatrosses in planing flight are hardly flexed at the joints. By contrast with such soaring birds of the land as eagles and vultures, however, their wings are generally bowed, rather than flat or sloping upward. Sometimes they seem as if made of whalebone held stiffly out, with weights at the tips to spring them down.

The great albatrosses commonly fly tipped up on one wing or the other. As they sweep over the sea, continuously rising and falling in arabesques, they tilt first one way, then the other. Sometimes they seem like swimmers, with long arms held rigid, who slowly roll their bodies from side to side so as to bring one arm down after the other in successive strokes.

Most observers report that the great albatrosses may sail for hours without a beat of the wings. I rather think that, if the birds could speak for themselves, they would say such a feat would be easy but not worth performing. As long as there is at least a moderate wind over waves, a great albatross has all it needs to remain aloft without flapping. In my observation, however, the sweeping arabesques of the albatrosses were frequently punctuated by a few easy beats, presumably for purposes of maneuver. These beats were like musical ornaments in the rhythm of tilting and circling, grace notes in an andante.

What I found most remarkable was the way the lower wing-tip of the tilted bird would move swiftly over the rough surfaces of the running waves — always so close as almost to touch them, but without ever actually doing so. It would conform to every irregularity, so precisely as even to flutter over the ripples. The only explanation I am able to conceive is that the wing-tip responds automatically to variations in the pressure of the cushion of air between it and the surface. Even so, the automatic precision of adjustment required to sweep tilted like this over the manifold and heaving irregularities of the sea, big and little, with the wing-tip almost scoring the surface, is astonishing. The same feat is constantly performed by the other species of albatross as well, and by the Giant Petrel.

The bill of a great albatross is conspicuous for its size, even in proportion to so large a bird. The bills of the other albatrosses are smaller in proportion, and the smaller Procellariiform birds have bills proportionately smaller still. Another feature is the extreme shortness of the tail, contrasting with the relative bigness of the webbed feet that extend beyond it. Undoubtedly such big feet are useful to the albatrosses in launching themselves from the sucking surface of the sea, which they can do only by springing their great bodies free and then pedalling hard over it.

Surely no bird is more completely pelagic than the Wandering Albatross, which may spend the first nine years after leaving the nest circumnavigating the earth without ever touching land, and which then, as a rule, comes to land for breeding only every other year.* Therefore one does not expect to find it, like the gulls, a city bird scavenging in man's harbors. However, on January 17, I was walking among the dockyards on the Wellington waterfront when . . . . But I may as well quote the notes I made at the time.

I walked down to the waterfront by the railway station, and at the slip of the Lyttleton ferry found not only two Giant Petrels swimming about the sterns of the great ships moored to the docks, but also an adult Wandering Albatross. I asked the albatross to stay right where he was, got a taxi at the station, picked up my camera at the hotel, and returned to find my bird still *in situ*. . . . I photographed him at 20 meters [65 feet]. At one point, when the Black-backed Gulls began swooping toward the stern of the adjacent steamer (where, perhaps, someone had thrown some food out), he raised his wings and, running along the surface against a mere breeze, just like a Fulmar or Cape Pigeon, took off for a few flaps and landed again at the scene of the possible feast. (But there was nothing.) . . . Through the binoculars I could distinctly see the nostrils, different from those of the Royal, the lack of a dark line at the cutting edge of mandible, and the bill that was pinkish to the tip, which was abruptly cream.†

* Fisher and Peterson, 1964, p. 30.
† In these notes I referred to this individual as a male because at the time I shared the general impression, supported by most of the literature, that the adult female can be distinguished from the adult male by a dark patch on her crown. Now,

I was also prompted by this albatross to set it down in my notes as a rule that "the bigger the bird, the bigger in proportion is its bill," adding "Look at gulls, petrels, hawks." To exemplify this, I cite the following: the bill of the Wandering Albatross averages about ⅕ its length; the bill of the smaller Black-browed Albatross (mollymawk) somewhat more than ⅐ its length; and the bill of the much smaller Southern Black-backed Gull somewhat more than ⅒ its length. The smaller gulls would be found to have proportionately still smaller bills. The rule appears to apply equally to all categories of birds, not just seabirds. I offer, here, a speculative suggestion of the direction in which an explanation may be found. The larger a bird the larger the size of the pieces of food it can carry or tear apart; the larger the pieces with which it copes, the larger in proportion to the size of its body its bill must be; and this requirement is the more readily met in that the weight of the bill does not increase at the same rate as its volume, so that the larger the bird the greater the proportionate size of the bill it is able to carry. I offer this as an hypothesis: let someone put it to the proof.

The Mollymawks

The species of mollymawks in the south temperate and sub-Antarctic seas are five. Three of them — the Black-browed, the Gray-headed, and the White-capped — because they range farther south than the other two, are circumpolar. The Yellow-nosed Albatross occurs only in the South Atlantic and Indian oceans (that is, west of Australia and east of Cape Horn), while Buller's

---

however, it has been virtually settled that this mark represents merely the relatively greater length of years that it takes the female to acquire the fully adult plumage with all-white head. See Tickell, 1968.

Albatross occurs only in the South Pacific (east of Australia and west of the Horn). All five are basically alike, varying in details. It is a curious circumstance, which may reflect convergent evolution, that in several respects they appear to be intermediate between the great albatrosses and the wholly unrelated species of black-backed gulls. They are midway in size between the great albatrosses and, for example, the Southern Black-backed Gull. Instead of having white backs in the adult plumage with black on the outer ends or hind margins of the wings only, like the great albatrosses, they have solid black mantles from wing-tip to wing-tip, like the gulls. And instead of short tails, beyond which the trailing feet extend, they have tails like those of the gulls that extend beyond the feet. They are also more like the gulls in that the length of the innermost section (or upper arm) of their wings appears proportionately shorter than in the great albatrosses — although the wings remain longer and relatively narrower than those of the gulls, as befits massive birds adapted to the winds of the high seas. Finally, they tend to hold their wings, in flight, rather more as gulls do, with a noticeable bend at the wrist — although in this, too, they are intermediate.

The first afternoon out of Wellington not a few mollymawks were to be seen; but, like the great albatrosses, they did not come close or follow in our wake. I attribute this to the fact that, being so near land as we still were, the space above and behind the ship's stern was preempted by the horde of Black-backed Gulls, although a few Giant Petrels (as large as the mollymawks) also followed, swiftly crisscrossing our wake close in, not to mention the quick and darting Cape Pigeons.

The following day, that of the morning fog and the overtaking wind, I saw an occasional Black-brow, but none chose to follow us more than momentarily. On the other hand, an occasional

White-capped Albatross emerged from the fog in the morning, and one followed us closely for a spell. It did this by way of belying its other vernacular name, Shy Albatross, which corresponds to its scientific name, *cauta*. Apparently, John Gould, who gave it its scientific name in the 1840s, was impressed by the fact that it stayed away from the ship in which he was travelling, and therefore he named it the Shy Albatross. It has not, however, been shy of the ships in which other observers have travelled, so that it is less misleading to call it the White-capped Albatross. ("I think it wrong," wrote Tristram Shandy, "merely because a man's hat has been blown off his head by chance the first night he comes to Avignon, — that he should therefore say, 'Avignon is more subject to high winds than any town in all France.' ")

It is a mollymawk of distinction. A dark streak through the eye gives it an air of seriousness. Its face is light gray below the eye (at least in the race, *salvini,* that honored the *Staten Island* with its attention), and this forms just enough of a contrast with the whiteness of the head above the eye to justify the epithet "white-capped." For the rest, it is completely white under the wing — except for the thinnest of black margins to set off the whiteness, and an artistically effective black spot where the leading edge of the wing joins the body.

The next day was Christmas, we had cleared South Island, and with the west wind blowing stiffly across our course we headed a procession made up chiefly of Black-browed Albatrosses. The vanguard hung over our stern rail as the gulls had on the first day, the rest streaming behind. As usual, the Giant Petrels crossed back and forth over our wake, while the Cape Pigeons, time and again, almost brushed the ship's iron flanks and stern.

The following day, after we left Campbell Island, there was no time when I could not count at least seventy Black-brows in our wake. One of them, distinguishable by a missing flight feather, circled us all day.

Throughout the next day, now among the icebergs, we were followed by from five to eight Black-brows. One alone followed the next morning, accompanying us right up to the frontier between the sea and the ice, but no farther. It was our last.

The honey-colored eye of the Black-brow is almost enclosed in a black patch, and bounded above by the long black streak of its "eyebrow," which seems to press upon it in a frown. This gives it the facial expression of a glowering pedant. The eyebrow and the all-yellow bill help to distinguish the species, but what does so chiefly at a distance is the fact that the white underside of the wing has an irregular margin of black so wide that the white itself appears simply as a long central lightening.

When garbage was dumped from the stern the waiting Black-brows, in their competition to get to it first, would collapse in the air, tumbling like balloons suddenly torn, their wings wavering above their falling bodies, their big feet extended for the crash.

Generally I saw one Gray-headed Albatross every day, but only one, until we got to the ice. None, however, followed the ship or came close up. Therefore, although I saw the species, I cannot say that I observed it. As I look at the total I find that I did, in fact, see every species of albatross that occurs commonly in these latitudes of the Pacific (Buller's Albatross being never more than a rarity).

The Light-mantled Sooty Albatross

To anyone who himself crosses the frontier between the sea and the ice, the reason why the great albatrosses and mollymawks do not is clear. The conditions on which they depend for their easy flight do not exist beyond it. The west-wind belt stops at the frontier — in fact, it creates the frontier, for the west wind is what arrests the northward drift of the sea-ice, causing it to accumulate in a ring against this barrier — and the easterlies that occur from the frontier south are relatively light. Moreover, the great plates of ice suppress the waves, flattening the sea except for a residual swell. Without the combination of big wind and big waves, any great albatross or mollymawk that crossed the frontier would find itself suddenly deprived of its normal aids to levitation. The Giant Petrels, more adventurous and aggressive, extend their range to the continent itself, even nesting at some points along its shore; but south of the frontier they can remain aloft, generally, only by beating their wings.

One albatross there is that crosses the frontier freely to range all the way down to the continent itself, but even among its kind it is an aerial prodigy.

The two species of the genus *Phoebetria,* the Sooty Albatross and the Light-mantled Sooty Albatross, are specialized for buoyant flight as no other species are, with the single exception of the tropical frigate birds. These latter are all sail and no ballast, for they have the greatest wing area in proportion to weight of any birds. This enables them to float like paper kites on the mere zephyrs of the tropics. The two species are second only to the frigate birds in this specialization. They have smaller bodies than any of the other albatrosses, and proportionately longer wings, proportionately smaller feet, and long pointed tails.*

Like the Yellow-nosed Albatross, the darker of the two sooties, because it does not go quite as far south as the circumpolar

* Since the measurements vary for individual birds, the following figures are only rough averages. In the Wandering Albatross and the Black-browed Albatross the wingspread is 3.28 times the length of the body minus the tail, while the equivalent figure for the two sooty albatrosses is 3.64. In the Wandering Albatross the tail represents 1/6 the overall length, in the Black-brow 1/5, while the equivalent figure for the two sooties is 1/3.

ocean, is confined in its longitudinal range to the waters east of South America and west of Australia. The Light-mantled, on the other hand, having the most southerly range of any albatross, is completely circumpolar.

The great albatrosses and the mollymawks, as distinct from the two sooties, are massive birds that depend on the momentum of their mass in a high wind — momentum being the product of mass and velocity. Living as they do in unobstructed space, they have little occasion for tight maneuvers or sudden stops. According to those who have witnessed it, when they land on their nesting grounds, which they can do only in flat open areas, they have difficulty reducing their speed enough, so that the Wanderers sometimes tip up on their noses and tumble over before coming to a stop. To take the air again they generally have to launch themselves from a height and into a wind. The two sooty albatrosses, by contrast, are notable for their deftness on the wing, which they have sometimes demonstrated by landing on the tip of a ship's mast. The lightness of their bodies, relative to the size of their wings, and, above all, their long cuneate tails, enable them to land gently enough on the ledges of their nesting cliffs. A great albatross, trying to land at the nesting site of a Light-mantled Sooty, would surely be wrecked.

One consequence of their aerial virtuosity is that the sooty albatrosses are not as dependent as the others on the combination of heavy wind and big waves for their support. They often fly higher, taking less advantage of the updraft against the waves or of the differential in the wind's velocity caused by its friction against the waves. Presumably the ratio between their weight and the area of their wings, as in the case of the frigate birds, makes it easier for them to ride light breezes. Under these circumstances it is not surprising that the Light-mantled ranges freely into the realm of pack-ice, calm seas, and light easterlies. If the other sooty does not do this as well, that is surely because its Light-mantled congener has already preempted the scene.

My first Light-mantled Sooty Albatross crossed our wake far behind just as the fog lifted on our second day out. It passed like a distant ghost and I saw it no more. I daresay that now as I write, in the middle of the austral winter following that austral summer, it is still gliding over the face of the waters, crossing the longitudes of the Pacific, the Atlantic, or the Indian Ocean, perhaps gliding around and around the world. If I could send it greeting, across the gulf of incommunicability, I would do so.

> But what I said it would not hear,
> And what I meant it could not know.
> Around a single globe we go,
> Each moving in his separate sphere.

Every day after that I repeatedly saw one, two, or three at a time, until I saw my last in the pack-ice just across the frontier between two worlds. Often one or two accompanied us for a time, but never did I see one actually follow. This is to say that they would circle us, sometimes fairly close in, sometimes in the middle distance. Sweeping high, sweeping low, tilting this way and that on motionless wings, they would come up from behind the ship, pass her as if indifferent to her existence — only to cross ahead, circle far back, and come up again. All this without any visible effort.

On the wing as on the nest they seemed creatures of art. In my notes for Christmas Day I have the following:

> Like the Wanderer, they did not simply follow in the stern but ranged alongside, close or far away. Especially when one sees the conspicuous white behind the eye, it is hard to be-

lieve they are not an invention by Walt Disney. . . . The
wings are too long, slender, and sharply pointed to be real;
the black bill is also long and elegant as the bills of other
albatrosses are not; I don't know what the bayonet tail is for
[this was before I had seen where the birds nested], but it is
fitting in the context and beautiful; and the pastel shading is
lovely. Of all fowl, this, surely, is the most elegant. Its wings
have the springy and bowed appearance of the Wanderers',
and its style of flight is the same; except that, the few times I
saw it flap, the wing-beats were rapid and sharp.

The Light-mantled Sooty Albatross, as I have said, is found in
the ring of pack-ice, beyond it, and even along the shores of the
continent itself. The most elegant of the albatrosses is the only
one that occurs in zones of the most hostile climate known to life
on earth.

Shearwaters and Gadflies

One would like to know all the shearwaters better. To the shipboard observer they are among the most elusive of seabirds,
paying no attention to ships at all, normally remaining so low
between the waves that the observer catches only occasional
glimpses of them in the confusion of the shifting sea. Their form
and the style of flight that has given them their name are distinctive. Picture a torpedo with excessively narrow blades extending
from amidships on either side, each blade forming a flat V with
the point forward. This bladed projectile shoots along the slope
of the running wave, tilting up first on one side then the other to
conform to the shifting masses of water against which the wind is
deflected. Typically, the underside is light, the topside dark, so
that, as the projectile tilts, it changes back and forth from black
to white against the glaucous sea. A large travelling flock seen at
a distance looks like clusters of lights going on and off.

The many species of shearwater vary from moderately small to moderately large. I have seen flocks of the small Manx Shearwater off the Aegean coast of Greece, twinkling against Homer's wine-dark sea. What I cherish especially, however, is another memory.

It was just after dawn on March 31, 1969, and I was perched in the forepeak of the S.S. *Ancerville*, approaching the main island of Madeira from the northeast, having come through the Straits of Gibraltar the previous evening. Ahead of us and somewhat to the left, the three peaks of the Desertas, those uninhabited rocks in the sea, were just rising above the horizon. Soon the main island of Madeira, too, began to grow out of the horizon ahead. The rhythmically heaving sea across which we lifted and plunged was covered by a moving carpet of Cory's Shearwaters, one of the larger species. They were coming from their nesting grounds on the Desertas, coasting along the slopes of the waves, crossing ahead of us. "For at least 2 hours," I noted that evening, "beginning when we came within sight of Desertas, the sea was covered with them, many passing just under our prow. Never have I seen such a wonderful silhouette, the bird sharp of outline and swift as an arrow, moving just over the rough running surface of the sea, tilting this way and that on set wings, first white then dark, with only occasionally a few easy wing-beats." For two hours, in the rising and plunging forepeak of the ship, the nearest birds passing below me as if unaware, I watched the spectacle — until at last we rounded the east point of Madeira and moved along the coast toward the port of Funchal.

Although shearwaters of one species or another occur over all the seas, I think of them as birds of temperate and tropical waters rather than of the high latitudes in either hemisphere. Here I must digress, however, to note that the vernacular terms used to distinguish the subgroups of the family Procellariidae — such as fulmarine petrels, gadfly petrels, and shearwaters — are often vague in their applicability to particular species. Only the members of the genus *Puffinus* invariably bear the name "shearwater," and if, taking the narrowest view, we should regard them as the only true shearwaters, it would follow that only one species, the Sooty Shearwater, occurs in Antarctic or even sub-Antarctic waters.

The Sooty Shearwater is one of only six species of birds (out of between eight and nine thousand in the world) that, nesting in the southern hemisphere as far south as New Zealand, then migrate to spend the southern winter beyond the tropics in the summer of the northern hemisphere. (The species that breed in the north temperate zone or higher and migrate to spend the northern winter beyond the tropics in the southern hemisphere would surely number in the thousands.) Five of the six belong to the one family, Procellariidae, the sixth belonging to the Procellariiform family Hydrobatidae. The Sooty Shearwater breeds in the islands south of New Zealand, as far as 55°S., but goes as far north as Alaska and Iceland during the southern winter.

For the first day and a half out of Wellington I saw occasionally, and at a distance, dark shearwaters or gadfly petrels, apparently of two species, that I could not identify certainly if at all — sometimes looking like great swifts, sometimes with slow wing-beats, sometimes with rapid; sometimes seeming to have light underwings (but one could not be quite sure). The larger of the two bedevilled me for the first two and a half days (after which I saw it no more), because I was able to tell that it had a light bill, and if I had not been a man of conscience I would have set it down categorically as that noble bird, the White-chinned Petrel (which often has little if any white on the chin), also known as the Shoemaker and the Cape Hen. In fact, I did put it down as that, but with the qualification that I was indulging in "one of those it-could-be-nothing-else identifications." So it remained, and so I report it here.

I was finally able to identify the smaller of the two species without qualification, by the silver on the underside of its wings, as the Sooty Shearwater.

The Sooty Shearwater, in addition to being, as I suppose, one of the most abundant and widespread of seabirds, migrating through both the great oceans from the edge of the Antarctic to the edge of the Arctic, is also one of the few seabirds that form immense and densely packed flocks, like those of Red-winged Blackbirds or of Starlings, but larger. Darwin reported seeing, off the coast of southern Chile during the voyage of the *Beagle*, "hundreds of thousands [that] flew in an irregular line for several hours in one direction. When part of the flock settled on the water the surface was blackened. . . ." Dr. Murphy reports "a single dense flock," numbering more than 10,000, "that passed us, the long-winged, graceful shearwaters flying high and low in the howling wind over the choppiest areas of water." He also reports another occasion when the ship he was in "plowed through a flock of Sooty Shearwaters that covered perhaps a square kilometer of the ocean. The day was calm, and the birds in the steamer's path flapped or 'ran' to either side, making frequent and frantic dives. . . . Again, I have seen more distant and undisturbed rafts of the birds moving along, half in air, half on the water, in pursuit of shoals of anchovies of pejerreyes. In such cases the rear of the flock would continually pour forward over the vanguard, so that the whole formation seemed to roll like a flattened hoop across the water."*

Every day, until we reached the ice frontier, I saw these shearwaters — usually single birds, couples, or small companies — and among the icebergs at the southern limit of their range I

* Murphy, pp. 668 and 672.

saw a flock of about a hundred densely concentrated, some resting on the sea, with scattered individuals as outliers.

As I had begun, so I ended, wishing I could know them better.

And so with the miscellany of petrels, big and little, sometimes called gadfly petrels, of which *Pterodroma* is the typical genus. Seabirds that, for the most part, allow themselves to be glimpsed only at a distance ought at least to have conspicuous marks by which they can be identified. The desirability of this was overlooked in the design of many, but not in the bird known as the Mottled Petrel or Peale's Petrel, which is one of the six that, nesting in the south temperate zone (Pacific only, in its case), and roaming as far south as the ice frontier, winters in the north temperate zone, even as high as the Aleutian Islands. It is said to fly rapidly in high arcs that lift it well above the horizon. Gray above, with an irregular dark band on the wings and back that, as in so many seabirds, forms a flattened **W**, it is basically white underneath and is most readily identified, in my experience, by a black line like a scar on the white underside of the wing.

On December 27, the day we crossed the Antarctic Convergence, one flew ahead of us and alighted on the water — only to take off again at our approach, running over the surface to alight again, this time out of our way. That evening we passed another, in the middle distance to one side, and the next afternoon another. Among the tabular icebergs that same evening I saw three together in the distance. As fortune would have it, then, the only member of the typical gadfly genus I was to see well enough to identify was the one that bears the specific name *inexpectata*.

The Prions Oestrelatous

Several authors have referred to Wilson's Storm Petrel as perhaps the most numerous species of bird in the world. James Fisher and Roger Tory Peterson speculate that it is the most numerous after the House Sparrow and the common Starling, both of which owe their present abundance to the human civilization that has assisted their spread around the globe.

To anyone who sees the prions or whalebirds of the southern seas in their millions, they seem all one species that he could well believe to be the most abundant in the world — for the shipboard observer, at least, cannot distinguish the differences (chiefly in their bills) that cause them to be generally regarded, today, as constituting five species. They are about the size of Turtle Doves, which makes them very small indeed against the boundless space they inhabit, and not altogether dissimilar in form of body, wing, and tail. A Turtle Dove, however, has a head separated from its body by a distinct neck, and its tail is seen as a separate appendage; whereas the body of a prion is a stubby torpedo, the head being simply a rounding off in front, the tail a tapering off behind.

Seen from above, the prions have a pattern of dark and light that, peculiar in itself, is common to a variety of seabirds (and only seabirds), including wholly unrelated species. Like the young of those seagoing gulls in the high northern hemisphere, the kittiwakes, like the immature Little Gulls of the North Atlantic, like several gadfly petrels of the genus *Pterodroma,* and like the Blue Petrel, they have a gray mantle across which a flattened W is inscribed by dark feathers that extend along the forward edge of one wing from the point to the wrist, then diagonally to

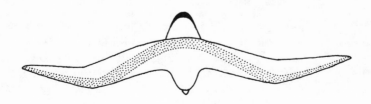

the rear edge of the wing at its juncture with the back, across the back, and so on across the other wing. Like the gulls mentioned, they also have black tips to their cuneate tails.

What is most remarkable about the five species of prion, to the anatomist and the evolutionist alike, are the forms of bill that chiefly distinguish them from one another. At one end of what may be regarded as a series of five is the Broad-billed Prion, with an extraordinarily specialized bill equipped with strainers on either side, like the whalebone in the mouth of a baleen whale, through which it expels the seawater it has taken into a pouch like a pelican's, thereby sifting out the organic matter that constitutes its food. At the other extreme is the Fairy Prion, with a relatively narrow bill that has no more than faint striations or rugosities where the Broad-bill has whalebone or its equivalent. The other prions have bills that appear to represent intermediate stages between the two extremes. It is as if, in living birds, one saw the stages of evolution by which mere striations had developed into important specialized organs. Dr. Murphy writes that the "group as a whole represents an excellent example of what might formerly have been termed orthogenesis"* — that is, evolution in a predetermined rather than an accidental direction. (Orthogenesis, even as a speculative conception, is so out of fashion in our time that no one can allow himself to acknowledge it as a possibility, even while he is offering "an excellent example" of it!)

Referring to the question of which is the most numerous species of bird in the world, Dr. Murphy writes:

> . . . an observer who has seen the flights of such southern forms as *Pachyptila* [the prion genus] filling the air like the flakes of a snowstorm, and stretching in all directions toward the circle of the horizon from daybreak until dark . . . might

* Murphy, p. 615.

be pardoned for extravagant assertions. The streaming rivers of the now-extinct Passenger Pigeons were doubtless composed of more densely packed birds; but this species travelled in concentrated formation, and was confined to the relatively small area of the North American continent. The whale-birds [another name for the prions], as represented by several species, apparently range through an almost unbroken belt of ocean, which is some thirty degrees of latitude in width and encircles the earth.*

I am grateful to Dr. Murphy (the last of the creative scientists whose creativity may be attributed to the combination of the scientific spirit with literary cultivation) for the addition of an excellent word to my vocabulary. He writes,

> The erratic gliding of these petrels is the most wild and airy type of flight among all birds; it might best be described by the term "oestrelatous" — goaded on by a gadfly. When the air is filled with a flock of whale-birds careening in the breeze, rising, falling, volplaning, twisting, sideslipping above the sea, now flashing their white breasts, now turning their almost invisible backs — they resemble the motes in a windy sunbeam.†

The first afternoon out of Wellington, once we got into open water, I began to see prions here and there — singles, couples, or three at a time — but always in the distance, low between the waves. In the vicinity of Wellington they were presumably Fairy Prions. The next day I saw none, and the day after only two separately in the distance. After we left Campbell Island, however, there were prions about constantly, singly or in companies of six or eight, darting and scooting among the waves, on rare occasions rising up high — once to cross over the ship. They had wings like those of doves, if narrower; and, like doves, they held

* Murphy, p. 489.
† Murphy, p. 485.

them partly bent rather than rigidly outstretched. They were quicksilver, flying swiftly but erratically, rapidly beating their wings and gliding, veering this way and that, tilting from side to side so that their white underparts twinkled, flashing on and off. Twice I saw prions mobbing a Great Skua, that predatory scavenger of the sea, following all its turns and twists, even rising high up with one.

By late afternoon and evening of the next day, when we had reached 57° or 58°S., the sea was thinly covered with them everywhere and constantly. I remarked in my notes that "if the sea is so covered for many miles they must number in the thousands of millions." They paid no attention to the ship at all, although so close on either side that the shipboard observer looked down on them. "They may sometimes have quite steady and rapid wing-beats," I noted, "like a small pigeon, and their form is a bit that of a Merlin. They bank first on one side, then the other, and are constantly changing direction abruptly. Three times I saw one alight on the water, head high, usually lifting its wings after a moment and darting off again. Two alighted repeatedly."

The day after, which was the one on which we met our first icebergs, "there was hardly a moment when one could not see some, and during most of the morning and half the afternoon they were as thick all about us as swifts on the Lake of Geneva on a cold day. Not infrequently, one will rise high in the sky, above bridge level, but still flying this way and that, changing course erratically. This erratic course makes them look very batlike in flight." These were presumably Antarctic Prions, which alone range this far south.

Beyond the frontier, which we came to the next day, I saw no more.

The Blue Petrel

The Blue Petrel is like the prions in size, in shape, and in markings, and it habitually flies in their flocks. The taxonomists, how-ever, tend to regard it as a gadfly petrel, related to those of the typical genus, *Pterodroma*. It was one of the species I was especially hoping to see, and so I remained alert every day for a bird that was most readily to be distinguished from the prions by the fact that its tail had a white rather than a dark tip. It was not until we had got among the icebergs that, looking down at the prions scudding erratically among the waves, appearing, disap-pearing, I saw one that seemed to have a white-tipped tail. "Striving on the tossing deck to confirm this with my binoculars," I wrote in my notes that evening, "I confirmed it absolutely, but lost any opportunity to observe anything else about the bird. So I have seen a Blue Petrel without observing it." A small bird low in the waves disappears as quickly as it appears.

Diving Petrels

Superficially, the five species of diving petrels, all belonging to one genus, resembling one another as closely as the five species of prion do, are utterly different from the other members of the order Procellariiformes. I have already given an account of them in Chapter II. At this point I should leave a page blank — for, although I spent five days in waters where they commonly occur, hoping and expecting to see them, it was not my fortune to have even so brief a glimpse of one as I had been allowed to have of the Blue Petrel.

Once we had entered the ice I could no longer hope to see any, for they do not, as we are about to do, cross that frontier.

Snow Petrel at nesting grounds near Cape Hallett

6. Across the Frontier

◆— AT THE BEGINNNING of Sutton Vane's play, *Outward Bound,* a miscellaneous company of passengers is aboard a ship that might almost be an ordinary liner on a transatlantic crossing. But the sky has an unreal light, and each passenger finds that he cannot remember how he happens to be where he is. Gradually, as they become acquainted with one another and learn that all are in a similar plight, it dawns on them that they have all passed a frontier, that they have left the world of the living and are "outward bound."

The same strangeness gradually possessed my mind December 29, the day we crossed the frontier between two worlds. When I came on deck at 7:30 A.M. we were sailing over a sea as blue as the Caribbean, but among the sculptured icebergs of some mythological realm. The sky was blue except for areas of thin cirrus. There was a breeze from the south. Five miles ahead and leading us was our sister ship, the *Burton Island,* which had come from south of Cape Horn for a rendezvous with us at four that morning. As the morning passed the cirrus disappeared, leaving the sky clear. Our position at noon was 66°25′S., 172°30′E., eight nautical miles (9.14 statute miles) north of the Antarctic Circle, which we crossed half an hour later. From now on there would be perpetual bright daylight, the sun never setting.

I have said that when I came on deck there were icebergs all around. There were also small blocks and plates of ice awash in the sea, rocked by the lapping waves. As the morning advanced we began to cut across one line after another of ice-floes, each wider and denser than the one before, until at last we were running through continuous pack-ice in the open track left by the *Burton Island*.

By mid-afternoon the sky had clouded and snow fell. Then the lower clouds passed, leaving a ceiling of high cirrus.

It was that evening — or in what should have been evening — that I at last began to lose the sense of being in a real world. The light was not normal. Although it was undoubtedly brilliant, objects looked dim in it. Everything was bathed in a ghost light that seemed to come as much from below as from above. The ice-floes extended to the horizon, with occasional wide leads, sometimes with open pools of gray water. And for the first time since we had left Wellington the sea was flat, except for a low swell that ran under the ice and the ruffled surfaces of such pools as were open enough to catch the breeze.

I say nothing at this point of the flying birds that were strange to me. The sense of having entered a world that was not the known world was intensified, however, by the sight of seals and penguins, bathed in the strange luminescence, on the ice through which we passed. Artists had sometimes imagined scenes like this, as Gustave Doré had in his illustrations for Coleridge's *Ancient Mariner*. But one had always supposed that they did not exist in reality — and for me some question remained, still, whether this one did.

The atmosphere, intensely cold, did not feel quite like anything I had experienced in the world now left behind. It was dry rather than oceanic. There was no haze to give atmospheric perspective to the scene, so that the ice-floes, the seals, the penguins, the ship ahead of us, although diminished in size by the intervening distance, remained no dimmer than what was up close.

From six in the evening until nine we moved through the thickest of the pack-ice in the open path left by the *Burton Island*. The ice itself was extraordinary, its white fields perhaps three feet thick, often pushed up into tentlike hummocks where adjacent floes had ground together or overridden one another. Their undersides, as one saw from their edges or from the bottoms of broken pieces partly upturned, were golden brown, stained with the microscopic cells of the vegetable plankton called diatoms. And, in the recesses formed by undercutting or by tented hummocks, some process of spectroscopic filtering caused the ice to glow with an azure light that deepened into cobalt.

At nine o'clock we emerged again into open sea, with only occasional irregular blocks and bits of ice floating here and there. We were inside the ring. At the same time the cirrus cleared away overhead, leaving the sun undisputed ruler over an elemental world of blue sky and blue water. The *Burton Island* in front and the *Staten Island* following, we continued steadily southward toward the continent ahead.

The next morning we were travelling through a generally ice-free sea under a low overcast. Snow fell occasionally. About noon we sighted, some forty-five miles to starboard, Cape Adare, and I had my first view of the Antarctic continent. The cape, as seen from the east, is a line of cliffs seamed with snow. It marks the corner where the shore of the continent turns abruptly south for a thousand miles to form the great bight that is the Ross Sea. During the rest of the afternoon, in the occasional glimpses of the continent to be caught between snow flurries, what one saw was dim black cliffs laced with white. They rose almost a mile out of the frozen white sea at their feet. Soon we were coming in closer, penetrating the continent's margin of pack-ice. At five o'clock, now enclosed by almost solid pack twenty-five miles off Cape Hallett, we slowed to a stop and the helicopters were made ready for our first landing on Antarctica. (I reserve the account of that, however, for the next chapter.)

It was midnight when we moved off again to resume our way south. The sun in the sky ahead of us was just breaking through the clouds. A tired but exalted passenger, returned from his first climb in the mountains of Antarctica, went below, deciding that the day was over for him whether the sun continued to shine or not.

The next day, New Year's Eve, I was on deck at 7:30. Except for the great white hump of Coulman Island to starboard, we might have been crossing the Mediterranean. All day the sun shone in a blue sky marked by streaming threads of high cloud. The temperature remained between 38° and 40°F. There was no ice except for a big berg that rose ahead of us in the early afternoon.

At this point, however, we swung around and headed back to Hallett. Word had come that the members of the scientific station there had forgotten to give us all their outgoing mail, so we were returning for it. That is how we happened to find ourselves again approaching, now on New Year's Day, the same iceberg we had been approaching the previous year, some twenty-four hours earlier. Again it was a sunny day with a light south wind. From midday on we were among icebergs. Soon the volcanic peaks of Terror and Erebus on Ross Island began to rise above the horizon ahead.

In *Sailing Directions for Antarctica,* published by the U.S. Naval Oceanographic Office, I find the following paragraph under the heading "Optical Phenomena":

In the Antarctic regions there is an almost complete absence of dust and other solid particles in the air, and the prevailing winds blowing off the continent are low in moisture content. These conditions favor high visibility and the mariner is warned of the error likely to be made in estimating distances, if this fact is not recognized and accepted.

When we first saw the white peaks against the blue sky ahead, our radar showed what their distance was. I took a photograph at the time, and when I now ask those who see it to guess the distance of the peaks their guess is usually twenty to forty miles. In point of fact, the distance measured by radar was 160 miles.

About four in the afternoon we suddenly entered pack-ice again, and a few hours later we were having to break our way in earnest. The ice was from four to eight or nine feet thick, with cracks or leads through which we turned and twisted, pushing the great floes slowly aside so that they cracked and rode up over their neighbors — until, as happened time and again, we were gradually brought to a full stop by the accumulated resistance. Then we would have to back away and try again.

Someone had remarked to me, before the voyage, that all possibility of sleep would surely end once the ship began breaking ice. This was plausible if one pictured her, as I had, repeatedly crashing into the ice and backing off to crash again. In point of fact, the motion involved is pure pleasure. The ship moves forward smoothly except for occasional little bumps as, widening a lead, she pushes the heavy floes aside. When her way is altogether blocked at last, she comes to a stop only gradually. Reversing to back off, and then moving forward again, involves no abruptness. Nor does the actual breaking of the ice that has blocked the way. On the undercut slope of her prow she rides smoothly up and over it until enough of her weight is on top so that it cracks, the broken plates to either side tilting to let her gently down into the water again. Lying in one's bunk, one feels frequently two or three easy bumps that give one the pleasant awareness of being in a moving rather than a stationary vessel, and occasionally one feels the front end rise and sink again as into a cushion.

What is endlessly fascinating is to watch the process from the bridge or the forepeak. The officer on duty stands in the open on one wing of the bridge in a state of excited alertness, shouting orders to the helmsman to turn the wheel hard this way or that. He is playing a game, estimating moment after moment which of the twisting leads will offer the best passage; but time and again a lead will angle so sharply that the ship is arrested or rides up over the floes. Then she has to back away and turn again. In itself, this is one of those activities that holds one's attention like the flames of a wood fire. While it was going on the members of the crew who were off duty crowded into the forepeak, simply watching hour after hour.

Absorbing as this was in itself, its interest was heightened by the frequent sightings of one or two penguins or one or two seals on the ice close in or far away. The sleeping Weddell Seals, especially, do not awaken easily, so that it was possible for the ship to pass one not far away, breaking the ice without breaking its sleep. One such seal, just to the left of the path we were breaking, woke up only when we were some ten feet away. Then — surprised, confused, and bellowing — instead of turning away from our path it was so ill advised as to try to cross it (while the men in the forepeak shouted and waved their arms), and was hit a glancing blow by the prow. (One should recall that these seals, and the penguins as well, presumably had never before seen a ship or a man.)

For me there was, in addition, the sight of all the flying birds that, no less than the penguins, represented the beauty and strangeness of the world we had now entered. But to the others aboard these were, for the most part, just birds — to be noticed, if at all, simply because a rather odd passenger was seen to observe them through his binoculars as if they were, for some reason, worth observing.

It means little to talk of day and night in this setting. For the next fourteen or fifteen hours after we came into the pack-ice the profile of the land grew ahead of us. The lower slopes of Terror on the left and Erebus on the right rose above the horizon, looming ever larger, until at last their island foundation was revealed in the form of the low, flat saddle of snow-covered land between them, with the minor peak of Mount Terra Nova in the middle. We passed Franklin Island to starboard, an irregular mound of snow bordered in part by ice cliffs; and then the dome that is Beaufort Island, sixty-three miles from Cape Bird at the northwest tip of Ross Island. There were wide areas of open water now, here and in McMurdo Sound along the west coast of Ross Island.

At 8:30 on the morning of January 2 a helicopter took off from the *Staten Island* to deliver the New Zealanders to their destination at New Zealand's Scott Base, then to deliver an American to America's McMurdo Station, two or three miles away. This was where the sea ended and the Ross Ice Shelf began. At 77°50'S., we had reached the southernmost point in the world for ship navigation.

The Ice Birds

The habitat of a species, the type of environment to which it belongs, defines it no less than the shape of its bill or the length of its tarsus. An albatross in a spruce forest is not an albatross. The live bird separated from its habitat is no more the whole bird than if a wing had been amputated.

The unique charm that the two birds I am about to describe have for me is, in part, their exclusive association with the world beyond the frontier. Within the category of seabirds, we may think of them as belonging to a subcategory, the ice birds, so rare that, in the strictest sense, it consists of only these two species among the flying birds of the southern hemisphere.

Captain Robert Falcon Scott and his company aboard the *Discovery* had their first experience of the ice frontier on November 16, 1901. Edward Wilson noted in his journal how, about the middle of the morning, they saw their first ice, a piece "the size of a soup plate." Within ten minutes there were bigger pieces all around.

> And then we passed the first stream of broken, brashy ice, and then another, and then quickly another and then an open stretch of dark grey water. . . . And now we had loose ice all around us and here and there great frozen hummocks, where slabs the size of kitchen tables were thrown one on the other anyhow and so frozen, with every hollow and crack and crevice a perfect miracle of blue and green light, and then came the ice birds — the Southern Fulmar, a beautiful bluish grey bird the size of a Common Gull, and then the black and white Antarctic Petrel, dressed like a domino, and then to crown all the Snow Petrel, pure white like a slim fantail, with black eyes and beak and the most graceful flight.

Neither the Snow Petrel nor the Antarctic Petrel normally gets beyond easy flying distance of the ice in which it lives. Their flocks, like flocks of pigeons, roam over the pack-ice, or they roost on the bergs around which they swarm like gnats. Moreover, the two species associate together, and many of the Snow Petrels I was to see were, in fact, accompanying flocks of Antarctic Petrels.

Both species are, like the Cape Pigeon, fulmarine petrels. This shows, when one sees them on the wing, in their tubular, neckless bodies. Unlike the Arctic Fulmar and the Cape Pigeon, however, they are adapted for flying over flat surfaces in breezes, rather than in high winds deflected from high waves. In my account of the Cape Pigeon I made a distinction between the relatively broad and flexible wings of gulls, suited to light coastal winds, and the narrow laths, adapted to gales, that are the wings of the Arctic Fulmar and the Cape Pigeon. Although everyone who sees the Antarctic Petrel for the first time, after passing through waters in which the Cape Pigeon is common, is apt to be reminded of the latter, the Antarctic Petrel is an airy bird that flies lightly with flexible wings. Like the Snow Petrel, which has the same manner of flight, it also feels free to mount the sky, for there is no advantage in staying close to the surface in the absence of a great wind deflected from waves. I saw Snow Petrels so high, on occasion, that they were mere sparkles against the blue; and the Antarctic Petrels, I understand, are equally given to the imitation of Icarus.

The pied pattern of the Cape Pigeon's plumage, its sharply contrasted black and white, is softened in the somewhat larger Antarctic Petrel. Its head and throat, and its entire back, are dark; its underparts, below the throat, white; its tail, above as below, white with a dark tip. The upper surfaces of its wings are dark along the front half and at the tips, but otherwise white. The undersides of the wings are white with broad dark leading edges and a thread of dark along the trailing edges.

Where I referred to the Cape Pigeon as "black and white" I have now described the Antarctic Petrel, rather, as "dark and white." The dark feathers, when still new after the moult, are "almost black brown" (as Wilson described them). They are the same color, still, in November, at the beginning of the Antarctic summer, and it is to be noted that in his journal, reporting his first sight of Antarctic Petrels on November 16, Wilson refers to them as "black and white." Under the influence of the summer sun, however, the black fades. It is a peculiarity of the Antarctic that, because of the scarcity of either moisture or dust in the atmosphere, the sunlight is highly actinic — which is to say that, when it reaches the earth at sea-level, its ultraviolet rays have not been filtered out to the extent that they have everywhere else. These rays tend to bleach the "almost black brown" feathers until, by the end of the season, they have faded to buff. The dark parts of the plumage, on the birds I saw at mid-summer, were a rich brown variously shaded.

The Snow Petrel is a somewhat smaller Antarctic Petrel with all-white plumage, black bill, and a dark eye that appears larger than it actually is because of the black feathers with which it is surrounded. The Arctic Fulmar, too, and other Procellariiform species with white heads, have black feathers that make the dark eye look twice its size. One could interpret this, unscientifically, as simply an expression of nature's artistry, for its aesthetic "rightness" is striking. At the other or utilitarian extreme, one might speculate that white feathers around the eye would reflect light into it, causing glare. Or one could speculate that an apparently large eye is intimidating where intimidation is desirable, although this would raise the question of why it should be so. My own philosophical disposition, in matters of this sort, is to apply the principle of complementarity that Niels Bohr applied not only to quantum physics but to the interpretation of all being as well. Just as the constituents of the atom may, with equal validity, be regarded either as particles or as waves, the two alternative ways of regarding them being complementary rather than opposed, so a specific peculiarity in a bird may have both a practical and an aesthetic justification, if we suppose that utilitarian values and aesthetic values, in the ultimate or God's-eye view, are merely different aspects of the same thing.

The Snow Petrel and the Antarctic Petrel are the only birds known to nest deep in the interior of the Antarctic continent. Because they lay their eggs in the crevices between the rocks of steep scree slopes, or on exposed ledges of cliffs, they are able to find nesting sites on the peaks, projecting through the ice, of the mountain-ranges that encircle the interior plateau of the continent. Nesting colonies of Snow Petrels have been reported 186 miles inland, and at altitudes above 6,500 feet.* The Antarctic Petrels, which nest in colonies of up to a million birds, have been known to nest more than a hundred miles inland.

Even today, the best pictures of Antarctic and Snow Petrels I know are the drawings and water colors that Wilson made during the *Discovery* and *Terra Nova* expeditions. In studying them before I went south I was puzzled, however, by what appeared to be a peculiar rearward extension of their bodies as shown in flight. The question in my mind was whether the birds were actually built that way or the artist had been at fault in showing them that way. The answer, when I at last saw the birds themselves, was that the artist had been right. The bird's tubular body in flight, as seen in profile, does not curve up from the belly to end at the sprouting of the tail. Instead, it continues in a more or less straight line to the tip of the tail, so that the body, in its thickness, appears not to end at the base of the tail but, rather, at its termination. I take it that the body is not actually longer than in other birds, but that the under tail coverts, much longer and

* Cline, Siniff, and Erickson, 1969, p. 710; Prévost and Mougin, 1970, p. 61.

heavier than in other birds, extend almost to the end of the tail.

I have told how, when I went on deck the morning of the twenty-ninth, I found the sea covered with icebergs fantastically carved. I also found that we were being accompanied not only by Cape Pigeons but by a mixed flock of Antarctic and Snow Petrels that often flew along our railings. Soon they were supplemented by my first Antarctic Fulmars, which became common, generally two at a time flying together.

I here quote from the notes I made that evening on the Antarctic Petrel and the Snow Petrel.

> *Antarctic Petrel.* A larger edition of the Cape Pigeon with a simpler design that has more white in it. . . . Before we really got into the pack, and after we emerged, it appeared generally in rather tight flocks up to fourteen, with a few Snow Petrels added. They generally stuck close to the boat, often circling it repeatedly at the height of the truck, sometimes passing within a few feet of my face at the railings, sometimes skimming the water. Inside the pack it was generally a case of two or three at a time, and at rare intervals.

> *Snow Petrel.* This ghostly lovely all-white petrel with black eye and short black beak . . . has a more gull-like, flexible wing than other petrels, although perhaps narrower than that of a gull. It flies with rapid wing-beats (faster than a gull), sailing occasionally and briefly. (The Ivory Gull must look very much like this.) It alters direction frequently. . . . It was single, in twos, threes, or fours, or associated with the Antarctic Petrels (which brought it nearer the boat). It continued common throughout the pack-ice, even when the Antarctic Petrel had become scarce. Twice I saw one land on a floe.

The Snow Petrel stands upright on its feet like a gull, differing in this from almost all (if not, indeed, all) the other Procellariidae, including the Antarctic Petrel, which rests in the typical squatting position on its tarsi. One wonders what occasion it might have, by distinction from the Antarctic Petrel and the Antarctic Fulmar, to walk about on the ice. It has also been known to alight on the decks of ships, perhaps taking them to represent something new in ice-floes.

December 30 was the day we sighted Cape Adare and landed at Cape Hallett, where I visited the Snow Petrels on their breeding grounds (as I shall recount in the next chapter). Wherever there was ice, small numbers of Snow Petrels were always about, and they were to be seen occasionally even in open water. There were always some associated with the flocks of Antarctic Petrels.

Antarctic Petrels appeared from time to time that day, especially when we were near the pack-ice. They were sometimes in dense flocks. One such flock, appearing like a black cloud, I estimated at five hundred to a thousand individuals. But I took a photograph of it also, and once home I set my daughter Julia to making a more studied estimate. Projecting the transparency on a large sheet of graph paper, she spent an evening counting the specks and making calculations in the most scientific fashion imaginable. The result was a solidly based estimate of 1,700 birds.

I saw no more Antarctic Petrels after the thirtieth, but about two hours after noon on New Year's Eve I happened to look up to see, as my notes put it, two Snow Petrels "winkling and twinkling high up in the blue sky above the ship — just passing over." Again on New Year's Day, especially after we got into the ice north of Ross Island, I saw occasional Snow Petrels fly past.

For the record, I note here that, while the Antarctic Petrels generally showed themselves interested in the ship, little companies of them circling her as close as possible, the Snow Petrels never paid us visits of inspection except when they were drawn to do so by the Antarctic Petrels with which they were keeping company.

The Other Fulmar

The reader will recall that the members of Scott's expedition in 1901 saw their first ice birds at the same time that the *Discovery* came to the outer edge of the ice ring north of the Ross Sea; and that I first saw the same three species mentioned by Wilson when the *Staten Island,* sixty-nine years later, also came to the outer edge of the ice ring. The Antarctic Fulmar, however, is less strictly an ice bird than the other two since it is not, like them, confined to the ice.

Anyone who is interested in birds may come to regard some one species as peculiarly his own, taking a special interest in it that acquires, with time, a proprietary character. Circumstances had led me to take such an interest in the Arctic Fulmar after observing it for weeks on its nesting grounds in the Shetland Islands north of Scotland — both in the spring of 1968 and that of 1970. I had spent endless hours studying it at the closest quarters, studying especially the virtuosity of its flight in the turbulent winds along the Shetland cliffs. I had read everything I could find on it, I had photographed it in every position and from every angle, I had sketched it, and I had published my observations in detail.

One reason for my special interest in the Arctic Fulmar was that it was the principal representative in far northern waters of the great seabird order that dominates the circumpolar ocean of the southern hemisphere and is native to it. The Arctic Fulmar is, in fact, the descendent of fulmars that strayed from the southern ocean to establish themselves in the northern hemisphere. Individual fulmars from high latitudes of the south, ranging the cold waters of the Humboldt Current up to the Equator, may well have continued as wanderers into the North Pacific and there, perhaps following other seabirds in their foraging and their migration, found in the Arctic a habitat similar to the one from which they had strayed. It would most likely have been inexperienced young birds that went astray like this. Becoming adapted to the seasonal cycle in the north as they attained maturity (a development that takes five to seven years in fulmars), they would have begun nesting on the cliffs of islands and coasts bordering the Arctic Ocean, spreading circumpolarly until, within the past century, they at last became the most abundant seabird of the northern hemisphere.*

Enough time has passed for the fulmars that went north and those that remained in the south to evolve into what are respectively two species today. But the differences between them remain minor, the similarities striking.

Because the northern species has been the only fulmar we have had in our hemisphere, it is natural that we have not felt any need to give it a distinguishing adjective, calling it simply "the Fulmar." The name most commonly given the fulmar of the south is "Silver-gray Fulmar," but this is unsatisfactory because the fulmar of the north is also silver-gray. "Northern" and "Southern," respectively, would be satisfactory adjectives, but, taking my choice among those used by various writers when the distinction has to be made, I prefer "Arctic" and "Antarctic." The fulmar of the north is truly an Arctic species, having been recorded closer to the north Pole than any other bird, even though the explosive proliferation of its numbers has lately forced it to find breeding sites as far south as the north coast of France; while

* Thomson, 1964, p. 549.

the fulmar of the south, which breeds only in the Antarctic, is truly an Antarctic species, even though in the off season it follows the cold currents northward to low latitudes.

The Arctic Fulmar, in its winter wandering, has been recorded as far south as 23°N. in the Pacific and 33°N. in the Atlantic. Dr. Murphy writes that the Antarctic Fulmar, after following the Humboldt Current to northern Peru in its own winter wanderings, sometimes goes even farther. "There are, at any rate, a larger number of records of this species in the North Pacific Ocean than of any of the other petrels ordinarily associated with the far south."*

While the Antarctic Fulmar is slightly smaller than the Arctic, I would not be altogether sure of how to tell the one from the other in the field, unless it was possible to see the difference in the bill, which is distinctly stubbier in the latter. Where the Arctic Fulmar has a patch of black feathers in front of the eye, just like the Snow Petrel, the Antarctic Fulmar has a less distinct patch of gray feathers, and I noted that the mantle of the Antarctic Fulmar seemed somewhat lighter than that of the Arctic, but with darker wing-tips. The remarkable atmospheric illumination of the Antarctic, however, so different from the dim light of the far north, would suffice to account for this impression.

With my proprietary interest in fulmars, I had been looking forward eagerly to the opportunity of observing the Antarctic Fulmar, of comparing its appearance and flight with that of the Arctic species, and I had every reason to expect that it would be common after we got to the ice. This expectation appeared to be confirmed on that climactic morning of December 29 when we came to the edge of the ice and found ourselves first in the company of the Snow and Antarctic Petrels, then in the company of

* Murphy, p. 598.

the fulmars as well. Generally two at a time and paying no attention to us, they passed in steady directional flight, alternately beating and gliding low over the surface, just like the Arctic Fulmars. But I was faced with the same unexpected embarrassment of riches as six days before, when we had emerged from Wellington Harbour to find ourselves suddenly among a variety of species that were new to me. Just as I had then given first attention to the Cape Pigeons that were close alongside, deferring a careful observation of the more distant albatrosses, which I could expect to be seeing for days to come, so I now gave first attention to the Antarctic and Snow Petrels ranging alongside, confident of the opportunities I would have later to study the fulmars. Once we were well into the pack, however, there were no more fulmars, nor was I to see any more at all after that. In any case, none came close enough, or none remained close enough long enough, to provide me with an opportunity for becoming as familiar with this species as with the other two ice birds.

.

The three ice birds were not the only new species for me that morning of the twenty-ninth. There was also another bird, as remarkable as any, that I was soon to see in abundance and at close range on its nesting grounds.

Wilson's Storm Petrel at its nesting grounds near Cape Hallett

7. Ice Birds in the Scree

WIND OVER WAVES is what supports the great albatrosses on the wing; but for birds as small as Starlings wind and wave can hardly be anything except a menace when they rise in their might. The smallest seabirds, some no larger than Barn Swallows, may be divided into two groups according to the way they cope with rough seas: the diving petrels and small auks that are swimmers more than fliers, and the storm petrels that are fliers first of all. In a high sea, when the waves careen one after another, auks and diving petrels avoid being rolled in the breaking crests by diving under each at the last moment. The storm petrels lift themselves to let each pass below. In either case, the birds must go for long periods, day and night, without rest.

A potential danger for all pelagic birds, except in the circumpolar ocean of the south, is that a great wind, persisting long enough, will at last drive them to destruction on a lee shore. From the largest albatross to the smallest storm petrel, seabirds ordinarily drift with the wind rather than strive against it. Fortunately, the most persistent winds are the light trade winds of the warm latitudes, while the great west winds of temperate latitudes are neither regular nor persistent. (Their prevalence is only a matter of annual averages.) When they do persist long enough, however, quantities of seabirds, finding themselves off a lee shore at last, are compelled to use all their reserves of strength to make head against them. When those reserves are finally exhausted, their emaciated bodies litter the rocks and beaches of some continental shore, or they are carried across the shore to perish in an alien world. Even mollymawks and Giant Petrels have been wrecked by prolonged winds on the west coast of Australia.*

In the face of this danger, the birds depend for their safety on keeping enough leeway. This presumably explains why some, perhaps all of the six species that migrate from temperate southern latitudes to pass the austral winter in temperate northern latitudes, do so on the western sides of the two oceans. The Wilson's Storm Petrels, which breed on the Antarctic continent and adjacent islands, migrate in the Atlantic off the east coast of South and North America, sometimes appearing in large flocks in the harbors of Rio de Janeiro or New York. It is only later that they appear on the European side of the Atlantic, having been carried eastward by the prevailing westerlies. Like the Sooty, the Great, and the Short-tailed Shearwaters, they appear to travel clockwise around the great oceans in the two hemispheres, crossing diagonally back toward the southwest as, riding the easterly trade winds, they transit the warm latitudes on their return to their breeding grounds.

The Coriolis effect bears on all objects that move over the earth's surface, but doubly so on these migrants, for they go with the winds that respond to it. Moving in accordance with a logic of which they are unaware, they are beautiful not only in themselves but in illustrating the order of nature as well.

•

Of the four families into which the order Procellariiformes is divided, if we set aside the family of miscellaneous petrels and

* Murphy, pp. 50–51.

shearwaters (Procellariidae), the remaining three present some interesting contrasts. As the albatrosses (Diomedeidae) are the largest of seabirds, so the storm petrels (Hydrobatidae) are the smallest. They are quite different, however, from the other family of minute seabirds, the diving petrels (Pelecanoididae). For the diving petrels live on and under the surface of the sea, almost like penguins, rising off it only to travel short distances in whirring flight and drop in again. Where one might compare them to flying fish, it would be more apt to compare the storm petrels to butterflies. Night and day they dance over the waves in fluttering flight.

I suppose that, except on their nesting grounds, the great albatrosses spend most of their time tilting above the surface of the sea, wheeling in great circles and drifting down the wind. The storm petrels, which appear to be as much nocturnal as diurnal, must also spend most of their time on the wing, night and day, but flitting and fluttering among the waves, hopping and springing and pattering over the surface with their feet, touching it here and there with their bills to pick up bits of organic matter — as tireless in flight as butterflies.

There are more than twenty species of storm petrel that, unlike the diving petrels and the albatrosses, are distributed over all the oceans from as far north as Iceland and Alaska to the Antarctic continent. Their observation from shipboard presents problems that the observation of the great albatrosses does not. Sometimes one gets a momentary glimpse between distant waves of what might have been a black moth. Fortunately, some species, including Wilson's, follow one's ship, dancing in little companies on the flat bubbling wake that is their dance floor. I recall occasions when I observed them under these circumstances while travelling between the east coast of the United States and Central America.

Then the game was to try to see, through one's binoculars, whether their feet extended beyond their tails, or had yellow webs between the toes, so as to be able to conclude that they were, indeed, Wilson's. (But one never could be sure of such details.)

The taxonomist, using his calipers on skins and skeletons, sees a wider variety among the storm petrels than is apparent to the observer in the field, for whom there is a basic storm petrel to which the majority of species conform with only minor variations. It is all black except for a white patch above the base of the tail (just like the European House Martin, and how many other swallows?), and a pale area on the upper side of each wing. The taxonomist may say that the British Storm Petrel belongs to an entirely different division of the family from Wilson's, and each of the two species may be said to have its own way of flitting and fluttering, but to the shipboard observer who does not already know them well they are the same, unless he is lucky enough to see, on these jiggling and darting creatures, that the feet would or would not extend beyond the tail if they were carried that way, or that the webs between the toes are, as the case may be, either black or yellow. Leach's Storm Petrel (belonging to still another broad division of the family) is the same, except for its particular way of dancing in the trough and the fact that its tail would show itself to be forked if one could ever see it that well.

It has been my good fortune to visit the British Storm Petrel on its nesting grounds in Shetland, to photograph it on its nest, and to hold the living bird in the palm of my hand. One night in mid-Atlantic a Leach's Storm Petrel, attracted and confused by the lights of civilization, dropped onto the deck of our ship, where I picked it up and examined it with delight — forked tail, polished black bill, and all — before tossing it out again into the darkness of the world before the Creation, from which it had come. On another occasion, in daylight, when we were threading our way through the Azores, I looked over the railing and straight down the iron flanks of the moving ship to see for a moment, close alongside, the one species of storm petrel, different from the basic type, that is readily identifiable. It was a White-faced Storm Petrel, gone as soon as seen.

I have no doubt that every species of storm petrel proves to be distinguished in its own way when one gets to know it.

In 1951 James Fisher estimated that Wilson's Storm Petrel was the most numerous species of wild bird in the world, but he later qualified this to make an exception for the House Sparrow and the Starling, both of which owe their present abundance to the spread of human civilization.* When a man of Fisher's authority offers such an estimate, surprising as it may be, it is not only to be taken seriously; one may be sure that it will be echoed by other authors until, over the years, it has gained a degree of general acceptance.

On Christmas Eve, in the waters just south of New Zealand, a little gray and white bird fluttering in the trough some distance away was presumably a White-faced Storm Petrel, the species I had seen so briefly in the Azores. On the day after we left Campbell Island I twice saw a storm petrel that I was able to identify surely, the second time, as the Black-bellied. It was not until we got to the pack-ice, however, that I saw, along with the other ice birds, Wilson's Storm Petrel. From the time we crossed the frontier until we had left Cape Hallett, individuals or companies up to four were to be seen frequently, flying steadily south, or a bit west of south, low over the ice and the water. They flew

* Fisher, 1951; Fisher and Peterson, 1964, p. 73.

like martins, flapping and gliding, sometimes beating about
erratically for a moment. One started to land on the ice, but
thought better of it, and another lowered its feet to skip over the
water. Always, however, they kept straight on course, without
deviation. They were presumably flying to relieve mates on the
nest at Cape Hallett or other points along the coast where they
have their nesting colonies. Mated British Storm Petrels relieve
each other every two or three days, and I would expect the period
to be about the same for these birds — unless, having to travel
farther over the ice to reach their feeding grounds, they should
consequently take more time between changeovers.

All species of storm petrel, where they have the choice, are
nocturnal at their nesting grounds, arriving or departing only in
the black of night. It is the same with all other small and most
middle-sized seabirds, the purpose being to escape their diurnal
predators — principally, in north and south temperate latitudes
alike, the skuas. At a breeding colony of British Storm Petrels in
Shetland, where I observed them, they made the changeover at
the darkest hour of the night (about 1 A.M.), but the darkest hour
on a cloudless night in July as far north as 60°N. was no more than
dusky. At the northernmost nesting colonies of the species, and
of Leach's Storm Petrel as well, in southern Iceland (about
64°N.), they must find even less darkness for the changeover, although the prevailing cloudiness of the North Atlantic must help.
It is plausible to speculate that these two species don't nest farther north because it would be too dangerous for them to change
over at the nest in full daylight, exposing them to the predation of
the skuas or jaegers that wait to catch them as they emerge from
their nesting holes or as they try to get to them.

Perhaps for the same reason, none of the diving petrels breed
south of 55°S. The Black-bellied Storm Petrel, which is circumpolar in the southern hemisphere, breeds south to 63°S. but no

farther, as is the case with the Antarctic Prion (although a colony, which has since disappeared, existed in 1913 at Cape Denison on the coast of the continent at about 66°S.).* This is to say, then, that no bird smaller than the Snow Petrel, with the exception of Wilson's Storm Petrel, nests as far south as the Antarctic Circle. It is perhaps not an accident that the limit of latitude, for the small birds, is the same in the northern and southern hemispheres — except for the peculiar case of Wilson's Storm Petrel. What prevents the nesting of all other small birds inside either the Arctic or the Antarctic Circle, where they would have to nest in full daylight, does not prevent this one species from doing so. I here quote Dr. Murphy on the puzzle this presents.

A most interesting point about *Oceanites* [i.e, Wilson's Storm Petrel] at South Georgia is . . . that this species, practically alone among the smaller water birds, enjoys absolute immunity from the aggressiveness of the skua (*Catharacta*). Lönnberg has recorded this before but my observations of the actual conditions were none the less a source of considerable surprise to me. The skua is to most of the birds, large or small, a wanton and relentless ogre. It is forever watching for neglected young penguins, cormorants, and even albatrosses; it attacks at sight the endemic teal, the diving petrel, and the *Prion*. To the last two species, it is such a terrible foe that they dare not show themselves in the fiords or over the land between daylight and dark; nevertheless, the skuas succeed in capturing so many of them that their dismembered carcasses strew the ground over their subterranean colonies. But *Oceanites* flies about with impunity in broad daylight. I have seen one almost brush a skua with its wing as the latter bird stood on a rock in the kelp fields, and both species sometimes fed together when stormy weather had washed away pieces of seal blubber from the supply floating alongside our brig.

Why does the skua ignore this petrel? It is surely as con-

* Prévost and Mougin, 1970, p. 74.

spicuous as the diver (*Pelecanoides*) and seemingly less difficult to capture than the fleet-winged *Prion*. The protective
character cannot be in an offensive taste, for the skua is quite
ready to pounce upon and devour a dead or disabled *Oceanites*. Possibly, however, its body affords too small a morsel to
warrant any effort on the skua's part. It is noteworthy that the
latter grants a like immunity to one other still smaller bird,
the pipit (*Anthus*).*

A difficulty with Dr. Murphy's speculation about the reason for
this storm petrel's apparent immunity is that none of the others
seem to enjoy it. However, this may be a relative matter, depending on local circumstances.

Wilson's Storm Petrel is, then, one of only nine species of birds,
including two penguins, that are known to nest, today, on the
polar continent itself. (If the Antarctic Prion no longer does so,
that may be because the skua was too much for it in the perpetual
daylight.) It nests in the crevices of cliffs and scree slopes all
around the edge of the continent, and perhaps it will someday be
found to nest as well, like the Antarctic Petrel and the Snow
Petrel, in high mountains of the interior. What might prevent it
from doing so, however, would be the distance and the height at
which individuals would then have to travel from and to their
feeding grounds during the intervals of their relief on the nest. It
must happen to Antarctic and Snow Petrels that they encounter
blizzards which delay or prevent their return to their high nesting
grounds in the interior, and perhaps the storm petrels never rise
at all to fly at altitudes far above sea-level, like the twinkling
Snow Petrels I had seen.

•

Cape Hallett is 69 miles south of Cape Adare on the precipitous
west shore of the Ross Sea, and some 415 miles north of the Ross

* Murphy, pp. 753–754.

Ice Shelf. Like Cape Adare it runs north, in cliffs rising almost a mile out of the frozen sea, to enclose a frozen bay surrounded by rock faces, glaciers, and scree slopes. Just on the inside of its tip there happens to be a flat spit of gravel that offers the only foothold at sea-level in the vicinity. This spit was completely occupied, when I was there, by a colony of over a hundred thousand Adélie Penguins (with its attendant skuas) mixed with a colony of fifteen human beings, the two species sharing the single plot available to them at the base of ice-coated mountain walls.

The penguin colony at Hallett is native and independent, without logistic support from abroad. The human colony, on the other hand, is under the joint auspices of New Zealand and the United States, both of which provide the support without which it could not survive. The purpose of the human colony is biological research, but there was a temporary lull in its scientific work at the time of my visit. No New Zealanders were there, and the scientific staff consisted of two young Americans — Malcolm Coulter and Charles Steffen, just graduated from Iowa State University — who had been left behind to collect eggs of Wilson's Storm Petrel for a comparative study of the consequences, for the reproduction of seabirds, of the chlorinated hydrocarbons that, having been sprayed over the northern hemisphere to reduce insect pests, had at last polluted even the waters that wash the Antarctic continent and the snow that falls on the South Pole.

The occasion for the *Staten Island*'s call at Hallett was not only to deliver and pick up mail but also to supply helicopter transportation for the two men to the nesting colony of the storm petrels, ten miles away, where the birds might by now be expected to have eggs.

It was five in the afternoon when the *Staten Island* came to a stop in solid pack-ice twenty-five miles from Hallett. The Captain and I got into wet suits (those suits made of rubber so thick as to be three-dimensional which frogmen wear) for the trip to the station. This sartorial precaution is a rule for those who embark in helicopters over water so cold (29°F.) that, if they should ditch without such protection, they could hardly survive long enough even for a prompt rescue. Then the helicopter, in its peculiar hovering flight, like some child's toy, took the two of us across the ice to deposit us on the beach among scattering penguins and men waiting before the great red packing cases, as they appeared to be, that served for the housing of the latter.

Upon landing, I was given my choice between using the hour and a half ashore to see the penguin colony or to accompany the two men, at their kind invitation, to the site of the nesting Snow Petrels and Wilson's Storm Petrels. Although I did not then know that I would ever again have such a chance to make the acquaintance of penguins, I chose the rarer opportunity and, within two minutes of landing, was aloft again, with the two egg collectors, on our way up the frozen bay. We put down on a flat shelf at the foot of a scree slope up which the three of us then scrambled pellmell — for the helicopter pilot had been emphatic in making the point that we had only an hour before we had to be back for the return trip to the station.

It was an excellent thing that I was wearing a wet suit and rubber thermal boots for that climb — which I daresay was no more than five hundred feet to the ridge that was our destination — because in the course of it I undoubtedly lost the extra pounds that Abi's cuisine had put on me. (When, back in the ship, I took off the wet suit, I had to empty the product of my dehydration out of it, pouring it down the drain of the bathroom shower.) So it was that, during my first hour on the Antarctic continent, I suffered from heat rather than cold.

Snow Petrels were flying back and forth along the contours of the scree slope, and the storm petrels were swarming, passing within two or three feet of us as if we were not there, constantly uttering a brief low-pitched sound without musical quality.

While the two men scrambled frantically among the tumbled rocks to find, in the time available, as many nests as possible of both species — so as to collect the eggs and, in the case of the storm petrels, the sitting birds — I had the best part of an hour's leisure to observe and photograph the birds under circumstances that come to few.

The storm petrels, in their manner of flight, varied between an even beating of the wings and fluttering, their glides being rare and brief. Swirling all about me, above and below, they gave the same impression of batlike flight that I recalled from the swirling of the British Storm Petrels at their nesting grounds in Shetland. Sometimes an individual, presumably near its nesting hole, would move slowly in hovering flight an inch or two above the surface, its tail fanned out and its wings merely quivering. One came to rest on the ground almost at my feet, in front of what I took to be its nesting hole, squatting not quite flat on its long tarsi, then fluttered away again. (As I write, this same individual may be fluttering between great waves off the coast of California.)

While all Procellariiform birds in flight carry their bills sloping down — as gulls, for example, do not — seeing these storm petrels so close I was struck by the fact that their little black bills, like crochet hooks, pointed down almost vertically. The other thing that struck me was that their wings, when fully extended, were more rounded at the tips, less pointed, than they are generally shown to be in the drawings and paintings one sees in the books. Finally, as in the case of the British Storm Petrels

I had seen at their nests in Shetland, it was surprising to see the size of the single egg laid by a bird so small. (Dr. Murphy gives average dimensions of the egg as 33.7 × 24 mm for a bird that has a total length of about 170 mm, of which some 63.7 mm is tail, leaving 106.3 mm, part of which is head and bill.) The egg, when ready to be laid, must fill a large part of the bird's body cavity. This may explain what has been a subject of speculation among ornithologists: why the females, in some species of storm petrel at least, are larger than the males.

Finally, I here testify for the record that, even under such ideal conditions of observation, it was not easy to observe either of the principal points of field identification. One could sometimes just tell that the feet extended beyond the end of the tail, but the fact that their webs were yellow was never visible to me.

The two men, in the course of perhaps three quarters of an hour, found ten nests of storm petrels in deep recesses of the scree, from which they took the eggs and sitting birds for the benefit of science. We also found several Snow Petrel nests far back in such recesses, from which only the eggs were taken. Both species defended themselves in typical petrel fashion by ejecting from their throats a reddish oil that covered the hands of the intruders. The Snow Petrels protested with loud caws or grunts. In one case, far back as it was in the darkness of its nesting recess, at the end of a sort of tunnel almost the length of one's arm, the white plumage of a Snow Petrel enabled me to photograph it still sitting where its egg had been. Presumably it would give up sitting when it had become fully conscious of the egg's absence, and I daresay it was not too late in the season to replace it.

If the storm petrels were immune to the depredations of the Great Skuas, a pair of which was nesting on the ledge where our helicopter had landed, the Snow Petrels apparently were not. Here and there on the rocks I found their beautiful white wings connected only by fleshless skeletons.

When we got back to the station, the Captain, out of the kindness of his heart, told me he would take the helicopter back alone, sending it for me after I had had an hour among the penguins. My two companions then took me on a guided tour of the penguin colony — but that is another story for another chapter.

Ross on Possession Island

8. Ross Island

➤ THE BIGHT called the Ross Sea is a thousand miles deep, most of it covered by the Ross Ice Shelf, a cake of freshwater ice larger than France and 600 to 1,000 feet thick, which floats on the underlying ocean although it is locked onto the land. The seaward edge of the shelf, an ice cliff up to 200 feet high, is the Great Ice Barrier referred to by successive explorers. All this ice is constantly flowing outward from the center of the continent, some four feet a day at its edge, where pieces break off to drift north in the form of tabular icebergs.

The Great Ice Barrier stretches over five hundred miles from 165°E. to 161°W. It marks the sector of the polar continent that is richest in the history of famous exploration. Here man first landed on it. Across the Ross Ice Shelf the South Pole was first reached by the Amundsen and Scott expeditions in the austral summer of 1911–1912.

Most of the history in which this sector is so rich is centered on Ross Island at the western end of the Great Ice Barrier. Scott's *Discovery* expedition of 1901 and his *Terra Nova* expedition of 1910 were based on the island, as was Shackleton's *Nimrod* expedition of 1907.

I have already reported with what ease the *Burton Island* and the *Staten Island* broke through the guardian ring of ice in only a few hours. But Captain Cook in the *Resolution* and Captain

James Ross in his specially reinforced ships, the *Erebus* and the *Terror,* had no power save the wind in their sails to push them through the floes. Nor was there any knowing what would be found as they penetrated deeper, or whether they would ever be able to return through the ice that closed behind them.

In Edward Wilson's journal for November 16, 1901, the day the *Discovery* came to the ice ring and the first ice birds were seen, he tells how the ship went

> on and on into thicker and denser pack and bigger and bigger floes, with big masses sticking up here and there, till at last we were hardly moving at all, for we had no steam up and were using only sail with very little wind. The scrunching and grating of the ship against the ice floes, the heavy thrust and drop or jolt that ran through the whole ship when we struck a particularly obstinate hump of ice were most strange. . . . At 11 we came to a dead stop and not a speck of open water was to be seen anywhere, so steam was turned on and the sails taken in and our head pointing N.E. we made our way slowly outward again. . . .

The next morning they again tried to make their way into the ice. Wilson noted that

> the strangest thing perhaps in the pack is the constant motion, and the gentleness of it, and yet the irresistible force of big masses of ice. The swell was very big, but the surface of the water was merely rippled like a lake, and in places not even rippled, so that the ice was beautifully reflected in the smooth water and yet this incessant immense swell rising and falling, like a breathing in sleep.

At midday, however, they again turned north and sailed back into open water, returning to New Zealand.

It was January 8 when they at last emerged into the open water inside. On January 9 they landed at Cape Adare, where they found Wilson's Storm Petrels nesting in crevices among the tumbled rocks.

A hundred and twenty-nine years earlier, on January 17, 1773, Captain Cook in the *Resolution* crossed the Antarctic Circle, the first on record ever to do so; but before the end of the day, finding his way blocked by the ice, he had to turn back. From a position south of Africa he sailed eastward around the continent and, with winter coming on, put into New Zealand, from which he again went south in November to continue eastward along the edge of the ice, looking for an opening. At a longitude just beyond the eastern end of the Ross Sea, he succeeded in making a second crossing of the circle on December 20, remaining south of it for three days before the ice again forced him back. Some 25 degrees farther east he crossed the circle a third and last time, reaching the farthest south ever attained before being turned back at 71°10′S. (Just before his ship came about, George Vancouver, then a midshipman hardly fifteen years old, climbed to the end of the bowsprit and cried out: "I am the farthest south man in the world.") In the first and third crossings alike, Cook had got to about a hundred miles from the shores of the continent; but he did not know it, and he could have got no nearer in any case.

There is some confusion, inherent in the situation, over the question of who first sighted the polar continent. By 1820 any number of sealers were poking about the ice-floes south of Cape Horn, where the Antarctic Peninsula points a long finger far across the Antarctic Circle into the Atlantic. Since the peninsula is continuous with the mass of ice which is the visible continent, it is generally considered "a piece of the continent, a part of the main." If one wishes, however, one may say that it is really only an island or a group of islands enclosed in a sheath of ice that is attached to the mainland. The question is how one shall use the word "continent" and how define "mainland" under circumstances that do not fit the meanings of these words as they apply to our familiar world.

We Americans maintain that the honor of discovering the continent belongs to Captain Nathaniel B. Palmer of Stonington, Connecticut, commanding the sloop *Hero,* who, sighting the peninsula on November 17, 1820, knew it to be the continent (if it was). But the Russian Admiral von Bellingshausen, already in February of that year, had seen the part of the peninsula, at its base, which we now identify as Alexander I "Island" (he had named it Alexander I "Land"), although there is permanent ice between it and the rest of the peninsula. In 1831, the British sealer and explorer, John Biscoe, saw and named Cape Ann, on what is now Enderby Land, which is considered part of the mainland even though we now know that a trough filled with freshwater ice, which is below what is technically sea-level, separates it from the rest of the continent.

Lieutenant Charles Wilkes, U.S.N., was the first to claim the discovery of the continent. In January 1840, heading an exploring expedition sent out by the U.S. Government, he sighted the coast west of Cape Adare, then proceeded westward along it for 1,500 miles, getting occasional glimpses of land through mist and snow. While his discoveries have since been accepted on the whole, the record is clouded by his claims, undoubtedly based on optical illusions, to have seen land where later navigators found none. Just one day after his first sighting of this coast, the French explorer Dumont d'Urville added to his glory as the discoverer of the Venus de Milo, twenty years earlier, the new glory of discovering what he named Terre Adélie (after his wife) on the coast that Wilkes was then engaged in exploring some 400 miles farther east. In fact, Wilkes's ship, the *Porpoise,* at one time passed within hailing distance of Dumont d'Urville's two ships, the *Arstrolabe* and the *Zélée* — an extraordinary occurrence in waters so remote.

The exploratory competition among Americans, English, and French, all under the auspices of their respective governments, was intense at the time. But the highest honors must go to the English, who planned and executed the greatest enterprise of all.

On New Year's Day 1841, Captain Ross, commanding the *Erebus* and the *Terror,* sailed south from Campbell Island. He crossed the Antarctic Circle and came to the edge of the pack, where he found Snow Petrels "flying about in great numbers." It was not until January 5 that wind and weather allowed him to enter the pack. After several hours, according to his report,

> the clear sea was no longer discernible from the masthead; with nothing but ice around, and fortunately a clear sky above us, we pursued our way through the pack, choosing the clearest 'leads,' and forcing the interposing barriers as they occurred; the way continued, if not to open before us, still sufficiently so to enable us to navigate freely amongst the ice, without danger or difficulty as we proceeded, at times sustaining violent shocks, which nothing but ships so strengthened could have withstood.

On January 9, at last, he emerged from the pack to find himself "again in a clear sea," and on January 11 land was sighted. "It rose in lofty peaks, entirely covered with perennial snow." He named this the Admiralty Range, and he named the projection of land at its foot Cape Adare. Because a combination of ice and surf prevented a landing on the mainland, Ross landed instead on a small island, which he named Possession Island, there to take possession of the newly discovered land in the name of Queen Victoria.   In fact, the first landing on the continent itself was not to take place until more than half a century had passed, but Cape Adare would be the site of it.

Proceeding southward along the coast of what he named Queen Victoria Land, Ross discovered Coulman Island, which he named after the father of "a lady to whom I was then attached, and whom I have now the happiness of calling my wife." In his account of this southward journey he refers repeatedly to the storm petrels (some of which may have been on their way to relieve their mates on nests at Cape Hallett) and to flocks of what probably were Antarctic Petrels although he called them Cape Pigeons.

On January 27 Ross landed on Franklin Island (where he observed "that the white petrel had its nests on the ledges of the cliffs, as had also the rapacious skua gull"), having now got farther south than anyone before him. Later that day he came in sight of the two volcanoes, one active and one dead, which he named Mounts Erebus and Terror. (This constitutes the discovery of Ross Island, although it was not then known to be an island.) The next day, as he approached it, he saw from the eastern end of the land (which he named Cape Crozier after the captain of the *Terror*) "a low white line extending . . . as far as the eye could discern to the eastward. It presented an extraordinary appearance, gradually increasing in height, as we got nearer to it, and proving at length to be a perpendicular cliff of ice, between one hundred and fifty and two hundred feet above the level of the sea, perfectly flat and level at the top, and without any fissures or promontories on its even seaward face." This was the first time a human eye had seen the Great Ice Barrier. To Ross's disappointment, it determined his farthest south, "for we might with equal chance of success try to sail through the Cliffs of Dover." He spent the next two or three weeks exploring the face of the Barrier eastward for some 350 miles, before the rapid formation of a new winter's ice forced him to retreat.

By February 16 he was again north of the northwestern point of Ross Island, which he had named Cape Bird after the senior lieutenant of the *Erebus*. Now, noting the deep bight that extended south between it and the mountains of Queen Victoria Land to the west, he named it McMurdo Bay after the senior lieutenant of the *Terror*. (Because we have since learned that it is a strait rather than a bay, it is now called McMurdo Sound.)

By the second half of February, when Ross at last turned north, it was already almost too late to escape from the increasing grip of the newly formed ice. Sometimes the ships were "more than an hour getting a few yards." (As he passed within distant sight of one cape on the coast of Queen Victoria Land, Ross named it Cape Hallett after the purser of the *Erebus*.)

The following November he started southeast from New Zealand in the *Erebus* and the *Terror* to discover the eastern end of the Great Ice Barrier. He entered the ring of pack-ice December 18; but this time, instead of traversing it in four days, he ran into difficulties that delayed his emergence on the inside until February 2, 1842, over seven weeks later. On February 23, when the season was too late for further exploration, he reached the eastern end of the Great Ice Barrier, where it abuts against the mountains of what is now known as the Edward VII Peninsula. Seeing the high undulations of ice on the horizon, but aware of the optical illusions that had misled other Antarctic explorers, he was so prudent as to mark on his chart only the words: "appearance of land." He had already accumulated enough honors so that he did not need to take credit for this further discovery, which was to be reserved for Captain Scott.

·

The peculiar history of Antarctic exploration and discovery is illustrated by the fact that the continent had been studied from offshore for over sixty years, and territorial claims had been made in the name of more than one nation, before any man ever set foot on it. With his two ships, Ross had stood only five or six miles off Cape Adare, and the next morning he had started for shore in a ship's boat to perform the ceremony of taking possession. But he had "found the shores of the mainland completely covered with ice projecting into the sea, and the heavy surf along its edge forbade any attempt to land on it." That was when, in circumstances of great peril, he had landed and performed the ceremony on Possession Island instead.

The first landing on the continent took place on January 24, 1895, when a Norwegian whaler, the *Antarctic*, under Captain Leonard Kristensen, came to rest among the floes off Cape Adare and sent ashore a boatload of seven men, the Captain included. Presumably the Captain was the first to step ashore, but the event is associated with another name, that of Carsten E. Borchgrevink. Born in Oslo, the son of a Norwegian barrister and an Englishwoman, Borchgrevink was living in Australia when the *Antarctic* touched there on her way south. In his determination to get to the polar continent he had shipped in her as an ordinary seaman, had followed his Captain ashore at Cape Adare, and had subsequently made a report of the occasion to the Sixth International Geographical Congress in London. He told the congress that he had thoroughly investigated the landing place "because I believed it to be a place where a future scientific expedition might safely stop, even during the winter months." He then offered to be the leader of such an expedition.

Accordingly, now as the leader of a British expedition, Borchgrevink again landed at Cape Adare on February 17, 1899. This event, on the eve of our present century, inaugurates the modern history of Antarctic exploration. Borchgrevink, with nine other men, passed the winter in a hut they built on the cape, while their ship, the *Southern Cross*, went north, returning for them in what is generally reckoned to be the following century, on January 28, 1900.* Continuing south in her, Borchgrevink landed near Cape Crozier, explored the Great Ice Barrier for some 350 miles, found a low place where he was able to land upon it with sledges and dogs, and even advanced southward 16 miles from its edge to the record latitude of 78°50'S. The penetration of the continent was being prepared.

•

Leaving Cape Adare on January 10, 1902, Scott's *Discovery*, to which we now return, proceeded southward along the coast of Queen Victoria Land past Coulman Island, and Wilson noted in his journal for January 19 that, although Mount Erebus "is as far now from us as Gloucester is from London (120 miles!), we can see it is in eruption in a mild way." Continuing through Mc-Murdo Sound, the *Discovery* company were disappointed to find on January 21 that the Ross Ice Shelf barred further progress. Turning back, they worked their way along the northern shore of Ross Island to the western end of the Great Ice Barrier at Cape Crozier. They then continued eastward along the Barrier, going

---

* In a strict mathematical construction, 1900 was the last year of the nineteenth century.

its whole length of over 500 miles, to arrive by the beginning of February at the point where it abuts against what Ross had reported as the "appearance of land," what Scott now named King Edward VII Peninsula. That done, they returned to Mc-Murdo Sound in search of winter quarters, exploring southward until they found a bit of a bay to winter in at the southwestern point of Ross Island.

This bay, which Scott called Arrival Bay, is now known as Discovery Bay. The narrow spit of land that bounds it on the north, Hut Point, is still crowned by the low square hut that the expedition erected on it for the storage of supplies. The whole area is occupied, today, by McMurdo Station, where a helicopter was to land a wide-eyed visitor sixty-nine years later.

In schematic terms, we may think of Ross Island as an equilateral triangle, between fifty and fifty-five miles to a side. Its west side runs south from Cape Bird to Cape Armitage, separated from the mainland by the width of McMurdo Sound, some thirty-five or forty miles. Its eastern angle is Cape Crozier.

As Scott discovered, this is not an island that one can circumnavigate, because the Ross Ice Shelf, closing McMurdo Sound between the mainland to the west and Cape Armitage, then abuts against the entire south shore to Cape Crozier. Where the shelf crosses McMurdo Sound from Victoria Land its edge is not conspicuous. The sound itself is frozen, and if one walks out on it from McMurdo one comes to a line at which the level is suddenly about a foot higher, so that one takes one step up to continue. That one step is from the saltwater ice of the sound to the fresh-water ice of the shelf. Against the south shore of the island, the northward flowing ice of the shelf crumples up to form pressure ridges. It is only from Cape Crozier, at the eastern end, that the edge of the shelf takes the familiar form of the Great Ice Barrier,

with its cliff face, which runs over 500 miles to its abutment at
the Edward VII Peninsula.

Cape Armitage, at the southwest corner of the island, is in fact
a long tongue of land, representing a steep and rocky ridge that
runs south from the main mass of the island. It is some twenty-
three miles long by less than three miles wide. The *Discovery*
expedition would have preferred to establish its base around the
point on the eastern side of the peninsula, where its expeditions
could take off directly across the Ice Shelf. Because the ship
could not round the point, however, there was nothing for it but
to establish the base on the west side and haul supplies across to
the east side — to what came to be called Pram Point after the
Norwegian boat, a "pram," that was also hauled across. The supplies were taken over what was called "the Gap" between the
steep cone of Observation Hill on the right and the more irregular
mass of Crater Hill on the left. Today, the American McMurdo
Station is on the west side, extending from Hut Point along the
shore of Discovery Bay to Observation Hill. The New Zealand
Scott Base is across the Gap at Pram Point.

Having arrived at Discovery Bay on February 8, 1902, the
Discovery company settled down to winter over, intending a
series of explorations as soon as spring was far enough advanced.

The most gifted member of both the Scott expeditions was Dr.
Edward A. Wilson, who was to die with Scott on the return
journey from the Pole in 1912. I shall not undertake a character
sketch of him here, but merely mention two respects in which he
was distinguished. He had the scientific spirit, which does not
belong to all who are scientists by profession. This is to say that
every natural phenomenon aroused in him a craving to find out
what the explanation was. (He was not the kind of scientist who
would close his eyes to a seal because he was an ornithologist

rather than a mammalogist.) He was also an artist, which is to say that he had an eye for natural beauty. When I say that he had an eye for natural beauty I mean more specifically that he was moved by the visible manifestations of what Werner Heisenberg has called "the central order" of nature. In these terms, artist and scientist turn out to be one. Isaac Newton, Charles Darwin, Albert Einstein, Niels Bohr, all the great scientists by vocation, as distinct from those who are scientists by profession merely, have been artists, searching for "the central order," and the artist in them has not been separate from the scientist.

Wilson, however, also had artistic talent. It is not a foregone conclusion that, if he had concentrated on a career as a water colorist, he would not have been among the great in that field.

Finally, he shared with Scott, Shackleton, Oates, Bowers, Cherry-Garrard, and the rest, an ethos that today seems increasingly quaint, for it belonged to their time and place rather than to ours. This was the ethos that set the highest value on what was called "character." Character involved calm acceptance of risk and the uncomplaining endurance of hardship in the pursuit of great aims, as well as standing by one's comrades at whatever cost to oneself. The members of both Scott expeditions, including the commander, depended on Wilson more than on anyone else — as all who left accounts of these great and sometimes terrible days testified. He seems never to have lost his serenity, even in suffering and death. When he lay dying in a blizzard next to the dying Scott, the latter wrote with his last remaining strength that "his eyes have a comfortable blue look of hope."

I mention Wilson at this point because his spirit is so closely associated with Discovery Bay, Hut Point, Castle Rock, Crater Hill, Observation Hill, Pram Point, the Gap — with the whole scene that is now the site of another base occupied by men of a different generation. We have Wilson's drawings and water colors of the scene as it was without the barracks and other structures of the present. And in his diary we have the account of how, through that first winter, he and his companions, living in the icebound *Discovery*, took their walks almost daily in a strange landscape of which the natural features remain unchanged today.

Emperor Penguin and chick

9. Life on the Brink

◆ NOTHING IS MORE REMARKABLE in our human nature than the way we take for granted the facts we have been brought up to, so that they seem obvious to us even when they are not obvious in themselves. (I think of a man I knew who wondered how people could once have believed the earth was flat.) If those of us whose first knowledge of penguins included the fact that they were birds could recapture the vision of the innocent eye, we would see how far from obvious that fact is in itself. Travelling beneath the surface of the sea they seem, in form and behavior, more like porpoises and seals. They have the same basic shape, and their forelimbs appear to be flippers rather than wings. Some species have the porpoise's graceful habit of repeatedly arching over the surface; and when, from ship or shore, one sees a company of penguins passing in this manner they look more like porpoises than like the birds of our ordinary experience. Seeing them out of water, on land or ice, the innocent eye might be at a loss to know whether they were birds, mammals, or something else. Even their coats appear to be made of the smooth hair that covers seals. These resemblances to seals and porpoises are interesting as illustrations of convergent evolution between birds and mammals.

The penguins are among the most primitive of living birds. This is to say that they are among those which have evolved the least since the birds branched off from the ancestral reptiles.

Their flightlessness, however, is not one of their primitive traits, for their avian forebears were flying birds (perhaps rather like the diving petrels) that, in the course of evolution, lost the power of flight. It is a penguin paradox that their closest surviving relatives on the tree of life are probably the albatrosses.

"Haeckel's Law," that the individual organism in its embryonic and pre-adult development recapitulates the evolution of its ancestors ("ontogeny recapitulates phylogeny"), is no longer accepted by biologists today, if only because it is so imperfectly true. Nevertheless, as one tendency among others, it is taken for granted by biologists, who conclude that the ancestral penguins flew because, *inter alia*, the modern penguins, in their embryonic development, acquire wing quills only to lose them again.[*] Edward Wilson, regarding the Emperor Penguin as the most primitive of all birds, speculated that its embryo might, in its development, provide an account of the evolutionary transition from reptile to bird. Therefore, with two companions, he went to extraordinary lengths and endured unique hardships, as I shall recount, in order to obtain eggs containing embryos.

•

The seventeen species of penguin, confined to the cold waters of the southern hemisphere, range in size from the Little Blue Penguin of Australia and New Zealand, 16 inches long, to the Emperor Penguin, which is 4 feet long and stands 3½ feet tall. The latter is the only bird that breeds exclusively along the edge of the Antarctic continent and its ice-shelves. It is also the only bird in the world, out of eight or nine thousand species, that breeds elsewhere than on land. No other species of higher animal, in fact, breeds in such forbidding circumstances — unless there are fishes

[*] See Goodwin, 1967, p. 14; and Austin, 1961, pp. 26–27.

in the oceanic deeps that reproduce themselves in circumstances equally extreme. It lays its eggs on the sea-ice as winter is setting in, so that its chicks, when they hatch two months later, emerge into a world of perpetual darkness in which the temperature may fall below —75°F. and the wind blow with more than hurricane force. It is also a world without food.

I mentioned in Chapter 1 that the shores of the Antarctic continent tend to correspond to the edge of the layer of life (sometimes called the biosphere) that covers the surface of our globe, for inland the environment is too extreme to support any life except such lichens or minute arthropods as somehow survive in sheltered places among rocks of the interior mountains. The Emperor lives here, on this brink of life. The fact that it breeds here at the time of year when the environment is most hostile, when nothing else above the surface of the sea can maintain an active life, is so extraordinary that Wilson and others at first viewed the evidence for it with incredulity. The logic behind it, however, is clear.

According to what is known as "Bergmann's Rule," warm-blooded animals tend to be larger in the cooler parts of their range. The reason is that, other things being equal, the larger a body the smaller the proportion of surface to volume, and it is only through the surface that heat is lost. The great size of the Emperor Penguin, then, represents its adaptation to a cold climate. According to another rule, however, the larger a bird is the longer the time required for the incubation of the egg and the raising of the chick. The Adélie Penguin, the only other penguin to nest all around the edge of the continent, weighs less than one fifth as much as the Emperor and so is able to complete the process of generation in three months — from the laying of the egg to the northward migration of chicks that have already become independent of their parents — where the Emperor needs six to seven months. If, then, the Emperor, like the Adélie, laid its eggs in the first half of November, its young would achieve independence at a time of increasing darkness and cold, when they were many miles across the sea-ice from the water in which their food occurred. As it is, having hatched in late July or August, the young become independent by late December, when the ice on which they were reared breaks into floes that carry them north as passengers.

The two species of penguin I have mentioned represent, respectively, the two alternative solutions to the problem of such marginal living as the environment allows. The Emperor, in the course of its evolution, has assumed a size that makes it less vulnerable to the cold, but that also exposes it to more extreme cold by preventing it from completing the breeding process within the limits of the summer season. The Adélie has assumed a smaller size that enables it to complete the process within the limits of the season, and so escape the extreme cold of winter, but at the price of being the more vulnerable to such cold as it must still endure.

The Emperor Penguin also illustrates another principle of adaptation, associated with Bergmann's Rule, known as "Allen's Rule." According to it, the limbs and other appendages of a warm-blooded animal tend to be smaller in cooler climates, thereby offering less surface from which the body heat may radiate away. (The ears of the Arctic Fox, for example, are smaller than those of foxes farther south.) A relative of the Emperor Penguin, so close that it may be thought of as a more northern form merely, is the King Penguin, which breeds on sub-Antarctic islands no farther south than about 55°. It is a smaller edition of the Emperor, four-fifths its length, with the same general coloration and markings, but with proportionately longer flippers, feet, and bill.

I note parenthetically, at this point, that both the phylogenetic relationship and the associated difference in geographical distri-bution between Emperor and King Penguins are matched in the Adélie and the Gentoo Penguins. The Gentoo, a close relative of the Adélie, which inhabits sub-Antarctic islands rather than the continental coast, has proportionately longer bill, flippers, and feet.

The Emperor Penguin may be regarded as the most truly Antarctic of all birds. While the Antarctic and Snow Petrels breed at equally high latitudes (roughly that of the Great Ice Barrier), and also confine their range to the pack-ice, the Em-peror Penguin is more specialized. It is, in fact, one of the most specialized birds in the world. One token of this is the fact already mentioned that it is the only bird in the world to breed elsewhere than on land; for only its specialized way of life, caus-ing it to breed in winter, enables it to breed on the sea-ice. How beautifully all fits together!

The Emperor is, I believe, the only bird in the world that does not make use of a nest, or something that serves for one, and does not have a nesting territory that it defends. As soon as the female has laid the single egg, usually in May, the male takes it and tucks it in between the top of his feet and a flap of skin that covers it like a blanket. He is thus able to walk about with it, however awkwardly. The fact that he has no resting territory from which he excludes others of his kind, even though that terri-tory were only three feet across (as in the case of the King Pen-guin), is part of the specialization, accounted for by the fact that the adult birds, their eggs on their feet, have to crowd against one another in a solid mass for protection against the cold and the wind. The proportionate smallness of the surface through which they lose heat, in consequence of their size, is further reduced when they are packed so tightly that only some 20 percent of the surface is exposed to the open air.

Adélie Penguins, like all other penguins except Emperors and Kings, normally lay their two eggs in nests and cover them with their bodies in the prone position. Occasionally, however, as when the eggs are laid in a cleft between rocks that does not allow room for the prone position, they stand erect with the eggs over or between their feet. One supposes that, among the ancestors of the Emperors and Kings, too, the erect position was only an occasional resort, but that evolution to meet changing environmental circumstances over the millennia at last made it their only method of brooding and incubating. They were then able to incubate their eggs and brood their young in more crowded conditions and even on the sea-ice, but it was impracticable to care for more than one egg or young at a time in this fashion.

In March, when all the other birds that nest on the continent, including Adélies, are heading north, the Emperors head south over the newly forming ice in groups that grow as they come together and as they gather new recruits along the way. In May or June, when the female of a couple has laid her single egg and the male has taken it on his feet, she and all the other females walk back to the open sea from which they have so recently come, "which by this time may be forty to sixty miles away beyond the northern horizon."*

At the beginning of the winter nesting season, the male penguins have accumulated so much fat that they weigh 76

* Quoted from Stonehouse's account of the nesting cycle, the chief source of my information here; p. 21.

pounds on the average, 18 pounds more than the females. During the two months or more that they may have to stand with the eggs on their feet in huddles of thousands they live on this reserve. Then the females, now fatter than the males, return and take the eggs on their own feet while the males set off for the open sea. Shortly thereafter the chicks hatch out, taking the place of the eggs on their mothers' feet. Although the females feed them from the full crops they have brought back from the open sea, not enough food is available for rapid growth at this stage. However, as the chicks slowly grow the two parents alternate brooding with foraging trips, until at last the young are big enough to get off their parents' feet and form huddles among themselves, leaving both parents free for the shuttle service to the open water, no longer so far away. By December, the ice on which they were born begins to break into floes that drift northward, carrying them along, a unique mode of migration. Now they find their own food in the sea and complete their growth at the height of summer under the best possible conditions. At the same time, the parents proceed to fatten themselves up for a new breeding season.

In Chapter 1 I commented on the "stubborn determination of life to perpetuate itself and extend its range" manifested by the extremes of environment and adaptation one finds in the Antarctic. The life cycle of the Emperor Penguin illustrates this.

•

The Emperor Penguin's reversal of seasons and migrations makes summer the poorest time for its observation, for then its numbers are scattered about the ocean and the pack-ice.

It was on December 29 at 66°S., as the reader may recall, that the *Staten Island* came to the pack-ice. That day I saw my first penguins, Emperors apparently full-grown but in the immature plumage, like that of the adult but less colorful. My first penguin ever was sharing an ice-floe with a seal. As we approached, it seemed nervous and uncertain in its reaction, finally flopping down on its belly and rowing away with its flippers for a few strokes, but stopping when we began to draw away again.

That day and the next we passed other immature Emperors on the floes, usually single individuals but sometimes two together, and these were the last I would see. At McMurdo Station on January 7 I was told of an adult Emperor that for several days had been standing on the ice of McMurdo Sound near the runway of the airport. (Williams Field, better known as "Willy Field," is the only floating airport in the world.) I took the helicopter from the Station to the airport and set off on foot across the ice in what must have been the wrong direction, because I did not find it. The Emperor Penguin, then, is one of the Antarctic birds, like the Antarctic Fulmar, that I can claim to have seen but not to know.

•

In the last chapter I told how the *Discovery,* running south from New Zealand, reached the pack-ice on November 16, 1901, but failed to get through and so turned back the next day. On a second attempt she got to the pack January 3, 1902, and this time continued through it. In Wilson's journal for the fourth he wrote: "After dinner we saw our first Emperor Penguins, two on a floe, some way off the ship. . . . They looked very large indeed for birds, much more like a small seal, the one lying down, but the other was on his hind legs." The next two were shot for the collection of birds Wilson was making, and "they proved to be young ones."

On April 5, when a company of Emperors were seen walking on the ice near Hut Point, Wilson wrote that they "were evidently making their way up north for the winter." It would have occurred to no one, at the time, that Emperor Penguins might go south for the winter.

By September 22 daylight had returned after the long winter's night. Wilson and Lieutenant Barne walked several miles up the coast of Ross Island, on the offshore ice, where they came on a group of fifteen Emperors. "We made our way to them," Wilson wrote, "and they came to meet us with evident signs of interest, and though they objected to being stroked and immediately tobogganed off on their stomachs if we tried to stroke them, they always came back at once and stood up again to enjoy our company. They were really most wonderfully handsome — bright lemon yellow all down the front, rich black heads, blue backs and rose pink and lilac beaks. The first birds we have seen this year. It was a great delight to watch them and we left them crying after us in a discordant cackle and following us at a stately dawdle."

On October 4 Lieutenant Royds left Hut Point with a party of six for Cape Crozier, to deposit a message for the relief ship that was to touch there when the ice broke up. The party returned on the twenty-fourth with the news that they had found at Cape Crozier, on the sea-ice below the Great Ice Barrier, what was the first rookery of Emperor Penguins ever seen by human eyes. In spite of the date, the parent birds were carrying well-developed chicks on their feet. Wilson commented in his journal that "they must lay their eggs very early indeed. . . ."

When the *Discovery* remained frozen in at Hut Point all summer, Wilson was not sorry at the consequent prospect of another winter in the Antarctic, partly because it would give him a chance to visit and investigate the Crozier rookery earlier in the season, when he might still find eggs to collect. In his journal for June 23, 1903, he wrote: "I have been ferreting out various things in all the books I can lay hands on, to try and get an idea as to how long the Emperor Penguin ought to sit on his egg before hatching it out. I have come to the conclusion that the egg must be laid in the middle of August." In fact, the egg is usually laid in May.

On the basis of his mistaken conclusion, Wilson left Hut Point with Royds and a party of four others September 7, arriving at the rookery on the thirteenth. "It was a very great surprise to us," he wrote, "to find that all the old ones had hatched their eggs and were already nursing chicks apparently every bit as old as those were that Royds and Skelton brought home the year before, on October the 18th, over five weeks later than we are now. I cannot understand this at all. . . ."

When the relief ships *Morning* and *Terra Nova* arrived at Ross Island on January 5, 1904, they carried instructions that the *Discovery* was to be abandoned if she remained icebound through still another summer. However, on February 14 she at last broke free, and soon after was on her way back to the world of normal human habitation — to end up where she is today, moored to Victoria Embankment in the heart of London.

When Wilson, with the second Scott expedition, left England in the *Terra Nova* on June 15, 1910, he had prominently in mind the prospect of reaching the Crozier rookery at a time of year when eggs of the Emperor could be collected, so as to supply a series of embryos by which, in accordance with Haeckel's Law, the "missing link" between reptiles and birds might be revealed. By this time he was reckoning that the eggs must be laid in the beginning of July. So on June 27, 1911, Wilson, Lieutenant

Henry Bowers, and young Apsley Cherry-Garrard left the base of the new expedition at Cape Evans, fifteen miles north of Hut Point, on what was to become the famous winter journey.

The classic account of this egg-hunting expedition has been given by Cherry-Garrard in his book, *The Worst Journey in the World,* while a briefer and more laconic account is in Wilson's journal.

What Scott was to call "the hardest journey that has ever been made" provides an extreme example of the hardships men can endure and still keep going. From Cape Evans around Cape Armitage and along the south shore of Ross Island to Cape Crozier is sixty-seven miles. For five weeks out and back, the three men made their way in the continuous darkness of night, with only occasional gleams of moonlight, having constantly to avoid falling into the crevasses that opened unseen at their feet, unable to find their way half the time, constantly climbing over almost insurmountable pressure ridges, sometimes making as little as a mile and a half in a march of eight hours, in temperatures that went down to the extreme of $-77.5°$F., in blizzards that immobilized them in their tent for days, frostbitten, hardly able to sleep, their strength running out. When, on the outward leg, it had become clear that there was no sense in continuing, they continued still.

What is most notable, however, is that, after reaching Cape Crozier only to be struck by a blizzard that carried away their tent, the only shelter they had, when any hope that they could survive seemed to have been foreclosed thereby, they still survived and got back.

They got back to Cape Evans with three eggs. When spring came, Wilson and Bowers went with Scott on the journey to the South Pole from which none of them returned. It was left to

Cherry-Garrard, now the sole survivor of the winter journey, to deliver the three eggs, more than a year later, to the Natural History Museum in Kensington. Although he had written to say at what hour he would come in with them, an Assistant Custodian made it clear, on his arrival, that the museum was not an egg shop, that it was not interested in eggs. Ushered into the office of the Chief Custodian, he found that dignitary engaged in conversation with a visitor and unwilling to be interrupted by a delivery boy with some penguin eggs. He took the eggs from his hands without a thank-you and told him he need not wait. When Cherry-Garrard asked for a receipt he was summarily dismissed with the reply that it was not necessary. He got his receipt, at last, only by stationing himself in the passage outside the Custodian's office and refusing to leave until it was given him.

In the fullness of time, the scientific examination of the three eggs was undertaken. The report, which is included in Cherry-Garrard's book, indicates that the embryos found in the eggs were of no great interest.

Lessing wrote: "Not the possession of truth but the struggle to attain it brings happiness to the seeker." That good and dedicated man, Leonard Woolf, entitled the sad final volume of his autobiography, "The Journey not the Arrival Matters." The phrase might serve as an epitome of the shining failures that constitute the principal achievements of Captain Scott and his heroic companions. In his final message, written as he, Wilson, and Bowers lay dying on the Ross Ice Shelf in their unsuccessful attempt to return from the South Pole (which Amundsen had reached just a month before them), Scott wrote: ". . . I do not regret this journey, which has shown that Englishmen can endure hardships, help one another, and meet death with as great a forti-tude as ever in the past." We must conclude that, in the final reckoning, it was not the eggs that mattered.

•

On January 6, 1971, 59 years, 6 months, and 25 days after the return of the Crozier party with their three eggs, I also made the journey to Crozier, and I made it along the same south shore, over the same pressure ridges and crevasses. The helicopter left its pad below Hut Point at three in the afternoon and landed me at Cape Crozier about three-thirty. The pilot had agreed that, on the return trip, he would fly me low along the Great Ice Barrier over the site of the Emperor Penguins' rookery so that I could get a close look and some photographs. While at the cape my time would be spent in the rookery of Adélie Penguins that was then active, and by dint of some pleading I got him to agree that I might take two hours for the purpose of observing it. This visit, however, was one of the most crowded experiences of my life, so that I was ten minutes late in returning to the helicopter, where the justly indignant pilot and his crewman were getting tired of tossing pebbles into the air and catching them. Under the circumstances, it was only right and proper that I should be deprived of the close view of a site that, among others, I had come twenty-five thousand miles to see. We were back at McMurdo in very good time for the evening meal.

10. *I Pagliacci*

➤ IN JANUARY 1841, when the *Erebus* and the *Terror* first penetrated the pack-ice, Captain Ross reported seeing "great numbers
of penguins of a different species from those we had met with at
Kerguelen and Auckland Islands." "These curious birds," he
wrote, "actually followed our ships, answering the call of the
sailors, who imitated their cry; and although they could not
scramble over the ice so fast as our ships sailed past it, they made
up for it when they got into the water, and we soon had quite a
flock of them in our wake, playing about our vessel like so many
porpoises." These, presumably, were penguins of the two species,
Emperor and Adélie, that ride the ice-floes but do not occur
north of the pack.

Cherry-Garrard, reporting the first entrance of the *Terra Nova*
into the pack, wrote: "Hardly had we reached the thick pack
. . . when we saw the little Adélie penguins hurrying to meet us.
Great Scott, they seemed to say, what's this, and soon we could
hear the cry which we shall never forget. 'Aark, aark,' they said,
and full of wonder and curiosity, and perhaps a little out of
breath, they stopped every now and then to express their feelings.
. . . We used to sing to them, as they to us, and you might often
see 'a group of explorers on the poop, singing "She has rings on
her fingers and bells on her toes . . ." at the top of their voices to
an admiring group of Adélie penguins'" (Cherry-Garrard quotes
this last from Wilson's journal).

Adélie Penguins porpoising

On January 11, when Ross was defeated in his attempt to land on the mainland at Cape Adare, there to take possession in Queen Victoria's name, and so landed on Possession Island instead, he found that "inconceivable myriads of penguins completely covered the whole surface of the island, along the ledges of the precipices, and even to the summits of the hills, attacking us vigorously as we waded through their ranks, and pecking at us with their sharp beaks, disputing possession." So the act establishing Queen Victoria's imperial sway did not go uncontested by the natives.

In January 1895, when Captain Kristensen effected the first human landing on the continent proper, at Cape Adare, he found the area where he landed under solid occupation by nesting Adélies. Wilson, after his first visit to Cape Adare in January 1902, wrote in his journal that the rookery contained literally millions of birds.

The rookeries of the Adélie Penguin are located at those points on the Antarctic coasts where a scouring wind prevents the permanent or deep accumulation of snow. By the time the birds arrive at the sites, in October, the stony ground, or the floor of guano accumulated from past years, is likely to be bare, so that the birds can proceed immediately with the arrangement of small stones to make nests. Murphy reports, however, that "the Adélies frequently get snowed under during spring and summer blizzards, and they have been known to live for weeks beneath the crust before they thawed out. No harm necessarily comes to the eggs from this. A returning cock appears to be made very angry, however, by the inability of his mate to leave the eggs when only her head is projecting through the crust of snow!"

From the first encampment of human beings along the edge of the Antarctic continent, which was at Cape Adare in 1899, men in the Antarctic have lived in an extraordinarily close relationship with Adélie Penguins. This is because we men, like the penguins, have chosen for our campsites such flat places as the wind has scoured bare of snow, and most of these, it appears, have been under prior occupation by the penguins.

When Hallett Station was established in 1956, the flat peninsula on which it was constructed was entirely covered by the rookery, which may have numbered half a million birds. Today a corner of the site is occupied by the cratelike structures in which men live and work, but the nesting penguins are all around and run about freely through the narrow passages between these buildings, human and avian pedestrians almost jostling each other as they go about their business.

It should be recalled that, in the fifty million years or more during which penguins have evolved — and there is every reason to believe that they evolved in the Antarctic — they have never, until the recent visits of man, had to adapt themselves to the presence above water of any creature capable of injuring them. (I except, here, such predatory birds as the skuas and Giant Petrels that take eggs or chicks left undefended by the adults.) The bird-life of the Arctic, by contrast with that of the Antarctic, has in the course of its evolution had to adapt its physiology and behavior to the threat of such predators as Arctic Foxes and Polar Bears, but there have never been any such predators in the Antarctic. Consequently, the penguins have developed no means of defence against such predators, no behavioral adaptations, no appropriate psychological responses. For them, danger of this sort exists only beneath the surface of the sea, in the form of Leopard Seals and Killer Whales, and in the course of their evolution they have become adapted to coping with it where it is found. Above the surface, however, no caution or precaution has ever been needed. Because the Leopard Seal does not hunt or feed out of water, a penguin will share a cake of ice with one in untroubled tranquility. We may be sure that an Emperor or Adélie Penguin out of water would have no hesitation in walking up to the wide-open mouth of a roaring Polar Bear, unable to apprehend the danger. In his journal for January 4, 1911, Scott reported how the Adélies at Cape Evans behaved in just this fashion with the Eskimo dogs tethered on the ice.

> They waddle forward, poking their heads to and fro in their usually absurd way, in spite of a string of howling dogs strain-ing to get at them. "Hulloa!" they seem to say, "here's a game — what do all you ridiculous things want?" And they come a few steps nearer. The dogs make a rush as far as their leashes or harness allow. The penguins are not daunted in the least, but their ruffs go up and they squawk with semblance of anger, for all the world as though they were rebuking a rude stranger . . . and then the final fatal steps forward are taken and they come within reach. There is a spring, a squawk, a horrid red patch on the snow, and the incident is closed. Nothing can stop these silly birds. Members of our party rush to head them off, only to be met with evasions. . . .

One of Scott's conspicuous traits was his sensitivity to the suffering of animals, and one can understand the spirit of exasper-ated agony in which he referred to these penguins as "silly birds." But the fact is that nothing in over fifty million years of evolution had given them any basis for knowing how to react to dogs or men.

In his journal for January 11, 1842, Ross wrote of "the great penguin," as he observed it in the pack-ice: "They are remarkably stupid and allow you to approach them so near as to strike them on the head with a bludgeon, and sometimes, if knocked off the ice into the water, they will almost immediately leap upon it again as if to attack you, but without the smallest means either of offence or defence." It would not have occurred to him, at the time he wrote, that this behavior of the penguins represented their natural association of danger with the watery realm only, and of safety with the realm above water, associations that had been confirmed over tens of millions of years; so that, when alarmed, their impulse was to avoid the water rather than make for it. Here is an early example of the poignant misunderstanding that, from the first, has existed between men and penguins.

Although the Adélies at the rookeries I visited were used to men, everything in their behavior still showed uncertainty about how to react to them. Probably because they are nearsighted, a penguin's first reaction to the approach of a man is likely to be to come close up for a good look. So it will run up to one, waving its flippers and barking, as if to greet an old friend. It may suddenly stop two or three feet away to peer first out of one eye, then the other, its flippers spread so wide that they point backward. It may seem at a loss to know what it should do next. Perhaps it will turn and run away a few steps, only to turn back again and run toward one; or it may run right up and pluck at one's trouser leg, then run away again. It has curiosity, but apparently no established awareness of possible danger out of water.

An exception to this last statement has to be made for its reaction to helicopters. At Cape Hallett, because the penguins are everywhere, the helicopters have to land virtually among them. The nearby birds scatter in all directions as the roaring machine settles down, some scudding on their bellies, flippers and feet working alike. Perhaps the experience of Giant Petrels and skuas has given them an awareness that danger may come out of the sky, or perhaps they share with all the higher forms of life a disposition to panic at any vast and noisy disturbance in the environment. The roaring descent of a helicopter is not wholly dissimilar to the roaring descent of a landslide or the rending fall of ice cliffs, natural phenomena that, in the course of their evolution, they have learned to fear.

If the reaction of penguins to men is ignorant, so for the most part is the reaction of men to penguins. They approach them as if they were mechanical toys or characters in an animated cartoon, and regard everything about them as a joke. The incomprehension between men and penguins, by its mutuality, is complete.

The penguins on their nesting grounds are engaged in a struggle to survive and perpetuate their kind under marginal conditions. They are engaged in basically the same struggle to maintain life as we men are, and this might properly engage our sympathy. (I think of Joseph Wood Krutch silently saying to those miniature frogs, the Spring Peepers: "Don't forget, we are all in this together.") But this would be to see them as the fellow creatures they are and, seeing them thus, to take them seriously.

When the four helicopters from the two ships landed at Hallett one could see how the crew members immediately classified the penguins, in their minds, as stage entertainment. One of these grown-up boys ran up to a nest, seized a squawking bird that was trying to cover and protect its chicks, and proceeded to waltz it about and to engage in mock wrestling matches with it, while his companions on the sidelines whooped and snapped photographs for the folks back home.

When I reported this spectacle to the Captain of the *Staten Island* his concern was immediate, spontaneous, and deep. He issued renewed orders that all hands were to avoid any unnecessary disturbance of the penguins on any occasion. I found that, like him, the other commanders and directors of the American activities in the Antarctic were alert to the conservation provisions of the Antarctic Treaty, applicable to the activities of all nations in Antarctica, and concerned to enforce them. In the long run, however, the protection of nature everywhere in the world depends on the acquisition by mankind in general of the understanding that "we are all in this together."

"It was the saying of Bion," according to Plutarch, "that though the boys throw stones at frogs in sport, yet the frogs do not die in sport but in earnest."

•

McMurdo Station and Scott Base, situated together at the tip of Cape Armitage, which constitutes the southwest corner of Ross Island, are occupied throughout the year. The only other sites of human occupation on the island during the summer of 1970–1971 was a six-man New Zealand station at Cape Bird, its northwest corner, and a three-man American station at Cape Crozier, the east corner, both occupied in summer only. There are large Adélie rookeries at both of these capes, and another at Cape Royds, halfway down the west coast between Cape Bird and Cape Armitage. This last rookery is the southernmost in the world, being farther south than the one at Crozier by some twenty-four miles. Cape Royds is where the *Nimrod* expedition under Ernest Shackleton set up its base, built the hut that still stands there, and passed the winter of 1908–1909. Halfway down from it to Cape Armitage is Cape Evans, where the second Scott expedition, which achieved the Pole, set up its base and built the hut that still stands. However, although both Cape Evans and Cape Armitage have flat ground that is exposed in winter, I know of no record of an Adélie colony at either, and I suppose the

Adélie Penguin rookery

reason to be that, at both, the adjacent water of McMurdo Sound is likely to remain frozen over through most or all of the breeding season. It is true that at Cape Hallett on December 30 the ice extended out several miles from shore, so that one saw long lines of Adélies traversing it in both directions, coming from or going to their colony; but this ice would presumably melt away before the end of summer, while that off Capes Armitage and Evans, in addition to being more extensive, is likely to remain all summer, as when it held the *Discovery* prisoner at Hut Point.

I owe it to the courtesy and helpfulness of those in charge at McMurdo that, during my brief stay, I was enabled to visit all the Adélie rookeries on Ross Island, which I have enumerated above; but I shall content myself here with describing my visit to the one at Cape Crozier.

The cape itself, at the easternmost point of the island, is where the slope of Mount Terror falls, partly in cliffs, into the sea. The Great Ice Barrier is anchored to these cliffs, and just above them is a volcanic cone, which the members of Scott's first expedition named "the Knoll," that rises a thousand feet above the sea. The helicopter from McMurdo buzzes over the south shore of Ross Island until, just short of Cape Crozier and the Knoll, it crosses inland toward the north shore, landing in a sort of high amphitheater among the rocks. To the north and east of the amphitheater the land slopes down into the sea, its slope extending to the heights dominated by the Knoll. The slope is solidly peopled with penguins, for it is the site of the Adélie rookery which was here already when the first explorers came (and for how long before?).

"Most of the south coast of Ross Island," I wrote in my notes of the flight, "welded as it is to the Ice Shelf, appears buried in snow that obliterates the connection; and out of the snow, which is crevassed along the slopes, bits of peaks or ridge stand out black. There is much black at the eastern end of the island, which the helicopter crosses south to north to land at the top of a slope that descends to the open sea."

The cabin that housed the three scientists then working at Crozier stands near the site of the helicopter's landing. The three were, in addition to a young Chilean ornithologist studying a nesting colony of skuas, Dr. and Mrs. Dietland Müller-Schwarze, whom I had come to know as fellow passengers on the flight from

North America to New Zealand. An animal-behaviorist who had studied under Dr. Konrad Lorenz, he was engaged, together with his wife, in a study of the adaptations that enable the Adélie Penguin to cope with the predation of the Leopard Seal.

The Müller-Schwarzes came to meet me and we stood a moment on this lofty height to survey the scene below. From close to where we were, the penguin-covered slope to the sea extended eastward until it was contained by a ridge that ended to the north in cliffs at the edge of the sea. On the ridge one could just see the post erected by the *Discovery* company on January 22, 1902, to mark the site where messages had been left by them for the relief ships that were to come the following season. The dark blue sea under the sunshine was free of ice except for one berg that, six days earlier, had calved from the Ice Barrier as if to celebrate the New Year. (The Müller-Schwarzes said that, in the middle of the "night" between December 31 and January 1, they had been awakened by what sounded like a cannon shot; and when they had arisen a few hours later it was to see this newly calved New Year's berg floating off their shore.)

Just below us, a Wilson's Storm Petrel was coursing like a swallow back and forth along the slope. Believing as I do that there must be a reason for everything in this world, although it is not commonly apparent, I was puzzled then and have been ever since to know why a bird that finds its food only in the sea was questing and quartering over a stony slope, a hundred to two hundred feet above sea-level, at a place far from its nesting grounds. Perhaps it found pleasure in the warmth and buoyancy of the air above stone heated by the sunlight.

Hardly had we started down the slope into the rookery when the Müller-Schwarzes called my attention to a drama taking place in the sea. At that moment a Leopard Seal not far offshore had caught a penguin. What I saw was the seal shaking the penguin's black-and-white body as a dog shakes a rat. The immense head of the seal would rise out of the water momentarily, and then the long curved back alone, like the back of a whale, would arch above the surface. A moment later, another Leopard Seal caught another penguin, and the same procedure was repeated, while half a dozen skuas waited on overhead to pick the bones that the seals left.

"The vigor and perfection of the Adélie Penguin," Murphy wrote, "which are continuously fostered by very high selective mortality, become apparent as one follows its life history." At its rookeries the Leopard Seals patrol the shorelines, facing out to sea. When a seal sees a company of returning penguins "porpoising" toward the rookery, it drops beneath the surface to surprise and catch its prey. Drs. R. L. Penney and George Lowry, who have studied the process at the Crozier rookery, have estimated that, in the course of a nesting season, the seals catch some 5 percent of the entire breeding population.

There is reason to believe that, while a Leopard Seal can swim faster than a penguin, the penguin, able to make tighter turns, can evade the jaws of death by dodging. Where there is only one penguin, however, the seal is apt to pursue it until it is exhausted and can dodge no more. Where there are many, the seal will turn from one to another until some individual weaker or less alert than the others is caught. So the individual penguins find a relative security in numbers. This makes individuals reluctant to be the first into the water at rookeries where the seals are waiting. They gather along the edge of the ice blocks that constitute the remains of the ice-foot, where the sea-ice was once attached to the shore, crowding ever more against the brink as more birds arrive, until at last one is crowded over the edge, whereupon the others leap in after it. The seal is presented with a sudden shower of penguins, an embarrassment of riches.

Many penguins escape from their pursuers by the ability to leap vertically out of the water and land, feet first, on top of a cake of ice as high as five feet above the surface (twice the penguins' standing height).

Down at the shore, when my hosts and I got there, a Leopard Seal was wallowing at the surface a few feet away, its dark body glistening as the back humped into the air or the great head was lifted to show the large and predatory mouth, quite unlike the mouths of all other seals, which feed only on the small and cold-blooded life of the sea. A line of penguins stood just above it on the ice-foot, extending their flippers back as if in surprise, or waving them slowly.

While photographing the scene I almost backed into a Weddell Seal that had been sleeping on shore until the commotion of us three, added to that of the penguins, woke it up. "Hello, old fellow!" I said. The way it lifted its head and looked at me gave an impression of indignation mingled with disgust, and at last, seeing that we intruders were apparently intending to remain, it heaved itself along the ice-foot and dropped off into the sea. (Leopard Seals kill and eat other species of seal, but I suppose the local representatives were on a penguin diet.)

•

At such sites as Cape Adare, Cape Hallett, Cape Bird, and Cape Royds, the migrating Adélies in October may have as much as a two-week march over the sea-ice, which they cross in endless files, before reaching their rookeries. The two eggs of each hen are laid in November, at an interval of three days, in the nest of stones. The whole business of coming ashore, establishing possession of a nesting site, finding the right or the wrong mate, building the nest, and finally producing the eggs, with all the fighting entailed, takes between two and three weeks, after which the male may be left alone to incubate the eggs for another two weeks, making a span of more than a month that he has to fast. Instead of drinking their usual seawater, the nesting penguins eat snow, of which the cock may sometimes fetch lumps from a distance for his mate on the nest. Once the eggs are laid, exchanges at the nest, at first running to intervals of two weeks, take place with increasing frequency. After somewhat more than a month of incubation the chicks, seeming as if clad in dark gray fur, hatch out. At about seven weeks old they acquire their juvenile plumage, like the adult plumage except that the throat is white. By late February they have attained the age of independence and are ready to go to sea on their own. At this stage, the Leopard Seals patrolling the shores face inland rather than seaward. The young, plunging in for their first wetting, remain on the surface, where their progress is slow, and the seals then have their fill with a minimum of effort. So it is that many adult penguins brave dangers and endure hardship for months only to provide a meal or two for the leopards of the sea. Surely, however, they are quite right to carry on as they were so plainly designed by nature to do, just as we men are also right in assuming that there is some ultimate if unknown purpose to be served by all this.

The chicks at Cape Crozier on January 6 must have been some three weeks old, for it is at about this age that, leaving their nests, they gather together, as the young Emperors also do, in nurseries of their own called crèches. At Cape Hallett on December 31 most of the young were in the nests, still ludicrously trying to remain under their parents although already too big to avoid coming out into the world; and now, a week later at Cape Crozier, the crèches were forming.

Human children who have to face difficulties in the process of growing up have the advantage that, once grown up, they may be better prepared by their experience to face such difficulties as await us all in the great world. The young of the Adélie Penguin do not lack this advantage. Let a chick stray but twelve inches from its nest and the parents in adjacent nests attack it mercilessly, biting it on the back, the head, the flippers, while it peeps frantically and struggles to escape. When the urge to form crèches leads a chick to move away from its nest it has to run the gauntlet of attacking adults, and it may not survive the experience. Moreover, if it strays from the center of its colony and parental protection it will surely be set upon by one or a pair of skuas, always in attendance, that may peck out its eyes and tear it to death to make a meal of it. There are other causes of death in childhood as well, such as starvation when a parent fails to return in time from foraging at sea and the parent on guard has run out of supply. In this peculiar realm where nothing ever decays, the ground of a penguin rookery is always more or less littered with the mummified corpses of chicks that did not live long enough to run the gauntlet of Sea Leopards. At the Cape Crozier rookery, as at the others I visited, the "aarking" of the adults formed a *basso continuo* for the constant peeping of chicks in distress.

The life of the Adélie Penguin is not truly the comedy that some observers take it to be. It is, rather, like the tragedy of Canio the clown, whose role it is to get slapped, his face frozen in its comical expression as he plays his part out to its fatal end and the bitter terminal line: *La commedia è finita!*

For all the suffering of the Adélie's life history, it remains true that one cannot look at any individual and see it except as one

Adélie Penguins

sees a circus clown, with his fantastic pantaloons and conical hat, the smile painted on his face like bravery itself. The adult Adélie is the solemn little gentleman with white shirtfront and black tailcoat, to which everyone wants to add a bow tie. What is irresistibly comical, like the clown's smile, is the eye, one on each side of the pointed black face, which looks like a round white stone with a black disk in the middle; and the habit the penguin has of never trusting completely to either eye, so that, turning its head first this way and then that, it uses first one and then the other for a stare of apparent astonishment at the object to be observed. What is equally comical is its habit of running up to the human visitor like some little Mr. Pickwick out of breath, flippers extended backward as if ready to hug him; then running away again, or suddenly deciding that, having seen the visitor out of one eye and confirmed him with the other, it may now go fast asleep on its feet in front of him, its bill tucked under one flipper.

The chicks in their charcoal-gray fur, while they do not have the same comic charm as the adults, are comical in their own way. They have immense bellies that overhang their feet, as if they were so many old Falstaffs. ("How long is't ago, Jack," Prince Hal asked, "since thou sawest thine own knee?") They might represent the senile and degenerate stage of penguinity rather than its hopeful youth.

Against the background of our human world the Adélie Penguins are bound to stand for a comedy that, against the background of their own world, is irrelevant.

.

Here I am thinking all these thoughts, relevant and irrelevant, while half running up the slope with the Müller-Schwarzes, among the wide-eyed penguins aarking and peeping, while he pours out his wonderful fund of knowledge on animal behavior, or picks up stones of rare geological interest for me to pocket; and all the time two impatient men under a helicopter are tossing pebbles into the air and catching them. By the time I reach them, breathing as hard as a penguin that has been running — waving to the Müller-Schwarzes, crying good-bye and thank you — our departure for the return trip is overdue.

➤ TEN SPECIES of bird are known to breed or to have bred on the principal mass of the Antarctic continent, and another nine on the Antarctic Peninsula. The ten include the two penguins I have just described and seven members of the albatross-petrel order, Procellariiformes.* That leaves one other species, the Great Skua.

The Great Skua is not primitive like the Procellariiformes, for it belongs to a higher branch on the evolutionary tree, being a member of the relatively advanced order that includes the gulls and terns. It occurs over the world's oceans and along its shores in several forms, which many authorities regard as varieties of one species.† Being by disposition more of a "lumper" than a "splitter," I shall so regard them here. As a species, then, the Great Skua is, out of some eight or nine thousand known species

---

* The seven Procellariiformes are the Giant Petrel, the Antarctic Fulmar, the Antarctic Petrel, the Cape Pigeon, the Snow Petrel, the Antarctic Prion, and Wilson's Storm Petrel.

† See Wynne-Edwards in Thomson, 1964, pp. 762–763; and Voous, 1960, p. 103. The reader should bear in mind that, in the continuous divergence of forms on the evolutionary tree, the question of how great a divergence must be before it may be regarded as representing the separation between species (rather than sub-species) is nominal rather than real. Although the traditional criterion has been that of whether different forms do or do not interbreed in nature, the reason for their not interbreeding may be nothing more than geographical separation; and this criterion, in any case, is so far disregarded by the authorities that some forms are universally distinguished as separate species even though they do interbreed in a state of nature — e.g., in North America the Golden-winged Warbler and the Blue-winged warbler. For current thought on this whole question see Mayr, 1970.

of birds, the only one that breeds in the high latitudes of both northern and southern hemispheres, although in the northern hemisphere its breeding is confined to the Orkneys, the Shetlands, the Faroes, and Iceland.

In the account I gave earlier of the albatrosses, fulmars, and petrels I mentioned that their order presumably originated deep in the southern hemisphere, where they dominate the circumpolar ocean today, so that the presence of a fulmar high in the northern hemisphere represents the straying of some of its members across the barrier of the tropics. By contrast, the order that includes the skuas, gulls, and terns presumably originated in the northern hemisphere, where it is dominant today; but some of its members eventually became established in the southern hemisphere, and it is likely that the Great Skua of the north is itself descended from ancestral skuas in the south that strayed back across the tropics into the North Atlantic to find new homes on the islands from Scotland to Iceland.

It is common, in the observation of birds, to be impressed by the "intelligence" of some species and the "stupidity" of others. We generally use these words to register unpondered impressions rather than scientific observations, and would be hard put to define either in precise terms. It seems to us stupid that a penguin, attacked by man or dog, should deliberately avoid taking refuge in the water; but the association of danger with the water, and with the water only, makes perfect sense in terms of the whole previous experience of the species. The case is the same with the albatross on land, for it has virtually no appropriate reaction to the potential danger represented by the approach of a large land beast like man. After all, even the birds we refer to as the most intelligent are presumably not reasoning creatures like ourselves, being governed only by intuitive reactions that represent hereditary adaptation to their proper environments. Consequently, one could not, on the face of it, expect those that seem to us the most intelligent to react to situations altogether alien to their hereditary experience in terms that represent the conclusions of a reasoning process.

All this is preliminary to remarking that anyone who visits the Antarctic is bound to be impressed by the contrast between the apparent stupidity of albatrosses, petrels, or penguins and the apparent intelligence of the skuas. With sufficient knowledge of the relationships involved, he will be inclined to explain this apparent difference by the fact that the former represent a more primitive, the latter a more advanced stage of evolutionary development. I daresay this is right. It is not that the skua has a reasoning intelligence, but that its psychological reactions, while still spontaneous and unreasoned, have become adapted to a more varied and complex environment than that in which penguins and petrels have evolved. The group to which the skua belongs, that of the gulls and terns, is not composed, for the most part, of pelagic birds, birds adapted to life far out in the ocean, like the albatrosses and petrels. It is composed, rather, of birds that live their lives along the shores of the sea or of inland waters, that belong to the edge between two contrasting environments. Their food may be found on land as well as in the water; they have to cope with land predators as well as water predators. They have to compete under more complex circumstances with a far greater variety of other life than do the primitive birds of the southern ocean.

If we except the extreme represented by certain deserts, the Antarctic continent and the surface of its surrounding waters must present, to birds, the simplest of all the large-scale environments on the face of the earth. (Contrast it with the environment

of a parrot living in the luxuriance of a tropical rain forest.) The environment occupied by the Emperor Penguin during its breeding season consists of ice and sky only, with open water perhaps many days' travel away, and there is no other life in it (except for such minute parasites as the penguins themselves may harbor). Between breeding seasons, the Emperor occupies the somewhat more varied habitat of the pack-ice — but it, too, is one of the simplest on earth. The albatrosses of the circumpolar ocean, below the latitudes of the pack-ice, while their environment may not be quite as simple as that of the Emperor and Adélie Penguins, still live in far simpler conditions than the majority of species in the group to which the skua belongs. Gulls and skuas, then, may be just as incapable of reasoning as the albatross shows itself to be when, unaware of danger, it allows itself to be picked up by a man rather than take flight. But a more varied, complex, and changeful environment forced the skua or its relatives, over millions of years, to continue their adaptive evolution at a high pace, suiting themselves to all sorts of conditions, while the environment of penguin or albatross imposed no like requirement. Therefore the impression an observer has of a contrast between the "intelligence" of the skua and the "stupidity" of the other birds is not without foundation. It may even be that, because the skua and its relatives have long had to be prepared to cope with relatively unexpected situations, they have in fact acquired at least the rudiments of such intelligence as we identify with the ability to reason. It is to be expected, at least, that they can learn faster than the more primitive species.

All the several forms of the Great Skua are about the size of Herring Gulls, but with bodies broader and heavier, and with broader wings. They are predominantly dark brown with a white flash across each wing that shows conspicuously when the wing is

South Polar Skua

extended. Built as they are, their flight always appears labored, nor do they ever, even in pursuit of other birds, seem to move otherwise than ponderously. It is surprising, then, to see how quickly they are able, in chase, to overtake some of the swiftest fliers of the sea. The explanation must lie in the sheer power of the pectoral muscles that work the wings and, by their size, give such breadth to the bodies. They are the stoutest of birds in more than one sense of the term.

Although the different geographical forms do not vary greatly in size, the largest, as well as the darkest, is the Brown Skua, which appears to be circumpolar (except, perhaps, for the wide quadrant of the Pacific east of New Zealand, where the absence of land over such wide areas may tend to exclude what is basically a coastal bird). Its breeding range is between the latitudes of New Zealand and those of the Antarctic Peninsula, roughly from 48° to 70°, and it occurs as far south as Ross Island. I here quote Dr. Murphy's description of it, which applies largely to the other forms as well.

> During the South Georgia Expedition of 1912–1913, I became extremely well acquainted with the Brown Skua, which has left, I believe, a more vivid impression in my memory than any other bird I have met. The skuas look and act like miniature eagles. They fear nothing, never seek to avoid being conspicuous, and, by every token of behavior, they are lords of the far south. In effect, they are gulls which have turned into hawks. Not only are they the enemies of every creature they can master, living almost entirely by ravin and slaughter, but they also have the appearance of a bird of prey in the general color of their plumage, the pointed, erectile hackles on the neck, the hooked bill, and the long, sharp, curved claws, which seem incongruous on webbed feet. They are tremendously strong, heavy, and vital birds which, in the air, look massive

rather than speedy. It is therefore somewhat surprising to learn that they can overtake in free flight such swift, long-winged petrels as the Shoemaker [the White-chinned Petrel] (*Procellaria aequinoctialis*). Energy is apparent in every movement of the skua — in its rapacity, in the quantity of food it can ingest within a few moments, and in the volume and continuousness of the screams that issue from its throat. Doubtless, its physiological processes are relatively rapid.

I first met the Brown Skua when the helicopter that was delivering Mike Gibson and me settled down at the meteorological station on Campbell Island. A number of individuals, even darker than the Great Skuas I remembered from Shetland, were standing about, unawed by the roaring helicopter or its whirling blades, let alone by the men among whom they were interspersed. But there was not a moment to stop and observe them. Instead, there were hands to be shaken, plans to be hastily improvised, rubber boots to be pulled on in a dark shed — and then we were off to visit albatrosses.

Five hours later, when we got back to the station, the helicopter was waiting to take off and again everything was rush. Nevertheless, in this valedictory moment an image of Brown Skuas fixed itself in my mind's eye, forever indelible. As we walked toward the helicopter between low, whitewashed shacks, the somber birds, all the darker for the whitewashed boards of their platforms and the light of the sky behind them, stood on the roofs indifferently surveying us in our passage. They seemed like feudal lords on their own battlements, looking down without respect or fellow feeling upon the ruck of common mortals moving past. It was they who owned the station, not the six human creatures who had been brought in to man it under their aegis.

The next day, at sea, I saw a Brown Skua attack in flight that other and much larger predator of the Antarctic, the Giant Petrel, driving it down onto the water.

•

If the Brown Skua is a medieval feudal lord, the South Polar Skua is a Renaissance prince. Instead of being dark brown all over (except for the white flash in the wing), it has a pale body, gray-brown, that contrasts with the dark and glistening plumage of the wings. Its neck, like the Golden Eagle's, is adorned with golden hackles. It is a bird beautiful as Tirzah, comely as Jerusalem, terrible as an army with banners.

Fear seems as unknown to the South Polar Skua as to the Brown Skua. I have already told, in Chapter 4, how on December 30 I accompanied two of the scientific staff at Cape Hallett by helicopter to the nesting sites of the Snow Petrels and Wilson's Storm Petrels some ten miles away across the frozen inlet. The helicopter landed where the steep slope rising from the inlet was stepped back to form a flat stony shelf, clear of snow and perhaps a hundred feet in diameter. A pair of South Polar Skuas, presumably associated with the colony of Snow Petrels off which they lived, had two eggs in a nest that amounted to no more than a scrape among the stones, perhaps thirty feet from where the helicopter landed. The two birds showed no fear of the formidable machine as it descended upon them, roaring and milling with its arms, but stood on their own ground, screaming, or rose and flapped so close that they seemed in danger of being caught by the revolving blades.

While all forms of the skua live largely on other birds, which they either kill or rob of their prey, they are not dependent on such predation. They can forage for themselves over the surface

South Polar Skua on the Ross Ice Shelf near Scott Base

of the sea, and they may live by scavenging about human settle-
ments, where they are consumers of garbage. So it is that, just as
skuas are found in attendance at every colony of Adélie Penguins,
they are also found in summer at every human settlement along
the rim of the continent. They nest in or at the edge of the
penguin colonies, living on penguin eggs and young. (It is not
uncommon for one skua to distract a parent penguin by harass-
ment while its mate goes after the consequently unguarded
young.) They were the only birds I saw at McMurdo Station,
where they were common, and here they were concentrated at
the garbage dump on the ice of Discovery Bay. Upon the first
arrival of man in the Antarctic, they promptly adapted them-

selves to his presence, with profit to themselves, just as the gulls of the north have adapted themselves to the artificial environment of man's cities.

The skua was the only Antarctic bird that I had been familiar with before going south. I had visited its nesting grounds on the moors of Shetland in July, at the season when the young were newly hatched and the parents repeatedly dove with full force on such intruders as myself, sometimes striking them on the head. In Shetland my defence had been to hold my camera tripod vertically over my head, thereby compelling them to keep that much distance. At Cape Bird on January 3, where the South Polar Skuas had newly hatched young, they repeatedly attacked and struck me — but this time my defence was a quilted cap. (It had the advantage over the tripod defence of leaving one's hands free to photograph one's screaming assailant coming in to the attack with the speed of an express train.)

At Cape Bird, as elsewhere, it was evident that skuas and Adélie Penguins took for granted their association, the skuas having their nests at the edge or in the midst of the penguin colonies, skuas and penguins often standing side by side in tranquility. Occasionally a penguin would drive a skua off, making it keep a greater distance, and once I saw two skuas attack a penguin conjointly from both sides, giving it such a buffeting that at last it ran away.

•

I now have to report an extraordinary fact about the South Polar Skua, for which it is hard to find even a speculative explanation. The record, which I am about to cite, shows that occasional skuas may be found anywhere in the interior of the Antarctic continent.

The reader is to picture this shield of ice, with a radius of some 1,300 miles, rimmed in large part by mountain-chains, the ice plateau of its interior generally eight to fourteen thousand feet high. Even in the perpetual daylight of summer it is cold beyond the extremes of normal experience, often swept by gales and fogged with blowing snow, with not an atom that would serve for nourishment over thousands of miles. For any kind of life, this is the most forbidding area on earth.

Wilson was the first to report the sighting of skuas far in the interior, and he offered a speculative explanation that, if it had any validity in the particular case, would hardly serve to explain other sightings reported since. In an account of the *Discovery* expedition of 1901–1904 he wrote:

> The Skua has no doubt good sight, but its sense of smell must be little short of marvellous. When on a sledge journey to the south with Captain Scott, on Ross' Great Ice Barrier, we camped in lat. 80°20'S., about 170 miles from open water, and 150 miles from the nearest spot which we knew to be frequented by the Skuas, we were surprised one day to see a bird hovering round our camp, till we realised that the wind was southerly, and remembered that the night before we had killed and cut up one of our sledge dogs to feed the others. Nothing but the scent of blood could have brought the bird those many miles. This was on December 10th, and the same thing happened again on our return when the wind was once more southerly, and the scent of blood was carried about the same distance, and brought on this occasion two Skua Gulls to our camp. They remained with us two days and disappeared, leaving us to finish our journey home alone. Three months of solitude were spent on this journey, so completely devoid of life that this was the only bird or beast of any sort that came to break it.*

* Seaver, 1937, pp. 144–145.

In Wilson's journal for January 2, 1912, of the polar expedition under Scott, he wrote: "We are now about 87°20'S. [i.e., 230 statute miles from the Pole and 10,000 feet high]. We were surprised to-day by seeing a Skua Gull flying over us — evidently hungry but not weak — its droppings however were clear mucus, nothing in them at all. It appeared in the afternoon and disappeared about half an hour later."

Scott, in his own journal, gave the following account of this incident. "A *skua gull* visited us on the march this afternoon — it was evidently curious, kept alighting on the snow ahead, and fluttering a few yards as we approached. It seemed to have had little food — an extraordinary visitor considering our distance from the sea." (The nearest open water would have been at least 600 miles away.)

Returning from their discovery of the South Pole, on January 9, 1912, at 84°26'S. Amundsen and his four companions came to a tower of snow blocks that they had erected on their way out as a beacon to guide them on their way back. This was on the Ross Ice Shelf halfway between its edge and the South Pole. In his report of the expedition he writes that, as they were continuing on their way,

> to our unspeakable astonishment two great birds — skua gulls — suddenly came flying straight towards us. They circled round us once or twice and then settled on the beacon. Can anyone who reads these lines form an idea of the effect this had upon us? It is hardly likely. They brought us a message from the living world into this realm of death — a message of all that was dear to us. I think the same thoughts filled us all. They did not allow themselves a long rest, these first messengers from another world; they sat still a while, no doubt wondering who we were, then rose aloft and flew on to the south. Mysterious creatures! they were now exactly half-way

between Framheim and the Pole, and yet they were going
farther inland. Were they going over to the other side?

Considering that only six expeditions had been deep into the
Antarctic interior by 1912, four separate sightings of skuas by
them made it seem probable that skuas travelled regularly
across the interior. And if they travelled regularly across the
interior, then there should have been not a few sightings of them
after 1955, when summer or year-round stations had been set up in
the interior. However, while reading up on the Antarctic in
preparation for my visit, I came upon no specific references to
skuas in the interior other than the early ones I have mentioned.
One item on my agenda for the Antarctic, then, was to find out
what I could about records of skuas in the interior since 1912.

After I got to Antarctica I learned what is undoubtedly the
principal reason for the paucity of published reports on skua
sightings since the first expeditions went into the interior. Most
of the scientists today are specialists in some one narrow technique, without broad cultivation or, what goes with such cultivation, the universal curiosity identified with the scientific spirit as
represented by Humboldt, by Darwin, and by Wilson. At Mc-
Murdo, for example, lunching with a scientist who had just come
from an interior station where he had been some weeks, I asked
whether any birds had been seen there. Yes, he replied, he had
himself seen birds there.

"What kind?" I asked.

"I don't know," he said. "I'm a physicist, not an ornithologist."

When I asked if he could tell me anything about what the birds
had looked like — their size, shape, or color — he answered that
he hadn't noticed, again adding that he was not an ornithologist
but a physicist.

(At a station in a dry valley of the interior, when I asked one of the resident scientists the reason for a spectacular peculiarity in the formation of the glaciers all around us, he answered: "I don't know, I'm a meteorologist, not a glaciologist." I was left to wonder what kind of a meteorologist it was who remained so uninterested in phenomena that were, after all, the products of meteorological circumstances. But the truth is that many of these scientists merely read instruments or act as attendants on machines that record on magnetic tape information that they don't have to understand themselves. Their readings or the tapes are then sent back home for the knowledgeable to interpret.)

There are notable exceptions to this lack of intellectual curiosity, and those who are responsible for the overall direction of the American Antarctic programs represent the opposite. When I got back from the Antarctic to pursue my frustrated inquiry by correspondence, their cooperation enabled me to uncover the following information, most of which has remained unpublished.

Item. In January 1967, the Station Scientific Leader at the South Pole, Dr. Richard B. Weininger, sent the following radio message to the USARP headquarters: "Bird, prob. skua, sighted and photographic [*sic*] vicinity geographic south pole 6 Jan 1967 2200Z."

Item. Dr. Alex Kennel, the Station Scientific Leader at the South Pole in December 1968, included the following in his "situation report" for that month:

> At 2100 G.M.T. December 19 a skua gull was sighted in the South Pole dump. Several close-up photos were taken, but it was impossible to tell if the bird had been banded. At any

rate it must not have enjoyed the environs, for the bird was not seen again after December 20 G.M.T. date.

In a personal letter, Dr. Kennel has written me as follows:

> December 19 was the day the Ninth Japanese Expedition traverse arrived at the South Pole for a one-week visit. Most of the station crew had gone out to the pole by about 0800 local station time (2000 G.M.T.). After much fanfare at the pole at the traverse arrival, all the men returned to the main station with the Japanese and American vehicles. I believe the skua was first seen as we passed the dump on this trip back to the station from the pole after the traverse party had arrived.
>
> The doctor took some pictures that afternoon. The bird was gone the next local time morning (say 2000 G.M.T. on 20 December) and was not seen again.
>
> In this Japanese traverse eleven men in three vehicles traveled from Showa Base to Pole Station via Plateau Station, which was still open at the time. The simultaneous arrival of the skua and the traverse suggests an obvious reason for its having been there. Unfortunately, I have no information from the Japanese about skua sighting along the traverse route.

The leader of the Japanese expedition, Mr. M. Murayama, has kindly informed me in writing that this bird had not come to the Pole with the expedition, but that he first saw it at the garbage dump there. He gives the date as December 23.

Item. I have photographs by Dr. L. Gary Holcomb of what is unmistakably a skua at the garbage dump of Byrd Station — which, at 80°01′S. and 119°31′W., is some 430 miles from the edge of the continent. The photographs were taken on January 6, 1971, three days before my own arrival there for a four-day visit.

Item. What is even more extraordinary than the presence of skuas at the South Pole and Byrd Station is their presence at Vostok, the Soviet station in the interior. Not only is Vostok as deep in the interior of the continent as the Pole, but at 11,444 feet above sea-level it holds the world's record for cold, −127°F. Nevertheless, a skua has twice been recorded at Vostok. The first occurrence was reported in the *Information Bulletin of the Soviet Antarctic Expedition,* number 55, 1965. I quote the following from a translation of that report in *Antarctic,* the bulletin of the New Zealand Antarctic Society, issue of June 1966.

> Vostok consists of a few small huts, surrounded by hundreds and thousands of miles of snow and ice, with not a single living creature to be found there. To the coast — the home of the native birds and seals of Antarctica — it is over 1,200 km.
>
> Workers at Vostok therefore were astonished when on December 15, 1964, a large dark-coloured bird appeared in the sky. It came from a northerly direction and seemed very tired, as it fluttered from place to place, often settling on the snow, drawing its feet up under it. The men tried to feed it, and it ate a tin of preserved meat, but it would not allow anyone near it. It appeared to be a great skua, one of the most widely distributed birds in the Southern Ocean. For two days the skua was the centre of attention at the station, and then it disappeared, without anyone seeing in which direction it flew off.

Dr. P. K. Senko of The Arctic and Antarctic Research Institute in Leningrad has been good enough to write me as follows about the second sighting:

> The second occurrence on the 15th of December, 1969 was not recalled in any detail. The station personnel had a very busy time getting ready for change of the wintering over

parties. The bird was around for two days (15 and 16 December), then it disappeared.

It should be remembered that both occurrences of the South Polar skua were observed a month before the arrival of a tractor-sledge train at Vostok Station. Thus there is no reason to associate them with the arrivals of the trains.

I submit that a species of bird which turns up at Vostok, as well as at the South Pole and the other localities cited, may be expected as a transient anywhere in the continent.

Many of the skuas that wander into the center of the continent do not, surely, survive to return to regions that support life, but it may be that some of them cross the continent from one shore to another. What impells them to embark on such journeys is a puzzle that is unlikely to be solved soon.

The puzzle is not confined to skuas, for both penguins and seals have been known to make for the interior of the continent — in their case inevitably to perish if they go far enough. Wilson reported Adélie Penguins on the Ross Ice Shelf some 68 miles from the sea. On December 31, 1957, the tracks of a penguin (apparently an Emperor) were seen by a party traversing the continent over 248 miles from the nearest known sea; and the next day a different traverse party, hundreds of miles away, came across the tracks of a penguin (almost surely an Adélie) at an altitude of 4,720 feet and more than 186 miles from the nearest known sea. Members of the party followed these latter tracks for about two kilometers, and according to Sladen and Ostenso the penguin was travelling "on an extraordinarily straight course [less than 2° deviation in any direction] that was taking it farther inland, roughly toward the South Pole." The mummified carcasses of seals have also been found in the interior of the continent or of its permanent ice-shelves.

Simply to conclude with the travel of skuas, I report that in March 1961 a South Polar Skua that had been banded in Antarctica was recovered north of the Equator in Udipi, Mysore, India. In May 1967, another that had been banded on the Antarctic continent was recovered, also north of the Equator, in the Caribbean.*

•

One can only speculate on the reason for the penetration of skuas, penguins, and seals into a region so extensive where no life can survive for long. I have already commented on the stubborn determination of all life to perpetuate itself and extend its range. The biological significance of the Antarctic continent is that it represents the frontier where life ends, its rim coinciding with the edge of the biosphere. The skua and the two penguins may be regarded as the pioneers who inhabit this outermost frontier.

Among crowded or colonial species of birds, the course of evolution has sometimes produced impulses leading to the dispersion that is necessary if the species is to spread or if inbreeding is to be avoided. The young feel an impulse, not unknown to the young of our own species, to leave the parental home, to push out into the unknown, to make a new life for themselves beyond the horizon. I daresay that, when young skuas or Adélie Penguins have reached the age at which they are ready to breed for the first time, they may find all the attractive nesting sites preempted by their elders. An unpondered impulse, then, may move them to head out from the home site in any direction. So new sites may be found, new colonies established, and the mission of the species to be fruitful, to multiply, and to fill the earth may be advanced. Perhaps the impulse that moves skuas and penguins to set out

* Sladen, Wood, and Monaghan, 1968, p. 225.

from the rim of the continent, sometimes in the direction of the South Pole, is not altogether unrelated to the impulse that impelled Captain Cook and his successors to seek a new world beyond the pack-ice. That such voyages of discovery, potentially so rewarding, are hazardous, that they take a high toll of life, is true for skuas, for penguins, and for men alike.

Only two species have made it, so far, all the way to the South Pole, the skua and man (undoubtedly in that order); but neither has any present prospect of establishing itself independently so far beyond the boundary of the biosphere.

Shackleton's ship *Endurance* frozen in the ice during the 1914–1917 expedition

12. To the South Pole

➤ MAN MADE his appearance among the other species of the earth between one and two million years ago. Although our own century, then, is only one of ten or twenty thousand during which he has been spreading over the globe, it is the climactic century in which he has at last reached its poles. While the airplane, invented in 1903, was bound to make the whole of the earth accessible to man, one may take a sporting satisfaction in the fact that he reached both poles (the North in 1909, the South in 1911) before it had been sufficiently developed to make its contribution.

•

At the beginning of this climactic century there was still no knowledge of what lay to the south of what could be seen from Ross Island, which was as far south as anyone had yet been. From there, all that could be seen was a barrier of high mountains, bounding the Ross Ice Shelf on the west, that continued southward to the limit of vision.

The aim of exploring the Antarctic in general could be justified by the scientific objective of enlarging human knowledge; but the aim of reaching the South Pole in particular could be justified only as a sporting aim, albeit one that entailed a symbolic achievement of the first magnitude. The man who seemed likeliest to be the discoverer of the Pole, Robert Falcon Scott, had a brooding sensitivity together with a habit of introspection that was hidden under the reserved exterior of a British naval officer. In him one detects the representative of a civilization that, in its self-consciousness, is beginning to show itself overripe. (He was self-conscious about what Columbus, Cook, Ross, and other earlier explorers appear to have taken for granted: the challenge to human will, to the inner man, that exploration beyond the frontiers of the known represented. The American explorer of some years later, Richard E. Byrd, would carry such self-consciousness to an extreme.) Scott resisted the sporting appeal in the planning and conduct of his two expeditions, justifying them by their scientific purpose. At the same time, however, he was conscious of himself as the bearer of a national heritage that went back to Sir Francis Drake. Personal endurance and achievement for the nation's sake counted for him. This made it impossible for him to be indifferent, on grounds of priority for science, to the everlasting luster that he and his band would add to the British crown by being the first to reach the Pole. We shall see that the man who got to the Pole only thirty-five days ahead of him, representing the more primitive heritage of the Viking tradition, was not affected by stirrings of the inner man.

It was in January 1901 that Scott's first expedition, in the *Discovery*, reached the southwest corner of Ross Island, where it settled down for the austral winter at Hut Point. The following November 2, when the sun was again shining, a party under his command embarked on an exploration by sledge southward across the Ross Ice Shelf, to reach the farthest south ever attained (82°17′S.) on December 30. Skirting the mountain-barrier that bounded the Ice Shelf to the west, he and his companions had discovered only that it continued ever southward, although with a tendency to curve toward the east.

During the southward journey of 1902 one of Scott's party, Ernest Shackleton, had fallen ill of scurvy, had become a burden, and had had to be sent home by a relief ship. Shackleton was a man of strength, of heroic determination, and of untroubled self-confidence, who must have felt his failure as a disgrace to be redeemed. He therefore organized his own expedition and, in 1908, returned in the *Nimrod* to McMurdo Sound. Prevented by the ice from sailing as far south as Hut Point, he established his base at Cape Royds, halfway down the west coast of the island. Here, at the edge of the Adélie Penguin colony that still flourishes, he built the large hut that still stands, sending the *Nimrod* back to New Zealand.

At the end of October Shackleton set out from Cape Royds with three companions to repeat the journey on which he had broken down. Within a month they had passed its farthest south. Continuing southeastward along the base of the mountain-barrier, they came to a glacier 14 miles wide that flowed 124 miles from the crest of the range to the Ice Shelf. This was the Beardmore Glacier, as it would later be named. In another month they had surmounted it and were the first men to stand on the high plateau of ice within the ring of mountains, 300 miles from the Pole. Continuing still, they got to 112 miles of the Pole before the shortage of food left them no choice but to turn back.

In late 1910 Scott, Wilson, Bowers, Cherry-Garrard, and the others sailed south in the *Terra Nova* on the second Scott expedition, which had a number of objectives, only one of which was to discover the Pole. On January 4, 1911, finding it impracticable to reestablish themselves at Hut Point, they made their landing on the ice off what Scott christened Cape Evans, halfway between Cape Royds and Hut Point. Here they built the hut, still intact, where they wintered while their ship returned north. It was from

Cape Evans that Scott, Bowers, Evans, Oates, and Wilson, follow-ing the old route and Shackleton's extension of it up the Beard-more Glacier, made their terrible journey all the way to the South Pole, only to find that the Norsemen had got there first. This was the journey on which all died — the three final survivors, Scott, Bowers, and Wilson, when after more than 1,600 miles only 11 remained between them and safety. But they were starved, their feet were frozen, and in the blizzard that continued undiminished day after day they could go no farther. So they lay down side by side in their tent to await the everlasting mercy of death.

Scott, as he waited, wrote with his dying strength the thought-ful letters that are now famous: to Wilson's widow, to the mother of Bowers, to members of his own family, and to those who had supported the enterprise that had come to this end. He also wrote the valedictory "Message to the Public" in which he said: "We are weak, writing is difficult, but for my own sake I do not regret this journey, which has shown that Englishmen can endure hardships, help one another, and meet death with as great a forti-tude as ever in the past." Today one reads this as a farewell in more than the ordinary sense, for it marks the end of the heroic age of exploration, in which men necessarily depended on their individual powers.

•

The impression one has of Amundsen, as one reads his own account of his expedition to the Pole, is of such an untroubled spirit as fortune sometimes favors above those who think too much. Exploration was a way of life to which he seemed to have been born, and he offered no more than lip service to its inci-dental heroism. He seemed to regard adventure as, first of all, fun. His Viking ancestors may have had the same attitude when

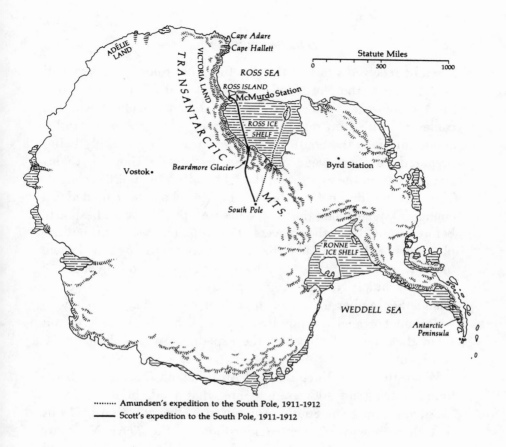

.... Amundsen's expedition to the South Pole, 1911-1912
——— Scott's expedition to the South Pole, 1911-1912

they sailed across the North Atlantic to the discovery of Vinland. One also has the impression, not unfounded, that he and his companions were native to the setting of snow and ice as gallant gentlemen in England were not.

In September 1909 Amundsen was making preparations in Kristiania (now Oslo) for a voyage into the Arctic, to discover the North Pole if possible, in the *Fram*, a ship loaned him for the purpose by the Norwegian Government. His capacity for daring improvisation, unhampered by inner conflict, manifested itself when he received word, at this juncture, that Robert E. Peary had beaten him to the North Pole. "Just as rapidly," he later wrote, "as the message [of Peary's discovery] had travelled over the cables I decided on my change of front — to turn to the right-about, and face the South." The *Fram* was still ostensibly being prepared for the voyage north. So his backers thought, so his companions on the expedition thought, and so the public thought. The only persons besides his brother to whom he confided his change of plan were the first officer of the *Fram* and, shortly before sailing, two other officers. Everyone else was told that the plan now was to sail around the Horn and north through the Pacific to the western end of the Northwest Passage — and on beyond.

The *Fram* left Norway August 9, 1910, arriving at the Madeira Islands September 6. Three days later, when she was ready to weigh anchor again, Amundsen called all hands on deck to tell them that the real object of the expedition was a dash to the South Pole.

When the *Terra Nova* reached Australia, on October 12, Scott found a telegram addressed to him that read, in its entirety: "Madeira. Am going South. Amundsen." Cherry-Garrard tells us that these few words were understood by the *Terra Nova* explorers to mean, as indeed they did, "I shall be at the South Pole before you." To this he adds, with the grace and gallantry of his breed: "It also meant, though we did not appreciate it at the time, that we were up against a very big man."

Amundsen, in his own account, wrote:

> I knew I should be able to inform Captain Scott of the extension of my plans before he left civilization, and therefore a few months sooner or later could be of no importance. Scott's plan and equipment were so widely different from my own that I regarded the telegram that I sent him later, with the in-

formation that we were bound for the Antarctic regions, rather
as a mark of courtesy than as a communication which might
cause him to alter his programme in the slightest degree. The
British expedition was designed entirely for scientific research.
The Pole was only a side-issue, whereas in my extended plan
it was the main object.

The epigraph of the chapter from which I have quoted the above
is taken from Rex Beach, and reads: "The deity of success is a
woman, and she insists on being won, not courted. You've got to
seize her and bear her off, instead of standing under her window
with a mandolin."

An example of how fortune was to favor Amundsen was in the
choice he made of an Antarctic base in consequence of a judgment now known to have been mistaken. Shackleton, in 1908,
had thought of establishing his base on the edge of the Ross Ice
Shelf at a point called the Bay of Whales, where it was low
enough to land on. When he got there, however, he found that
miles of it had broken away. Judging rightly that the shelf rested
on water rather than land, he did not take the risk that, having
established his base camp on it and dismissed the *Nimrod,* the
part on which the camp stood should break off and float away.
Amundsen, however, did choose to establish his camp, which he
called Framheim, on the edge of the shelf, here at the Bay of
Whales. "Although I had a very great regard for Shackleton," he
later wrote, ". . . I believe that in this case his conclusion was
too hasty. . . ." If he had waited "a few hours, or at the most a
couple of days," when he visited the Bay of Whales and decided
not to make his camp there, "it would not have taken him long to
determine that the inner part of the bay does not consist of floating barrier, but that the Barrier there rests upon a good, solid
foundation, probably in the form of small islands, skerries, or

shoals. . . ." If Amundsen had known that he was, in fact, wrong, he surely would not have taken the risk he unknowingly did take. He established his camp on the ice and, by good fortune, the risk was not realized. (The Bay of Whales no longer exists today, its shores having calved away since Amundsen's time.)

On October 20, 1911, Amundsen set out from Framheim with five men, four sledges, and fifty-two Eskimo dogs. "At first we had made up our minds not to drive more than twelve to eighteen miles a day," he wrote; "but this proved to be too little, thanks to our strong and willing animals." Beginning November 8, they were regularly making "a daily march of about thirty miles." (This would be a remarkable daily distance for a man walking on greensward in some earthy paradise, and I should think it not unremarkable skiing over snow.) On the seventeenth they came to the foot of the mountain-barrier. They might well have reached it in a part of its extent where it was insurmountable, but luck continued with them. "The land under which we now lay," Amundsen wrote, ". . . looked perfectly impossible, with peaks along the barrier which rose to heights of from 2,000 to 10,000 feet. Farther south we saw more peaks, of 15,000 feet or higher." However, they went right on up the slopes, climbing steep glaciers where they had to harness twenty dogs to each sledge, taking the four sledges in two relays. "It only took us four days from the barrier to reach the immense inland plateau. We camped at a height of 7,600 feet."

Bad weather held them up for four days now, but on November 25 "we were tired of waiting, and started again." On the twenty-ninth they came to another range of mountains athwart their way and, by December 3, had surmounted it too. On the fourteenth they halted, "as according to our reckoning we had reached our

goal." They had covered some 870 miles from their base of
Framheim, averaging 15½ miles per day (even with the four-day
halt taken into account).

They spent some three happy days refining their observations
and casting out in various directions to make sure that the precise
location of the Pole would be included in the area traversed.
Then they turned back and, now averaging 22½ miles per day,
reached Framheim January 25, 1912. They had met some bad
weather, and some difficult conditions requiring detours, but
when one reads Amundsen's account one has the impression that
the whole journey was a holiday lark.

•

It was not so with the fatal Scott expedition. Writing ten years
later, Cherry-Garrard summed it up, saying: "I now see very
plainly that though we achieved a first-rate tragedy, which will
never be forgotten just because it was a tragedy, tragedy was not
our business." The epigraph to the chapter in which this erst-
while classics scholar at Oxford recounted the tragedy was not
from Rex Beach but from the seventeenth-century poet George
Herbert:

> And now in age I bud again,
> After so many deaths I live and write;
>   I once more smell the dew and rain,
> And relish versing. O my onely light,
>   It cannot be
>   That I am he
> On whom thy tempests fell all night.

Ten years later, contrasting the success of the Amundsen expedition with the failure of the expedition on which he served,
Cherry-Garrard judges that the latter tried to do too much in too

Scott Expedition at the South Pole.
Left to right: Oates, Bowers, Scott, Wilson, Evans

complicated a way, making experiments that "any rather con-
servative whaling captain might have refused to make." "We
were discursive," he writes. "We were full of intellectual interests
and curiosities of all kinds. We took on the work of two or three
expeditions."

There is no need to repeat here the memorable outpouring of
Cherry-Garrard in the philosophical but bitter last chapter of *The
Worst Journey in the World*, entitled "Never Again." The Englishmen, trying to make heart do for muscle after the limit of
muscle had been passed, had worn themselves out even before
they set off across the ice to the Pole. On all these journeys,
which were too many and too hard, they quickly had to do

without dogs and pull the sledges themselves, sometimes making no more than two or three miles a day with immense effort. On top of this, where Amundsen had had good luck they had bad luck, the worst of which was the unmerciful weather that finally stopped them forever, and so close to salvation.

After the *Terra Nova* had left Scott and his men at Cape Evans she sailed eastward the length of the Great Ice Barrier to land a party on King Edward VII Peninsula, but found it impossible to do so. Returning along the Barrier then, on February 1, 1911, she came to the Bay of Whales, prepared to make the landing there. To the astonishment of all hands, a ship was already in the bay — the *Fram*. There were exchanges of visits between the surprised members of the two expeditions; courtesy, consideration, and discretion were shown on both sides. Then the Englishmen, having found their landing-site preempted, sailed on to tell Scott at Cape Evans.

On January 16, 1912, exhausted and only a few miles from the Pole, the members of Scott's expedition came upon the traces of the Norwegian expedition. To all except Wilson this was shattering, robbing them of the satisfaction they would otherwise have had out of their arrival next day at the Pole itself, now bearing like a memorial monument the insignia of the Norwegian triumph. "Great God!" Scott wrote in his diary, "this is an awful place and terrible enough for us to have laboured to it without the reward of priority."

•

Every man, aside from his inborn qualities, is the product of his cultural background — which is to say that he is in part a product of his times. No one would have expected the ancient Vikings to manifest a general intellectual curiosity. By contrast, the cultivated members of the Scott expeditions did manifest it; and indeed it was in nineteenth-century Europe that this chief glory of mankind flourished as rarely before, declining with the years of our present century. Today we have still another breed of men. Surely they are good men for their purpose, highly trained in the technical procedures that belong to one or another branch of specialized investigation, or in the operation of machinery. But they are for the most part without general education or the ranging curiosity with which such education endows the mind. One could not say of the officers and scientists in the Antarctic today what Cherry-Garrard said of the company of his day: "We were discursive. We were full of intellectual interests and curiosities of all kinds."

After the Homeric explorers come the Greeks of the Golden Age, and after the Greeks the Romans.

•

The image of the South Pole I had had in mind was that of the "awful place" referred to by Scott, reinforced by the photograph of the five afflicted explorers looking like men who have come to the end of hope and endurance alike. I imagined grayness, the fog of blowing snow, and the air that froze what it touched. Today my picture is different. In my journal for January 4, 1971, I wrote: "This was not at all the setting in which I pictured Scott, Wilson, Oates, Bowers, and Evans upon their arrival on January 18, 1912. It had not occurred to me that they might have found themselves so bathed in sunlight and glory."

The area of the South Pole is among the driest on earth — as well it might be, for it is the best part of a thousand miles from the sea, the prevailing katabatic winds flow outward from it (being replaced by air from above), and the temperature always remains far below the freezing point, so that the atmosphere contains no water vapor. I understand, moreover, that snow almost never falls from the sky, although it blows like smoke along the endless plain.

Moreover, while the Sahara, the Gobi, and the American Southwest may be equally dry, only the atmosphere over the Antarctic continent is free of dust, so that the snow, even if years old, remains still as white as when it fell. It follows that there is a lack of atmospheric perspective, of the tendency for objects to become dimmer as well as smaller with distance. A man standing half a mile away looks like a homunculus standing much nearer by. One sets out to walk to an object that seems no more than three minutes away and takes twenty to reach it.

.

It is unreal to talk about time of day at midsummer in the Antarctic, for the sun circles endlessly without ever approaching the horizon. (At the Pole it never even varies its height, except with the changing seasons.) Human activities at McMurdo, for example, tend to continue around the clock, the mess hall serving a meal at what is called midnight just as it does at what is called midday. Airplanes, wherever they may be going, are as apt to leave or arrive at 2 A.M. as at 2 P.M. Nevertheless, all hands wear watches and, glancing at them from time to time, retain the outlandish habit of distinguishing between day and night.

It was ten o'clock in the morning, then, when the Hercules cargo plane at Willy Field moved forward on its skis, gathering speed until it lifted off the Ice Shelf and rose into the sky, heading south. My fellow passenger was a young, gentle, and modest Roman Catholic priest, Father Crawford, whom the U.S. Navy had flown down from New Zealand for the Christmas season to celebrate the mass at various stations. He and I took turns sitting in or standing by the seat which the commander of the airplane had kindly given up to us. We flew up the Beardmore Glacier, past mountain-peaks that projected through the snow, and out over the high plateau. (I shall not here describe the scene and setting because the business we have in hand, now, is to get to the Pole.)

So it was that, three hours after leaving McMurdo, the great plane slid across the white floor and came to a stop. There was a huddle of huts like crates, there were pylons for radio antennae, there was the garbage dump that is bound to be so conspicuous a feature of every interior station (since garbage in Antarctica cannot be buried and must remain, in that eternal cold, forever imperishable), and at the entrance to what is called Amundsen-Scott Station a line of fifteen flagpoles with the flags of the fifteen nations that conduct activities in the Antarctic fluttering in a light breeze.

Not only are all directions here north, all present the same scene. It is Euclidean, made up of two elements only: the white floor below and the blue sky above, separated by a line that might have been drawn with a ruler. There is no modification in the brilliance of the white or the intensity of the blue as they approach the line of their joining. In all the rest of the world there can be no other scene where nature is as simple, as abstract, and as complete in the purity of its perfection.

The temperature, if not abnormal, was far above the local average during my nine hours at the Pole, remaining between $-10°$ and $-15°F$. (It did not get above $-21°F$. while Scott was there.) And, as I have said, there was no more than a breeze running over the snow, just enough to ruffle the fifteen flags.

After we had, like marmots, gone down a tunnel for a visit to man's little world below the surface, and had sat with the station's company at chow, Father Crawford and I emerged again to be taken by an enclosed and tracked motor vehicle to the wooden stake that had been set up to represent, as it were, the axis of the earth projecting through its surface. From there we were driven across the snow to where a one-tenth model of a projected new station, to replace the present one, had been constructed.

Here I excused myself to walk back alone to the Pole, which looked so near but took me so long to reach. The snow was dry underfoot, not absolutely flat but undulating almost impercep- tibly. Moreover, there were wind-ripples, inches high at most. At each step one's foot sank in crunchingly about an inch.

I was dressed in specially designed Antarctic clothing that left no more than the center of my face exposed. Only when, in walk- ing, I turned away from the sun and into the breeze did I have to hold my mittened hand over my nose because of the cold. To take photographs I could expose my hands for a minute or two.

All this time I was in a state of exhilaration that was a sort of ecstasy. It was not only the purity of the scene — so pure, it seemed, as nothing else on earth. The air was like some clarify- ing liquor of the gods, a draft of which confers immortality.

If the scene and the air of this Olympian world accounted in large part for my peculiar exhilaration, I attribute it also in part to the knowledge that, in the midst of this unexpected perfection, I was walking about on what we think of as the bottom of the earth. I had told my family, before leaving for the Antarctic, that whether I got to the Pole or not made little difference, since all it would entail was the satisfaction of the little boy who remained in the grown man. I now testify that never in his remarkably long life was the little boy given so much satisfaction.

This abode of the gods was also a geometrician's paradise. I had been told that the stake marking the Pole had been planted in the ice a year before with a margin of error of 20 feet, but that an annual drift of 60 feet, accounted for by the flow of the ice, would since have displaced it by that amount. The actual Pole, then, was somewhere in a ring that had the stake as its center and a radius of forty feet on its inside, of eighty on its outer rim. Determined to circumnavigate our terrestrial globe, I started out from the stake in a clockwise spiral, walking for over two hours around and around it, each time farther out, until there could be no doubt left that I had circumnavigated it any number of times. As I did so I gained an hour every 15 degrees, but lost all the accumulated gain each time I crossed the International Date Line, when I had to set my calendar back a day.

If I had been a person of abnormal sensibilities I might have been conscious of weighing more at this axial point of the globe than when, crossing the Equator eighteen days earlier, I had sustained the full centrifugal force of travelling at more than 1,000 miles per hour around a circumference of 25,000 miles — in addition to the centifugal force consequent upon the movement of the earth in its orbit at 67,000 miles per hour which, because it was nighttime, when I was on the outside of the spinning and orbiting earth, also countered the earth's gravitation. Here, if I was not actually turning on my own axis, I was close to doing so. (On the other hand, one's weight is less at 10,000 feet than at sea-level, since one is that much farther from the earth's center of gravity.) Had I been a person of such sensitivity, moreover, I might also have been conscious, as I walked, of the Coriolis effect, stronger here than anywhere else except the North Pole, which tended to deflect me always to the left (see Appendix A). However, godlike though I was for the moment in mind and sensibilities alike, I had no physical consciousness of the pressures involved in my exceptional geometric situation.

What I wanted to do, beyond all measure of desire, was to walk away forthwith over the endless plain, all the way to McMurdo; for in this world of divinity I could hardly imagine that it would not be a glory all the way. But the little boy was safely encased in the grown man, who managed to keep him under control. After my hours on Olympus I descended again to the world of my fellow men, entering the darkness for mortal food and drink in a hot and windowless room that might have been a cellar in Manhattan, my ears now assailed by barracks language shouted above the throbbing and wailing of the juke box.

When, about ten o'clock in the evening, I emerged to board the airplane back to McMurdo, a cover of cloud had come out of nowhere to screen infinity from the sight of the undeserving.

> Whither is fled the visionary gleam?
> Where is it now, the glory and the dream?

Once more we flew over the white plain, then among the peaks, on down the length of the Beardmore Glacier, and out over the Ice Shelf. It was one o'clock on the morning of the fifth when we landed at McMurdo, only fifteen hours after having left it.

> The Rainbow comes and goes,
> And lovely is the Rose;
> The Moon doth with delight
> Look round her when the heavens are bare;
> Waters on a starry night
> Are beautiful and fair;
> The sunshine is a glorious birth;
> But yet I know, where'er I go,
> That there hath passed away a glory from the earth.

Victoria Land: the Transantarctic Range

13. Snow Mountains, Ice Plains, and Oases

◆— IN THE OPENING CHAPTER I described the Antarctic continent as a circular shield of ice that flowed outward in glaciers between the containing mountains and spread as ice-shelves over the marginal seas. I suggested that it was academic to ask how much of the land under the ice might be called continental and how much might be said to consist of islands or archipelagos, since the question whether the underlying land was above or below sea-level had no practical significance where the sea could not penetrate. In an academic context, however, one may properly be academic.

To the geographer who is concerned with the history of the earth, as to the geologist, Antarctica is divided into two distinct parts, two separate continents joined together, which are best called Greater and Lesser Antarctica. The seam between them is marked by one of the world's great mountain-ranges, the Transantarctic Range. It begins at its Pacific end in the mountains that bound the Ross Sea on the west, from Cape Adare to McMurdo Sound. It continues southeastward along the edge of the Ross Ice Shelf, and then on across the shield to the Weddell Sea and the Filchner Ice Shelf. Its scalloped horizon on the other side of McMurdo Sound, as seen from Ross Island, has the steep and jagged outline of all mountain-ranges too new to have suffered much erosion as yet — like the Himalayas, the Alps, the Andes, and the Sierra Nevada in California, by contrast with the Jura,

the Alleghenies, and the Rockies. It was this range that we
skirted when we flew to the South Pole, crossing it, at last, where
the Beardmore Glacier flows through, to fly on over the unbroken
ice of Greater Antarctica, over the polar plateau.

The highest peak in the Transantarctic Range, which stands
alongside the Beardmore Glacier, is Mount Kirkpatrick, 14,800
feet high; but it is not the highest peak in Antarctica. That distinction belongs to the Sentinel Range of the Ellsworth Mountains, at the base of the Antarctic Peninsula, in which the Vinson
Massif rises to 16,860 feet.

The bulk of the shield we call the Antarctic continent is constituted by Greater Antarctica. It is older than Lesser Antarctica,
which is essentially a continuation, by way of the Antarctic
Peninsula, of South America. (The relative youth of Lesser or
Andean Antarctica is consistent with the fact that it has the
highest peaks, erosion having had less time to act here.) If one
were suddenly to strip the ice cover from Lesser Antarctica the
sea would flood in over it, leaving little but islands consisting, for
the most part, of the mountains that now rim it on its seaward
side.

I am about to report my visit to a station in Lesser Antarctica,
but before I do so I must give an account of the Transantarctic
Range as I saw it from the airplane flying to the Pole and back,
and again between McMurdo and Cape Adare on the flight back
to New Zealand. What one sees from the air is what one would
see flying over the Pennine Alps and the Mont Blanc range if they
had been all but drowned in snow — if all the intermontane
valleys, including the valleys of the Arve, the Trient, and the
Rhône, had filled up with snow to a level above which only the
upper ridges and peaks stood. But there is a virgin purity about
the scene here that represents, only in the smallest part, one's

knowledge that no man or beast has ever been among these peaks or left a footprint on the snow plains between. In the mountains of the rest of the world the snow, except after a fresh snowfall, is stained with rock dust and the debris of erosion. This appears not to be the case here, partly because of the absence of dust in the atmosphere, but partly also, I would guess, because erosion must be a particularly slow process where the temperature never rises to the melting point. (It is the trickling of melt-water into every crack and cranny of the Alps, when the midday sun shines upon them, followed by its expansion as it freezes at night, that causes an erosion made visible and audible by scree falls, and that covers the upper snow slopes with constantly renewed masses of fallen stone.) Finally, the clarity of an atmosphere devoid of dust contributes to the impression that this is a world freshly made, as yet undimmed by any process of aging.

Looking down from so high above, I think to myself that these mountains are waiting for me to come and climb them — but I never shall. This is as close as I can ever come to the world that preceded Original Sin. In an hour the mountains are left behind as we fly on over the polar plateau — or as, on the return trip to New Zealand, we fly out over the Pacific.

.

Although the sun was high, the time was actually an hour before midnight on January 8 at McMurdo when I got word that the first of a series of refueling flights to Byrd Station was to leave in two hours. The custom is to fly what are called "double shuttles" from McMurdo to Byrd as from McMurdo to the Pole. Each is a six-hour round trip, and since twelve hours is the flying time allowed the air crews before they must rest, the two runs of the double shuttle have become customary. This meant that I could fly to

Byrd on the first round trip, remain six hours, and return on the second.

Byrd Station in Lesser Antarctica, halfway along a line running from Ross Island to the Bellinghausen Sea, is at 80°S. and on approximately the same longitude as Los Angeles. While its altitude above sea-level, 5,020 feet, is more than 4,000 feet lower than the Pole, the thickness of the freshwater ice there is 8,680 feet — which is to say that at Byrd the land itself is 3,660 feet below sea-level.

When the present Byrd Station was built in 1960–1961, replacing an older one twelve miles away, the experiment was tried of building it under the ice. Trenches, immense and deep, were cut by heavy machinery, prefabricated buildings were lowered into them, and then the trenches were bridged over by the ice and the snow, restoring the natural surface above. Although a community of some eighty persons (in summer) is thus hidden under the ice, making this the largest station in the interior, all one sees from above is some projecting structures that house scientific equipment, the navigation aids and associated shacks of the air-strip, the inevitable garbage dump, and a cavernous opening that slopes downward into the nether realms, with a warning sign before it that quotes from Dante's *Inferno:* "Abandon hope all ye who enter here."

This experiment, however, has at last had to be recognized as a failure, forcing the prospective abandonment of the present station. I am sorry to report this because there is something particularly cozy about living in a well-lighted and air-conditioned community hidden under the surface of an endless snow plain. But the ice of the whole continent is, after all, flowing slowly outward to the sea with a force that nothing can resist, and the heat from the buildings, by melting the ice ceiling above them, brings it constantly lower, threatening to crush them, so that an inordinate number of man-hours have to be spent in cutting the ice back.

The flight from McMurdo was over cloud at first, then on over the featureless white plain. Such a plain, seen from 20,000 feet above, gives an impression of immensity that dwarfs the imagination of one who has previously seen only its representation on the map. It is clear that men with sledges, crawling over its surface day after day, could push ahead for a month and still seem to have got nowhere. As we drew toward our destination, at last, a blanket of lamb's-wool clouds, more conspicuous by the shadow of its ragged edge on the snow than in itself, appeared ahead and below. Then the long downward glide began, continuing until the airplane penetrated the blanket and, a moment later, slid over the snow to a halt. The time was 4 A.M.

Just as we clambered out of the airplane's cavernous interior, a sudden wind struck, filling the air with blown snow. There were men at hand — muffled up, leaning against the wind, turning their faces away from it — to unload the great bird and to connect a black hose to the tank of diesel oil it carried in its belly.

Directing these operations in the midst of the blizzard was a man who remains affectionately in my memory, like one of the more admirable characters in a novel by Dickens. Lieutenant Hoyt, U.S.N., the Officer in Charge, was a big boyish man with glasses who was in a state of the most ebullient good humor imaginable at all times. Everything that happened, good or bad, and virtually every word spoken, caused him to shake from head to feet with irrepressible laughter. He shook with laughter, now, because the blizzard made unloading so hard. He shook with laughter because, after I emerged from the airplane, I started off in the wrong direction, so that he had to run after and retrieve me. He shook with laughter because another refueling airplane, unannounced and unexpected by anyone, came in just behind ours. He shook with laughter because a blizzard was blowing, as he would certainly have shaken with laughter because one was not blowing.

The entrance to the station led down to a broad hall for trolls under the ice, a tunnel that ran at right angles to the entrance. On either side frozen foods were piled high, a demonstration of the fact that housekeeping in the middle of Antarctica is easier to the extent that artificial refrigeration is not needed. At each end of this open hall another tunnel went off at right angles, both tunnels occupied by cratelike buildings, one after another. The communications building, the galley, the powerhouse, and the snow melter were in the tunnel that opened opposite and a bit to the right of the entrance from the outside. The other tunnel, opening at the other end of the hall, contained the living quarters and the meteorological building. The main hall and the two tunnels or corridors leading off it were illuminated by electric bulbs and were lined, in part, with corrugated iron. At the far end of the tunnel that contained the living quarters, however, another and narrower tunnel, unlined, led to various outlying scientific installations. The temperature in this tunnel was that of the surrounding ice, about $-20°$F., so that, however bundled up one might be, one was moved to hold one's mittened hand over the exposed parts of one's face. In the other tunnels the escape of heat from the buildings, contained by the tunnel lining, kept the temperature higher, although still well below freezing.

Since it was expected that my stay would be short, Lieutenant Hoyt proposed to wake up the Station Scientific Leader forth-with, so that I could be shown the scientific work under way. But it was five in the morning by then. Not only did I not want to interrupt anyone's sleep, my generosity in this respect was abetted by the fact that I had myself been up twenty-three hours, during which I had visited, by helicopter, both Cape Royds (the site of Shackleton's hut and of a penguin colony) and Cape Evans (the base of the second and last Scott expedition). At my request, then, I was shown to a bunk in a cubicle where I rested until seven.

As the speed of travel and its facilities increase, we find ourselves going constantly farther and having constantly less time when we get there. It may be that in years to come we will be able to visit the North and South Poles all in one day, but we will be lucky to spend five minutes at either and perhaps there will no longer be any time at all for sleep.

All this is belied, however, by what happened to me next.

After breakfast it transpired gradually (as in *Outward Bound*), by way of rumors and uncertain reports, that instead of having only six hours at Byrd I was to enjoy an indefinite stay. This would give me the unexpected opportunity of seeing what day-to-day (perhaps week-to-week) life was like in the interior of the continent. If only because of the unexpected arrival of the flight that followed hard upon our own, it transpired that the station was now fueled up to 80 percent of its capacity, so that no further flights were scheduled. Somebody, directing operations, had changed his mind.

Four pleasant days now went by, their pleasantness moderated only by some anxiety that I would miss my flight back to New Zealand, that I would miss the activities in prospect for me there, and that I might miss, as well, the only military passenger flight back to the United States from New Zealand that was scheduled for months to come. At the end of four days, however, when this latter possibility had become a clear prospect, an airplane came from McMurdo and out I flew.

It can only be a nuisance for those who administer Antarctic activities to have on their hands a guest with a schedule to make (including lectures to give in Switzerland). I here pay them the tribute of saying that, although this must have been so, none of them allowed me to see any sign that it was.

There were amenities to be found under the ice during those four days. One was a small library with many novels and, as well, books on Antarctica, some technical and some narrative. The Science Building had a lounge for the scientific staff, with sofa and easy chairs, in which one could listen in comfort to a large collection of records on the phonograph. It was alone in this lounge beneath the ice that I discovered, like someone who discovers divinity, the posthumous voice of Enrico Caruso. I have since tried to find, in Europe and North America, the recordings on which I heard it, but they appear not to exist. It is just as well. For us mortals, the experience of being lifted to the level of the gods can only be fleeting — as it had been at the South Pole. Nor can we expect such experience to be repeated, even though all the outward circumstances are re-created. I daresay that if I listened to the same records today I would no longer hear what, for the unheralded moment only, I had been permitted to hear. It is just as well, for no mortal could long sustain the experience.

There was an office, too, with desks and paper. The consequence was that friends of mine on remote northern continents were to receive long letters that had been postmarked on what seemed another planet.

In making up the catalogue of amenities I must not omit the galley. Eating well is not one of those naval traditions that go back over the centuries, but the Navy food was excellent wherever I went, and better at Byrd than anywhere else. Galley and mess hall were all one room, not very large, the galley occupying the far half, the tables for eating the near. One went to the far half to fill one's plates and cups (again and again in my case) with the luxurious variety of food and drink exposed to one's plunder. When at last one could eat no more, one took plates, cups, and utensils back to the big sinks, where one washed them and put them away. Plain living and high eating was the rule in Antarctica.

All the scientific staff were expected to take their turns at two duties, known respectively as "house-mouse" and "snow-melter." House-mouse duties were those of sweeping and swabbing these subglacial premises. Snow-melter duty was the consequence of a paradox.

Stations like Byrd, surrounded by over 90 percent of all the frozen water in the world, are constantly having to struggle with a penury of water. This requires a drastic economy in its use. It also requires the continual operation of a snow-melter. This contraption, at the far end of the tunnel that housed the galley, consisted of a great tank, perhaps a dozen feet high, by the side of a diesel furnace that melted the snow dumped into it. An endless-chain shovel (i.e., buckets on a moving chain) sloped up to the brim of the tank from a chamber in the ice that communicated with the outdoors by a wide chimney overhead. Bulldozers above pushed the snow in solid chunks into the chimney, so that they dropped down into the chamber. Whoever was on snow-melter duty, then, shovelled the chunks into the buckets, which carried them up and dumped them into the tank. There was a general unwillingness to burden a visiting drone with any duty, but the conscience of the drone took the opposite position. Consequently, on the fourth day he did his stint at the snow melter, foreseeing that it might become his principal duty in his indefinite continuance as a member of the community, that it might be his way of earning his keep. Then, on the fifth day, the airplane came and took him back to McMurdo.

The first day, in the morning, I was conducted about the

station for a view of the scientific work being done in terrestrial magnetism, in seismology, in cosmic radiation, and in VLF (very-low-frequency noise). After that, for my remaining time at Byrd, I alternated spells of reading and writing in the lounge with walks in the world above. In one direction was the airstrip, marked by navigational equipment and an empty hut at one end. In another was the garbage dump, where I went most frequently, moved by a forlorn hope that the report of an unidentified bird, seen there some days before, had aroused in me. (This was the skua, reported in Chapter 11, which I have since identified as such by the photographs Dr. Holcomb took.) In still another direction was the line of projecting towers and masts belonging to the various installations for making scientific observations.

Because of the danger that one might lose one's way in thick weather, never to return, there were handlines running from stake to stake for perhaps half a mile from the station in every direction. Especially when the wind blew up a fog of snow, I made a point of remaining within sight of these handlines, and there were times when I remained within touching distance. Beyond the immediate confines of the station, however, it was curious to walk in a world where all directions were the same and distance made no difference. One might as well walk in a circle, over and over again, as in a straight line.

In all these walks, without being conscious of it, but simply out of established habit, I was constantly looking for life or signs of it. Of course there was none, except occasionally such human life as was represented by a tracked vehicle moving about near the station — and this was not what I had in mind. I did not become conscious of how great an emptiness this made for me until, at one o'clock on the morning of January 13, the airplane from Byrd was coming in to its landing at McMurdo. Then I saw through the window, with a sudden and surprising excitement, skuas flying back and forth below.

•

The Antarctic continent is not unique in its ice cover, for Greenland bears a like burden. What is altogether unique in Antarctica, however, is the isolated existence, at a few points, of deep valleys that never have any covering of ice or more than a sprinkling of snow, summer or winter — the so-called dry valleys, also referred to as "oases" although they are, in a literal sense, deserts. The scientific accounts suggest that no one, as yet, fully understands this remarkable phenomenon.

Some explanation is provided simply by a local lack of precipitation — and, indeed, parts of the dry-valley region that I visited, and am about to describe, have been called "the driest on our planet."* Consequently, any snow that falls into them evaporates, as do the tips of the glaciers that start down their sides. I do not mean that the snow or ice melts, becoming water that evaporates in its turn. For the most part, snow and ice evaporate directly, going from the solid to the gaseous state without passing through the liquid.

A complementary explanation is that strong winds, blowing down the valley walls, heat the air at the bottom by compressing it. It remains true, however, that the mean annual temperature of the dry valleys west of McMurdo Sound is about $-4°$F.

Finally, the heat of the sun, during the season when it shines, is absorbed by the exposed soil and rocks, where it would otherwise be reflected back by snow and ice. So the very absence of snow and ice contributes to perpetuating their absence.

Because there is some melting at the glacier snouts when the

* A. T. Wilson, in Holdgate, p. 21.

sun is high, small streams start in summer, forming a lake at the bottom of each valley. In keeping with the paradoxical nature of this aberrant environment, these lakes are coldest near the surface, warmest in the depths. Lake Vanda (which we are about to visit in these pages), is 218 feet deep, and the temperature of its bottom water is 77°F., offering at least a lukewarm bath if one could enter it from below. The surface temperature is much nearer freezing. This inversion of what we regard as normal is accounted for by accumulating salts, carried in the streams from the glaciers, which make the bottom water saline, and therefore relatively heavy, by contrast with the fresh water above. The accumulated solar heat is retained in the salt water below, rather than being dissipated upward by the process of convection that takes place in lakes which lack this peculiar difference in weight. The difference inhibits the vertical circulation of the water.

Finally, although these oases are, in reality, stony deserts, they do contain some life in the midst of the surrounding lifelessness. They support a primitive flora so sparse as to be quite inconspicuous. In shallow dishes of still water algae may be found; and there are some bacteria in the soil. This would hardly constitute an oasis in any temperate or tropical country, but it does here.

The only one of the few known Antarctic oases that has been studied is the one known as the McMurdo Oasis, where New Zealand maintains a scientific station of some half-dozen men. The site, on the shore of Lake Vanda in the Wright Valley, is across McMurdo Sound from Ross Island and some twenty-five or thirty miles inland. There are three large valleys, with smaller ones interspersed, through which the Onyx River in summer follows a winding course of eighteen miles, broadening into a lake in each valley. But this summertime river runs inland, rather

Glacier tongue in a dry valley

than toward the sea, and is at last lost, evaporating in the dry atmosphere. After the height of summer the whole river dries up, and the lakes are sealed over with ice pending another season of renewal.

I venture here the categorical statement that there are no other scenes on this earthly planet as unearthly as those of the dry valleys, which occur so unexpectedly in the midst of the endless snow and ice. In this realm of eternal winter they look like summer — as if, hidden away among the Antarctic mountains, one should find a tropical rain forest.

About nine on the morning of January 7 the helicopter took off in the brilliant sunlight to fly transversely northwest across the frozen surface of McMurdo Sound to Queen Victoria Land and inland to Vanda Station. We flew between 200 and 400 feet above the ice, so that we could see the Weddell Seals, often attended by skuas, sleeping about the occasional holes in it. Cumulus clouds lay on the mountain-peaks ahead but were tending to dissipate as we approached and, at last, flew up through a series of valleys leading in from the sound.

For most of my life I have, in my travels, amused and instructed myself by playing a game that one may call "Where Am I?" Assuming that one has been dropped onto the earth from the moon, the object is to determine where one has landed. One does this by observing the scenery, the vegetation, the bird-life, the methods of farming, the architecture, et cetera. (The written or spoken word, however, is excluded as evidence.) Generally one determines first whether one is in a temperate or tropical zone, or at a high altitude in the tropics, and gradually (in my case, chiefly by the observation of birds) sees how far one can narrow down the area — perhaps to the point of being able to say, for example, that one is not far south of the Baltic, or in the southeastern United States, or in northern Australia. The only place I have ever visited that would have defeated me completely, if I actually had dropped on it from the moon, is the McMurdo Oasis. I don't know how I would have avoided the conclusion that I had landed on the wrong planet. In the scene before me I would have found something in common, I daresay, with the moon from which I had just come. I would also have been reminded of deserts in Colorado, Wyoming, and Utah, with their buttes and mesas, but it would have been a reminder only.

As anywhere in the Antarctic interior, the lack of atmospheric perspective misled one in the judgment of distances. Standing on the shore of Lake Vanda, I might have tried to throw a stone across it, in which case I would have had a surprise — for I was told that it was, in fact, three miles to the other side. The walls of the valley rose 6,ooo feet. Glaciers lapped over their tops and started down their slopes, but were abruptly cut off, as by a knife, before they had descended more than a quarter of the way. (The descending mass of ice comes to something like an invisible wall, beyond which it evaporates.)

The colorfulness of the scene was extraordinary in a realm otherwise all black and white. The rock strata varied in their hues, but for the most part seemed remarkably bright — partly, I am told, because continuous cold inhibits the chemical weathering that would otherwise dim them, partly because the sun imparted its own brilliance to them, and partly because the visitor had become unaccustomed to color in the landscape. The floor of the valley, although it was only rocks and pebbles, seemed in bloom.

The six hospitable New Zealanders took us into their neat cottage by the shore of the lake, gave us coffee and cakes, and then showed me through their laboratory, with its instrumentation to record solar radiation, earth radiation, earthquakes, and weather data.

Outdoors again, I would have been glad for time to climb the valley walls. But it would have taken days, and the hour of departure was already at hand.

On our flight out we carried packaged sewage and garbage for disposal at Scott Base. I am glad to say that at Vanda Station, in Antarctica's only equivalent to a garden spot, the scenery is unmarred by any garbage dump.

Stopping at the foot of the Commonwealth Glacier, which towered as a wall of ice above the little helicopter and the little men, I was given the chance to photograph it. Then we flew back across McMurdo Sound.

It was the next day that I was taken to visit Cape Royds and Cape Evans, before unexpectedly flying to Byrd Station for my four days there. And at 1:30 in the morning of January 14 the Hercules airplane took off from Willy Field to fly north over Victoria Land, over the Pacific, and up the east coast of New Zealand's South Island, to land at Christchurch, at 9:30, amid the luxuriance of foliage, flower, and bird, and in the balmy atmosphere of the New Zealand summer.

14. The Teeming Ocean
and Its Whales

❧ VIRTUALLY THE WHOLE SURFACE of our planet is crowded with a life so abundant and varied — from the worm on the ocean floor to the elephant on the savanna, from the microscopic cell under the soil to the eagle in the sunlight — that we can hardly comprehend it as the single whole it is. In a large view of time and space, however, the many are one, being the progeny of a single ancestral form. From a beginning lost in time, the entity called life has been constantly spreading out, pushing its way into every crevice and cranny. The variety of its forms today represents simply adaptation to the varied environmental circumstances it has encountered in the course of its expansion. With one exception, it has fitted itself into every niche.

The only major environment to which life has not been able to adapt so far is ice. Consequently, the mantle it has formed over the rest of the globe stops where the teeming ocean laps the shores of the Antarctic continent. Only in the continental expanses that surround the South Pole is our planet bare of life over a wide area.

Nothing is more interesting to observe than the edge between two environments. The edge between the ocean and the glacial continent is of special interest because it presents the unique contrast of a lifeless realm with an immediately adjacent ocean that swarms with the most abundant oceanic life anywhere on earth.

Oceanic environments may be compared to those of a tropical rain forest. The forest extends vertically above the surface of the earth, 125 feet or more. Aloft is sunlight, below perpetual gloom. The complex of life that inhabits the sunlit canopy, and is largely confined to it, is quite different from the complex at ground level, and there may be still another complex that occupies the intermediate zone.

Rain forest and ocean are the only environments on earth that have distinct vertical components above ground level. In the case of the forest, we men normally have access only to the life at the bottom. Walking among the great boles and roots in the filtered twilight, one hears overhead the sounds of birds and beasts one can never see to identify. I have also had the experience of flying in an airplane just over the surface of a rain forest that I was familiar with at ground level, viewing spectacular forms of life that were never seen at all from below.

By contrast with the rain forest, which offers a limited and peculiar set of environments, the ocean provides the widest complex of environments on earth. A single body of water in which the land masses are islands, it covers over 70 percent of the earth's surface, its average depth is over two miles, its extreme depth almost seven miles. For our own air-breathing species its lower parts are, of all regions on earth, the most inaccessible. They, in turn, are inhabited by creatures of darkness that could not even suspect the existence of the illuminated upper world in which we ourselves live.

Pelagic life, the life of the open sea, suffers from a limitation that does not exist for life on land, or even for life along the ocean shores. Its only vegetable forms are microscopic single cells, and it is on the vegetable forms, directly or indirectly, that the animal forms feed. Only the vegetable forms can synthesize, and thereby make available to the animal forms, the energy of sunlight on which all life depends for its nourishment, not excluding that in the total darkness of the ocean's floor. But there are no trees, shrubs, or herbaceous plants in the open ocean, only microscopic cells in the wash of the waves. (The seaweed of the Sargasso Sea is hardly an exception, for it has merely drifted away from shore moorings and cannot reproduce itself.) The ocean's floor is too far below for large plants to root themselves in it, and there are reasons why they could not survive a rootless life in the winds or currents at the ocean's surface.

When it comes to animal life, however, by far the largest forms inhabit the ocean rather than the land. A Blue Whale may be 100 feet long and weigh 150 tons. An animal that big, if on land, would not be able to carry its weight around, but there is no limit to the body weight that water will support. All that nourishes the Blue Whale, however, albeit by way of intermediate organisms in the food chain, is the plant life that takes the form of the microscopic cells. Considering the loss of nutrient energy at every stage of the food chain, the 150 tons of the Blue Whale represent many times as many tons of these cells. We shall, however, return to the whales and the food chain.

Where the life of the rain forest grows up from the ground, the life of the open sea begins at its surface and extends downward. It begins with the microscopic plants, which must remain near the top to absorb the energy of the sunlight. In the surface layer they form pastures on which minute forms of animal life and small fish graze. Successively larger forms — arthropods, jellyfish, squids, vertebrates — feed on the smaller; and so, link by link, the food chain is extended to the point where a small fraction of the original solar energy supports seals and whales, storm petrels, albatrosses, penguins, and skuas. The food chain, like the genetic chain, binds all this varied life together, making it one.

From the surface, where it absorbs the strength of the sun, this life filters downward, through intermediate layers in which great and little fish dart or drift, until at last it reaches a cold, black, unchangeable world inhabited by weak-bodied monsters, some of them all mouth and stomach, some carrying lamps — monsters that share with us a common ancestor in time beyond recall. The floor of the ocean deeps is the uttermost margin, the habitat most remote from the source of life. The beings that populate it depend entirely on leavings of the higher life in the form of such crumbs as ultimately sink to their level.

Writing in the mid-1930s, I made a statement about the world's ocean that would not be tenable today.

> It is some consolation, if you are as much troubled over the increasing subjection of nature by man as over the subjection of man by nature, to reflect that two-thirds of the globe's surface remains an unconquerable wilderness. By a welcome paradox, the sea, in which all is drift and continual change, is nevertheless the most abiding feature of the earth. It is still the sea of Genesis. The American continents have been so scarred in the past four and a half centuries that the contemporaries of Columbus would hardly recognize them if they returned, but the ocean they crossed would give them no clue to the lapse of time.

Today I have to recognize that this is not true — if only because the contemporaries of Columbus would be bound to ask, "Where are the whales?" Moreover, they would find oil on the surface and, to the extent that they were able to investigate such matters, they would find the whole biology of the ocean changed, in part by chemical pollution that has at last spread even to the shores of Antarctica — even, for that matter, to the snow that falls on the South Pole.

•

While life on land is most abundant in the tropics, thinning out progressively toward the Poles on either side, the opposite is true of marine life. Relatively sparse in tropical waters, it becomes progressively more concentrated toward the Poles. It prefers the high latitudes.

If we men were, like dolphins, creatures of the sea, what we would need to have explained to us would be the strange preference of terrestrial life for the warm surroundings. Part of the explanation to give an intelligent dolphin would be that, in a circumambient medium penetrable by sunlight and of virtually no density, where nothing floats, vegetable life is able to root itself in the floor of its habitat. This enables it to develop gigantic forms with specialized organs that spread out to catch the radiation from the sun. However, the demands that the gigantism of these forms makes on the environment, in terms of the requirements for their growth, are met with increasing difficulty as the latitudes get higher because of the thermal instability of air by contrast with water, its inability to retain heat. Where the temperature of the sea, even at the North Pole, never falls below freezing except at the surface, the air outside the tropical and subtropical zones is apt to fall far below freezing, at least seasonally, and this tends to inhibit the growth of the gigantic vegetable forms peculiar to the land, as well as creating adverse conditions for animal life by covering the ground to great depths with a white precipitate in the form of microscopic ice crystals. This is why the vegetable forms are necessarily most abundant and most effective at gathering solar energy in the tropics. Here, by their size and density, they create rich local environments of their own that sustain myriad forms of animal life — forms, however, limited in the size they can attain by the absence of an all-encompassing medium capable of supporting their weight, which they have therefore to support themselves on special limbs developed for the purpose. These are among the disadvantages associated with the struggle to survive outside the natural or, at least, the original medium for life.

In fact, however, there is a paradox in the preference of pelagic life for the high latitudes. Since all life, oceanic no less than terrestrial, depends on the radiant energy of the sun, which pours more abundantly over the tropics than over the high latitudes, one would expect the oceanic as well as the terrestrial life to be

most crowded in the tropics. Indeed, one would expect the surface of tropical waters, over large areas, to be green meadows, floating carpets of the microscopic plant cells that are the vegetation of the open sea. The quantity of sunlight, however, is not all that counts. Life also requires phosphate, silica, and other minerals, which are most abundantly available where they are supplied to the ocean's surface by a constant upwelling of the cold bottom waters. Such upwelling occurs in some degree along all continental coasts, making the offshore marine life richer than

Minke Whale
among the ice floes

that of the open sea, and is most notable along the west coasts of South America and Africa. The cold Humboldt Current, so called, is really a constant upwelling and overturning of bottom waters along the west coast of South America, as a consequence of which conditions associated with the cold waters of the Antarctic extend all the way to the Equator, where they are manifested, *inter alia,* by a penguin native to the Galápagos Islands. Perhaps the richest marine environment in the world, then, is that in the low latitudes off the coasts of Perú and Ecuador. Even though this environment is basically coastal rather than pelagic, I should amend the generalization I made earlier that marine life is richest in the high latitudes. Marine life (I should have said) tends to be richest wherever cold surface waters occur, and such waters occur chiefly in the high latitudes.

The circumpolar Antarctic Ocean, extending out from the continent some 2,000 miles and therefore constituting a pelagic rather than a coastal environment, is the only great oceanic area enriched, like the surface waters of the Humboldt Current, by a constant overturning of waters, here set in motion by the outflow of melted ice, by the currents that respond to the Coriolis effect, and by the inversion of weight brought about where the colder fresh water from the continent encounters the warmer salt water from the north.

Another reason for the greater hospitality of the cold waters, at least to animal life, is that such life requires oxygen, and the colder the water the greater the amount of oxygen it can hold in solution.

Finally, I note a condition that is confined to the highest latitudes. At these latitudes sunlight is available continuously for half the year, while for months of the remainder there is continuous darkness. Above the Antarctic Circle the meadows of microscopic plants are absorbing sunlight and the animals are absorbing the plants continuously around the clock for half a year at a time. The debris from all this activity is raining down continuously on the underworld of the ocean, where it is carried to the bottom feeders, at last, by the strong currents of the over-turning waters. Then, through the long winter months, the source of life is cut off, darkness is continuous, the meadows perish, some of the animal life emigrates, and the rest lives on the stores of food left over from the long summer's day. Whether such a slow alternation of day and night, each a season long, confers a net advantage or disadvantage is a matter for specula-tion and investigation. It is, in any case, one of the most peculiar and conspicuous features of the polar environment

I mentioned in Chapter 6 that the pack-ice through which our icebreaker smashed its way was golden brown in the bottom half, as could be seen when broken pieces were upended to show their edges. This golden brown represented the basis of the abundance that distinguishes life in the Antarctic Ocean, for it was produced by the frozen remains, packed solidly together, of microscopic diatoms, chief among the single-celled plants from which the food chain begins.

If oceanic life is more abundant in the high latitudes, it is also less varied. There are more individuals but fewer species. The reason is to be found in the difference between a faster pace of life in warm waters than in cold. "The warm-water temperatures of the tropics," Rachel Carson wrote, "speed up the processes of reproduction and growth, so that many generations are produced in the time required to bring one to maturity in cold seas. There is more opportunity for genetic mutation to be produced within a given time. . . ." On the other hand, the longevity that results from the relatively slow processes of life in cold seas means that more generations overlap, in consequence of which the total populations of the fewer species are greater.*

•

An account of the food chain in Antarctic waters that omitted any mention of krill would be equivalent to an account of Hamlet without the Prince of Denmark. For all the whales except the toothed whales, for dolphins and porpoises, for what is by far the commonest of the seals (the Crabeater), for penguins, and for many of the fish and the flying birds, krill is "the staff of life" — more so than bread ever was for any human community, even in the days when it was the chief item of human sustenance. Krill is the whaleman's term for members of the genus *Euphausia*, shrimp-like crustaceans, bright red and up to 2½ inches long, that make shrimp soup of the Antarctic surface waters over large areas. By far the most abundant, it appears, is the Lobster Krill, so that it is to this species that the term ordinarily refers.

To the southbound biologist, the Antarctic Convergence is not so much the line where the cold fresh water flowing north sinks under the warm salt water flowing south as it is the frontier where the Kingdom of the Krill begins. When nesting Adélie Penguins march off, the members of a pair turn by turn, to forage in the ocean, what they return with is crops full of krill, which is disgorged into the mouths of the hungry nestlings. The red stains on the shirtfronts of virtually all the adult Adélies I saw represented krill juice spilled in the process. W. E. Pequegnat has estimated that a growing Blue Whale consumes some three tons of krill per summer's day. I myself have waded through thick carpetings of dead and faded krill washed up on the shores of Ross Island. "The krill," writes Dr. Murphy, "symbolizes life in

* Carson, 1951, p. 22; Murphy, *Scientific American*, September 1962.

the Antarctic more aptly than any penguin does. It is the key organism in the shortest food chain of one of the most abounding provinces of life on earth. Feeding directly on the one-celled plants of the sea, the krill in turn supports not only fish but also penguins and vast populations of winged seabirds, seals and whales."*

The reader has now been introduced to an Antarctic environment that supports, more conspicuously than any other in the world, such of the whales as remain and seals that lead a life no less strange than that of penguins.

•

What has been, in effect, a campaign of extermination against the world's great whales — a campaign now in its final phase — presents a history of human cupidity and cynicism so ugly that one hesitates to enter upon it. As the species have been approaching extinction, it is evident that the whalers, backed by their national governments, especially in the case of Japan and the Soviet Union, have deliberately followed a policy of reaping what profits they can in the present without regard for the future. ("In the long run," the saying goes, "we are all dead.") The cynicism consists especially in such pretenses as that of agreeing, in the name of conservation, to limitations on the annual catch in excess of what it would be possible to catch anyway. Today, whatever remnant of the Blue Whale population remains is probably too small for recovery, even though the killing now stopped completely, and other species are also in what seems likely to be their final decline. In 1946–1947 some 10,000 Blue Whales were taken in the Antarctic; the figure for 1965–1966 was 594; and whether any remain at all to be killed today no one knows. The

* Murphy, 1962.

recently abundant Right Whales and Bowheads have now come to the edge of extinction. As the most profitable species have declined to remnant populations, the whalers have concentrated on the next most profitable, so that the order of extermination may be said to represent, at least, the use to which man has put the godlike capacity for reasoning that, among all the species on earth, is his alone. And when at last the whales are gone, we can console ourselves that, because we have enjoyed the consumption of margarine and fertilizer made from their carcasses, they will not have died in vain.

In the eighteenth and nineteenth centuries, when whales were pursued only in sailing ships and rowboats, and then at great risk, they always had a sporting chance to escape. Today, spread-out whaling fleets with helicopters to locate every whale in a sixty-mile radius, with cannon mounted on catcher vessels to fire explosive harpoons into their bodies, and with factory vessels to process the corpses on the spot, the matter is greatly simplified: for the men no longer run any risk and the whales no longer have any chance. It will be too bad when no whales remain; but those who have exterminated them will at least be able to retire on the profits.

I surmise that until modern times the oceans, over large areas, abounded in whales, so that they were to be seen from shipboard on all sides; and the Antarctic Ocean especially, with its pastures of krill, must have been alive with them. I remember, as a little boy in the 1920s, crossings of the North Atlantic in which, from just outside New York Harbor to Cherbourg, it was our sport to watch for the jets of steam that betokened the spouting of a whale, and sometimes to get a glimpse of a black back rising under the spout, only to sink again. Certainly the sight was not so rare that our scrutiny of the surrounding seas was not frequently rewarded. Even by then, however, the North Atlantic populations must have been seriously depleted.

I would have thought it had occurred to no one, as early as the middle of the last century, that the abundance of nature was exhaustible, that man might actually exterminate common species altogether by his hunting of them. However, in *Moby Dick*, published in 1851, Herman Melville refers to an inquiry "often agitated by the more recondite Nantucketers. Whether owing to the almost omniscient lookouts at the mastheads of the whale-ships, now penetrating even through Behring's Straits, and into the remotest secret drawers and lockers of the world; and the thousand harpoons and lances darted along all continental coasts; the moot point is, whether leviathan can long endure so wide a chase, and so remorseless a havoc; whether he must not at last be exterminated from the waters. . . ." However, contemplating the widespread abundance of the whales, and considering how few whales forty men in a sailing ship can catch even in a four-year voyage, he concludes that the whale is "immortal in his species, however perishable in his individuality."

There are several ways to define the loss that the world has suffered with the progressive disappearance of the whales. I am glad to say that only one of these ways is represented by the definition implicit in a recent scientific paper. After mentioning that the Antarctic stocks of whales have, since 1904, been reduced to a tenth of their former size, the author points out that, in the absence of certain restrictions instituted by the International Whaling Commission, "the decline would have taken place more rapidly with an estimated loss of more than £50 million worth of products actually obtained in the more recent years." Here the weight of whales is given in pounds sterling.

•

I have been referring to "whales," but the meaning of the term is not precise. There is an order of mammals called the Cetacea, just as there is an order of birds called the Columbiformes; and just as the term "pigeon" is generally used to designate the larger members of the latter order (the smaller being commonly called "doves"), so the term "whale" is generally used to designate the larger members of the Cetacea (the smaller being commonly called "porpoises" or "dolphins"). If we are talking scientifically, we identify all the living cetaceans as belonging to either of two suborders: that of the baleen whales, with whalebone instead of teeth, and that of the toothed whales, which includes with the Sperm Whale the porpoises and dolphins. In my references to the disappearance of the whales, it is to the great cetaceans that I refer, not to the porpoises and dolphins.

The mouths of the baleen whales are filled by an arrangement of fringed Venetian blinds (made of whalebone) that strains krill and other small animal forms out of the seawater flowing through it; and since none of them, not even the Blue Whale, could swallow anything larger than a man's fist, none of them is the "fish" that swallowed Jonah. A baleen whale in the Antarctic may collect a ton of krill a day by merely cruising through the krill pastures with mouth open. While whales are free to wander from the Arctic to the Antarctic, and from the Atlantic to the Pacific, some of them being among the greatest of travellers, the krill pastures make the Antarctic especially attractive to the whale-bone whales.

The Sperm Whale generally inhabits the world's warmer waters, but in the southern summer adult males, deserting their families, visit the Antarctic Ocean. This species is remarkable on several counts. Although an air-breathing mammal like all the other cetaceans, it may descend a mile to rake the bottom of the ocean with its toothed lower jaw, and remain under an hour between breaths. It feeds largely on squid, some of them bigger than a score of Jonahs put together. There is reason to think it may be able to communicate over distances measured in miles. Finally, it has the largest brain of any animal of any kind whatever, not excluding either the reader of these words or their author.

Because cetaceans and men inhabit entirely different worlds, there can hardly be such communion between them, and such mutual understanding, as there is between men and dogs. Lately, however, by a deliberate effort to achieve an understanding relationship with dolphins kept in swimming pools, where men can enter into close and leisurely association with them, it has been discovered that they are intelligent in ways that no one had expected. Is it not possible that, if we could enter into such relations with Sperm Whales as we enjoy with dogs, we would find that they were creatures of sensitivity and intellect? The possibility might be borne in mind by those who hunt them down to weigh them in pounds sterling.

What is undoubtedly the most conspicuous, and perhaps the most abundant, of the cetaceans that inhabit the Antarctic Ocean is the so-called Killer Whale, which is in fact an outsize member of the dolphin family — a dolphin, that is, which grows to a length of over thirty feet. It is ferociously predatory, hunting in packs and taking even the great baleen whales as its prey. The following account of a brush with Killer Whales is from Scott's diary for January 5, 1911, when the *Terra Nova* had arrived at Cape Evans.

> Some 6 or 7 killer whales, old and young, were skirting the fast floe edge ahead of the ship; they seemed excited and dived rapidly, almost touching the floe. As we watched, they suddenly appeared astern raising their snouts out of water. I

had heard weird stories of these beasts, but had never associated serious danger with them. Close to the water's edge lay the wire stern rope of the ship, and our two Esquimaux dogs were tethered to this. I did not think of connecting the movements of the whales with this fact, and seeing them so close I shouted to Ponting, who was standing abreast of the ship. He seized his camera and ran towards the floe edge to get a close picture of the beasts, which had momentarily disappeared. The next moment the whole floe under him and the dogs heaved up and split into fragments. One could hear the 'booming' noise as the whales rose under the ice and struck it with their backs. Whale after whale rose under the ice, setting it rocking fiercely; luckily Ponting kept his feet and was able to fly to security. By an extraordinary chance also, the splits had been made around and between the dogs, so that neither of them fell into the water. Then it was clear that the whales shared our astonishment, for one after another their huge hideous heads shot vertically into the air through the cracks which they had made. As they reared them to a height of 6 or 8 feet it was possible to see their tawny head markings, their small glistening eyes, and their terrible array of teeth — by far the largest and most terrifying in the world. There cannot be a doubt that they looked up to see what had happened to Ponting and the dogs. . . . Of course, we have known well that killer whales continually skirt the edge of the floes and that they would undoubtedly snap up anyone who was unfortunate enough to fall into the water; but the facts that they could display such deliberate cunning, that they were able to break ice of such thickness (at least 2½ feet), and that they could act in unison, were a revelation to us. It is clear that they are endowed with singular intelligence, and in future we shall treat that intelligence with every respect.

The remains of fourteen seals and thirteen porpoises have been found in the stomach of one Killer Whale. All the flying birds of the sea and the penguins are included in the list of their prey.

•

I have already said that, in a cosmopolitan view, life is one. The ancient Greeks did not know how big the universe was when they allowed themselves to believe that the measure of all things was man. Even within the confines of this little planet, however, it takes a narrow view to distinguish man, so confidently and completely as we commonly do, from the rest of life. Evolution has been going on for five hundred million years now, and it is no more than two million years ago that we men made our appearance. What grounds are there for being so sure that we represent the completion of the process? Wait another five hundred million years and we may see that the highest achievement of the process, at that time, is some immeasurably more developed species, possibly descended from *Globigerina,* a microscopic protozoan that now drifts with the waves of the sea, awaiting its day. I find it more plausible to believe that, within the confines of this planet at least, life is the measure of all things. That is as far in narrowness as I am willing to go.

Let us cherish the whole of the life to which we belong, not just the one part that is ourselves. Surely Joseph Wood Krutch was right to say to the Spring Peepers, in his confrontation with them: "Don't forget, we are all in this together." We and the peepers and the *Globigerina* are all brothers, descended from a common ancestor and striving together toward an end we cannot know.

But there are discontinuities in the expression of our brotherhood, as Dr. Krutch realized when, peering through his microscope at protozoa in a drop of water, he became aware of his inability to enter their world. He could see that world only from a distance through the agency of a microscope, as one might see life on Mars through the agency of a telescope. "It is not," he wrote, ". . . that these creatures are much unlike us, except in size, for their strangeness is not a matter of difference but merely

of the discontinuity which a great disparity of magnitude estab-
lishes. Like us they are composed of protoplasm, and this implies
the very closest and most essential kinship. . . ."

No such absolute discontinuity exists between us and our
closer relatives, the great whales. (They are so close that, in a
God's-eye view, the distinction may seen negligible.) We are
alike warm-blooded mammals that have two eyes and a mouth,
that breathe air, that mate in the same way, and that suckle the
young we produce for our replacement generation after generation. (Motherhood, especially, is remarkably similar in whales
and men.) We are the same mortal flesh. Each of us has what is
merely his own variety of a single brain. Each of us has a
language, so that to some degree we might converse with each
other, entering into a communion ever closer than that between
us and dogs. But we know the elephant, for example, much better
than the whale, being often on terms of the closest friendship
with it, because, like us, it happens to inhabit the land.

Now, however, we have begun to enter into friendly relations
with certain of the cetaceans. In 1955, at the town of Opononi on
the coast of New Zealand, a wild dolphin, quite on its own initiative, took to cultivating the acquaintance of swimmers and
boaters, playing with them and even making friends with particular individuals, as in the case of a little girl whom it allowed to
ride on its back. There have been other well authenticated in-
stances, not a few, in which dolphins, in spite of the difference in
habitat, have demonstrated a kinship with men and an enjoyment
of their company. The U.S. Navy recently trained a dolphin to
carry mesages and tools to designated underwater locations, and
to go to the rescue of divers who, having got into trouble, called
them by prearranged signals.* If such association is possible with

* Soper, 1969, p. 167ff.

dolphins, what possibilities might there not be in cultivating relations with one of the great whales, which we might find to be more nearly our brother in intelligence than any other creature.

When Captain Cook, the first man ever to do so, sailed into the Antarctic seas, the great whales must have been pasturing in numbers all around him, like the quadrupeds that still crowd the grasslands of east Africa. They swam close alongside his ships, for they could hardly yet have learned the fear of man. Today, all that is left of them are the vestiges that some of us still weigh in pounds sterling.

Here is the entire tally of one constant observer on an eight-day sea-voyage, from Wellington to McMurdo, across 2,600 miles of ocean.

Item. On New Year's Eve, off the Antarctic coast south of Cape Hallett, I twice saw a whale blow repeatedly without itself appearing above the surface.

Item. My notes record that, later the same day, "a large cetacean leaped on several occasions, with an interval of at least a minute between, almost vertically from the water. It was dark above, light below, had a large dorsal fin, and seemed to have a rather pointed snout." This was probably a Killer Whale.

Item. My notes for the next day read: "Saw a school of Killer Whales, perhaps a dozen, all blowing and arching their backs above the surface to show the very large dorsal fin, below which there seemed to be a white area. Later saw several whales with smaller dorsal fins, which appeared all black."

This is the entire harvest of my search for whales in the South Pacific and Antarctica. Let us turn, then, to the seals.

15. Mammals of Sea and Ice

➤ IF THE DIFFERENCE in habitat makes communion with the whales difficult for us men, the case is not the same with the other great division of oceanic mammals. For the seals are at home in both worlds. They belong, moreover, to the same group of mammals as those of our fellow creatures with which we have the most intimate relations. Their whiskered muzzles, if nothing else, reveal their membership in the order to which the dogs and cats belong, that of the carnivores. Some, like our common Harbor Seal, appear so human when they poke their heads above water for a look around that they are sometimes mistaken for human swimmers. On occasion, Harbor Seals, Sea Lions, and other members of their suborder form relations of intelligent and perhaps affectionate association with us men, like those we enjoy with our dogs and cats. What their relations may be with whales, in the other world of their habitation, I don't know. They do, after all, feed in the same pastures, like antelopes and elephants on the African plains.

As a scientific experiment for the year 3,000 I suggest the transplantation of a human brain into a seal, so that it can, by whatever means may be devised, tell us about the whales and the world it shares with them.

Seals, along with all the rest of us, represent the drive of the single entity that is life to penetrate and fit itself into every hole

Elephant Seal

and corner of the planet, even though to do so entails some adaptations so extreme that, in the absence of incontrovertible evidence, any sober student of life in its more ordinary forms would properly regard them as old wives' tales. So it is that the southernmost species of mammal in the world, although air-breathing like the rest of us, spends the Antarctic night foraging on the sea floor under the ice that rims the continent, and even ranges southward under the Ross Ice Shelf. The seals, then, no less than other groups, represent by their own extraordinary variety the variety of environments with which this mundane sphere challenges life.

Leaving aside the Walrus of the Arctic, which constitutes a family by itself, the seals, like the whales, fall into two groups, commonly called the "fur seals" and the "true seals." Since this nomenclature implies that the former are impostors, I shall call the latter by their alternative name, the "hair seals." The fur seals depend on a thick pelage to keep them warm, where the hair seals, like the whales, although they have a thin coat of hair, depend on blubber. The fur seals have external ears, lacking in the hair seals, so that the two groups are also known as the "eared" and the "earless" seals. The most notable distinction, however, resides in the fact that the fur seals can raise themselves on all four limbs for locomotion on land, swivelling their hind flippers around under their bodies so as to lumber along at an awkward gallop. The blubbery hair seals, by contrast, appear to have more body and less limb, being in this respect more like the cetaceans. Unable to gather their hind limbs under them, they make their way on land or ice by humping and undulating their whole bodies, fore flippers perhaps pushing a bit, hind flippers simply dragging.

It seems clear that, of the two groups, the hair seals are the more adapted to the water, the fur seals to the land. This is not just a matter of locomotive procedures. The lack of an external ear in the hair seals adds to the streamlining that counts in the water but not on land. Finally, fur, which provides the best kind of insulation against cold air (feathers excepted), hardly serves as protection against cold water that soaks through it to the skin. All the other mammals of the sea — the cetaceans, the sea cows, the Walrus, and the hair seals — could testify that, for life in the sea, blubber is the thing.

Moving back and forth between two worlds as they do, the seals of both groups are confined to shore waters or areas of sea-ice that afford floating platforms. It is among the ice-floes, rather than in the iceless mid-regions of the earth, that they are most numerous. They participate in the relative abundance of the colder sea waters.

The tendency of the polar regions to be rich in individuals and poor in species is well exemplified by the seals of the Antarctic. There are only four species that are strictly and characteristically Antarctic, but those four include the Crabeater, which may be the species with the largest population of any seal in the world. The others are the Weddell, the Leopard, and the Ross Seals. They are hair seals, and are the most specialized of all for aquatic as opposed to terrestrial life. This may be seen superficially in a number of features: their relatively large size, which makes the retention of body heat easier and is hardly a disadvantage in a medium that supports unlimited body weight; the thickness of their blubber; and the relative smallness of their limbs, which are too small to be of much use in supporting their heavy bodies on land or on the ice, but are just right, in the water, to act as stabilizers (front limbs) and propellants (hind limbs). There are evident points of convergent evolution between these species and the cetaceans, as also between them and the penguins. Species that become adapted to like habitats acquire like features of adaptation. They come to resemble one another in peculiar ways.

The four Antarctic species normally never leave the ice at all. One supposes that, with the likely exception of the Leopard Seal, which does occasionally wander farther north, they had better remain alongside the ice that is their only sure refuge from the Killer Whales. The Crabeater, Leopard, and Ross Seals normally lead floating lives from birth to death, the cows bearing their pups on the floes and caring for them there until they are old enough to go in swimming. The Weddell makes itself at home on or under the fast ice, including the ice-shelves, as well as in the pack.

Only these four, I have said, are strictly and characteristically Antarctic. This qualification omits the Elephant Seal, which has wider geographical associations, and which confines its breeding to islands around the edge of the Antarctic or farther north, even as far as the Falkland Islands off the east coast of South America. Although it may frequently wander as far south as the Antarctic continent, this is hardly enough to give it full standing as an Antarctic species, any more than records of the Leopard Seal off the South African coast make it an African mammal.

This great beast of the ocean, which is one of the hair seals, has the distinction of being by far the largest seal in the world. Bulls have been known as long as twenty-two feet, and they may weigh as much as 5,000 pounds. The cows are so much smaller that they might almost belong to another species. It is the bull's capacity to inflate his proboscis until it bears some resemblance to an elephant's trunk curled in on itself that accounts for the common name. A race or a closely allied species of Elephant Seal was once abundant off the Pacific coast of North America, but relentless hunting reduced its numbers to what is today only a remnant population on the island of Guadalupe off the coast of Lower California.

On January 11, 1904, Edward Wilson and others were walking along the coast of Ross Island at Cape Royds when they came upon "a very large seal" resting on the beach. "I saw at a glance," Wilson wrote in his journal, "that he was no Antarctic seal." What he turned out to be was an Elephant Seal, a young bull twelve feet long with a girth of some ten feet at the shoulders. Cape Royds is as far south as a seal can normally go without travelling inland or under the solid ice. What, one wonders, was this young bull doing so far from home?

The Elephant Seal breeds in dense colonies composed of the biggest bulls and their harems. A young bull that is still only twelve feet long has no chance to establish himself in such a colony, and this may move him to embark on such travels as might, at last, bring him up at what is the end of the world. In many species, including our own, *Wanderlust* is a characteristic of young males. Perhaps the wanderer does not specifically dream of a harem beyond the horizon, but there is a lack of satisfaction with circumstances at home that makes him restless. Or perhaps there is just the urge to explore, which may have some manifestation in the mind of a young Elephant Seal as in that of a Captain Cook.

My acquaintance with the Elephant Seal is limited to the one brief encounter on Campbell Island that I reported in Chapter 4. I did not, in that inadequate introduction, find it the loveliest of seals. That adjective I reserve for the Crabeater which, although confined to the pack-ice of the Antarctic, may also be the most numerous seal in the world today — partly because it was not accessible to the seal hunters of earlier generations, who reduced the Elephant Seal of the north and other once abundant species to remnant populations.

Relatively long and slender, the Crabeater is gray in color, fading to creamy white in older individuals. It is a swift swimmer, sometimes travelling in groups that porpoise (like Adélie Penguins, like porpoises themselves), repeatedly arching all together over the surface of the water. (Species that become adapted to like habitats acquire like features of behavior.)

This species, like the Blue Whale, lives almost exclusively on krill; and, just as the Blue Whale has fringed whalebone slats instead of teeth to filter the krill out of the pouring seawater, so this krill-eater, miscalled the Crabeater, has teeth that have evolved into nothing more nor less than devices for filtering krill.

I say that the Crabeater is normally confined to the pack-ice, but no species can be sure that its young, at least, will always remain within bounds. The mummified remains of Crabeaters, estimated to have been dead over 2,000 years, have been found in the dry valleys of Victoria Land. Like the young Elephant Seal, they adventured up on the shore of the continent, but long before there was any chance that they would find man there. It may be that, at the moment when certain ancient Greeks were speculating about the possibility of an Antarctic realm far beyond the earth's torrid zone, a young Crabeater was hunching his lonely way inland up the valley of the Onyx River — with who knows what in mind.

On that day when the ship in which I was being transported out of the real world first entered the phantom world of the pack-ice, when the Antarctic Fulmars, the Antarctic Petrels, and the Snow Petrels suddenly appeared all about us, when at the same time I saw my first penguins and seals riding the ice-floes — on

Leopard Seal

that day, and in that passage through the pack-ice, most of the seals I saw, usually singly but sometimes two together, sometimes sharing a floe with one or two penguins, were Crabeaters. Like everything else, they were bathed in the brilliant dimness of a radiance without relief. Whether in their paleness they were real or phantom was a question without relevance to a world that appeared to have, itself, only a ghostly reality.

The Leopard Seal also spends the greater part of its life among the floes of the pack-ice, although many individuals, at least, pass a season along the shores of the continent, attaching themselves, like the skuas, to the Adélie Penguin colonies on which

they feast. The term "lovely" would be as inapplicable to the handsomeness of the Sea Leopard as to that of the Siberian Tiger. With the Elephant Seal and the Walrus, it is one of the three largest seals in the world, exceeding the latter in length although not in weight. It has a powerful long body that tapers elegantly to the hind flippers, a large head clearly separated from the body by a neck, which is unusual in seals, and a wide mouth armed with distinctly carnivorous teeth. It is a racing seal, as any such predator must be to catch its prey, and has been known to attain the momentum needed to shoot out of the water onto ice-surface eight feet above. It is dark topsides, light below, and more or less spotted all over; but those I saw, as I saw them — against ice-floes from the ship or, as at Cape Crozier, wet in the water close at hand — simply looked dark and shiny.

The land Leopard can hold large prey with its claws while it tears off chunks small enough to swallow. The Sea Leopard can only thrash its prey about (which is why it needs a neck), but it has a gullet large enough to swallow at least an Adélie Penguin whole. As I saw for myself, its procedure is simply to shake the body out of its skin, which is quickly done, and then gulp it.

I suppose that Killer Whales, although they hunt in packs, must at least hesitate to attack the most formidable of seals as long as there is any other prey available. This may explain why the Sea Leopard is not as exclusively attached to the vicinity of the ice as the other three Antarctic species. For the fact is that stragglers are recorded north of it. The availability of penguins, rather than its own safety, may well be the chief factor that keeps it about the pack-ice.

Who can say that inside the head of a Sea Leopard there is not an intelligence equal to that of a dog, of a Sea Lion, or of a dolphin?

Observations of the Ross Seal have always been rare, and while it is undoubtedly the least common of the four Antarctic species it may be that difficulties of observation make it seem rarer than it is. There is reason to believe that it prefers hard-packed ice where ships are less likely to penetrate, and inexperienced observers are likely to mistake it at a distance for the Weddell Seal. Although I cannot claim to have seen it, I find in my notes a reference to a seal on an ice-floe, seen from the *Staten Island,* that "looked to me like Ross's." (If it had looked to me like a Crab-eater I would presumably have set it down as such. So it is that a bias in favor of the common species always enters into our identifications.)

·

The statement with which I began this chapter, that we have a common meeting ground with seals as we do not with whales, applies less to the three Antarctic seals I have so far discussed than to any others. It is hardly convenient for us to join them on the rocking ice-floes where they spend their lives in order to cultivate their acquaintance at leisure. Consequently, we know little about how they pass their lives and conduct their vital activities. The case is different with the fourth of the Antarctic seals. Dr. Gerald L. Kooyman of the Scripps Institution of Oceanography, giving an account of the species in the *Scientific American* of August 1969, has written: "Probably more is now known about the Weddell seal than is known about any other marine mammal."

This is a paradox, because the Weddell Seal inhabits the outermost verge of the biosphere, living the year around at the brink where further life at last becomes impossible. A breeding colony has been found at 79°S., some 288 miles inside the edge of the

Ross Ice Shelf, at a point near Roosevelt Island where there are rifts in the ice, which means that the seals find their food in the utterly dark waters beneath the shelf and so far from the open sea. One wonders how they got there in the first place. There is also a colony at White Island, some ten or a dozen miles south of McMurdo Station.* However, the very fact that this species is found on the fast ice, where we men can set up camp as we cannot in the pack, makes it the most accessible of the four. The additional fact that it has developed remarkable adaptations to the most extreme of environments has made it an object of special scientific curiosity.

Especially in winter, when the air is far colder than the water, the Weddell Seal passes most of its time under the ice. For breathing it depends on holes that it keeps open by the use of teeth especially adapted for the purpose. But it is able to spend at least an hour under water without breathing, during which it may travel several miles, and it is known to descend to a depth of 1,950 feet. How it finds its food of fish, squid, and crustaceans in the black darkness, especially during the long winter's night, no one knows.

The cows come out onto the ice in August, through holes of their own making, to give birth to their single pups, which lie alongside their mothers on the ice until, when two or three weeks old, they go down the holes into the water below.

As in the case of the Emperor Penguin, the Weddell Seal is able to live and function under such marginal circumstances only by virtue of extraordinary physiological and behavioral adaptations. Since this general account is no place for a technical exposition of these adaptations, I here confine myself to registering the fact of their sheer beauty in terms of the fitness and delicacy of

* Gerald L. Kooyman, in letter to author; and E. C. Young in Holdgate, p. 498.

particular responses to particular challenges of the environment. The Weddell Seal in the wintry darkness under the Ice Shelf and the Emperor Penguin in the wintry darkness above it are the two outstanding examples of the highest orders life has developed so far, mammal and bird, at the ultimate frontier. Who can say that life, on this sphere lost in space, is not beautiful, heroic, and tragic?

Like the Emperor and Adélie Penguins, until the advent of man the four Antarctic seals never knew an enemy above the surface of the sea. (This accounts for the fact that, while newborn seals of the Arctic species have white coats to make them inconspicuous to foraging Polar Bears and Arctic Foxes, the newborn of the Antarctic species are, in their darkness, as conspicuous as can be against the snow and ice.) The Weddell Seal, when out on the ice, is so far from remaining alert to possible danger that, as I reported in Chapter 6, it is capable of sleeping on an ice-floe while an icebreaker, crashing through the pack, bears down on it, awakening so late that it is struck by the ship's advancing prow before it can make its escape.

The three seals that are generally confined to the drifting pack-ice are not in a good position to mass together in dense colonies of millions, like the Northern Fur Seals in the Pribilof Islands, or in colonies of hundreds of thousands, like the Elephant Seals on their breeding grounds, or even in small groups. Being more firmly based, the Weddells do congregate at certain places in loose groups, composed chiefly of cows. Such groups occur in summer on the fast ice just offshore, where the rising and falling tide breaks its grip on the land, leaving pressure ridges and cracks between them through which the seals can come up on deck or go below. But individuals are found here and there and everywhere, on shore or sleeping near holes in the ice.

Weddell Seal and pup

In 1902, when man first arrived this far south (in the *Discovery* under Captain Scott), there were Weddells congregated on the Ross Ice Shelf at Pram Point, across the peninsula from the

present McMurdo Station, where New Zealand's Scott Base now is — and, indeed, they were so thick along the south coast of Ross Island that Wilson, in his journal, reported "literally thousands of them in herds of a hundred or more, stretching away out of sight." These seals were, to the explorers, what the Turkeys had been to the Pilgrim Fathers during their first New England winter. They have continued ever since to provide all the dog food — although now, happily for the seals and their admirers, motor vehicles have at last made the dogs obsolete.

The herd of Weddell Seals at Pram Point was still there sixty-seven years later, and perhaps it had been there for 10,000 years before. So large and cylindrical as these great beasts are, with fore flippers that are hardly more than excrescences on their flanks, they look like small whales stranded on the ice. They are there for no other purpose than to sleep, a purpose to which they give themselves with a thoroughness that is impressive. It is obvious that they have no fear of us men when we manage to wake them up, but they generally show themselves annoyed. Some react with displays of bad temper, some make off in what appears to be a spirit of philosophical resignation, and some simply go back to sleep. The placidity of some individuals is demonstrated by the fact that scientists have attached tubes to the nipples of nursing mothers and drawn off their milk while they continued to sleep.

It was January 2, in the morning, when the helicopter from the *Staten Island* delivered me to McMurdo Station. In the afternoon I crossed the Gap, as the *Discovery* explorers had called it, to Pram Point for a visit with my New Zealand friends at Scott Base. As soon as I got to the shore and saw the seals lying out on the ice I recklessly began trying to make my way across the cracks and crevices of the pressure ridge to join them. The Deputy Director of the base rushed after to save me from my folly — and then, in an equally kindly spirit, supplied boards by which I could cross the worst gaps to get onto the fast ice.

The following is from my notes on my meeting with the seals:

> The first problem in photographing any was to wake it up, for one could stand three feet away and shout at it, and only gradually, after a while, would it open its eyes and lift its head to look at one. Individuals then reacted differently. Some, after a long reluctance and wakening process, would undulate off (one rolled over and over, away from me, tending to pivot on its tail). Others would bark and hoot. One chattered its jaws like the albatrosses at Campbell clapping their bills, hooting at the same time. Others would remain largely undisturbed, allowing me to photograph their heads close up.

•

When I think how brief my visit to Antarctica had to be I remember scientists who told me that, although they had spent several seasons on the continent, and had even wintered over, they had never seen a penguin or any other wildlife except the skuas at McMurdo. Their experience was to be flown in to McMurdo from Christchurch, seeing nothing on the way, and from McMurdo to stations in the interior where there was no life, returning as they had come.

Beside the skua, however, there is one other Antarctic species that one can hardly help seeing, if only from a distance, as one flies in or out of McMurdo. When we took off from Willy Field at 1:30 on the morning of January 14, the scattered bodies of the Weddell Seals could be seen lying on the ice off Pram Point. A few others were visible as specks on the ice of McMurdo Sound before the airplane got too high. In a few minutes, however, we were over the mountains and glaciers of Victoria Land, and after another hour or two there was only the open Pacific. My visit to Antarctica was over.

Snow Petrel

Epilogue
A Report to the Greeks

◆ THE SPHERICAL SHAPE of the earth had already been a matter of speculation among the ancient Greeks when Aristotle first gave it proof. The sun was known to shine perpendicularly on the Equator, making the equatorial belt torrid, and to shine at an ever flatter angle over the surface that curved northward, causing the climate to become ever cooler in that direction. By the simple logic of geometry, the same must be true as the earth's surface curved southward from the torrid zone. On this basis, the existence of a coldest zone about the southern extremity of the earth's axis, as about the northern, was a matter of plausible speculation.

The geographical knowledge of the Greeks did not, however, extend even as far as the Equator, and they could easily believe that as one approached the Equator the torrid zone became so fiery that men could continue no farther. And so the cooler realm beyond would remain forever unknown.

In the absence of knowledge, we men have always populated the world with mythic creatures of our imaginations, with phoenixes and rocs, with sea serpents and dragons, with mermaids, sphinxes, harpies, and gryphons. We have filled the vacuum of our ignorance, not only with legends handed down from generation to generation, but also with the tall tales of travellers.

Imagine, now, a traveller who returns from the realms beyond the torrid zone, reporting that he has made his way past desert islands, across frozen seas, over mountains greater than any hitherto seen, up glaciers as wide as many days' march, and across endless snow plains to the southern extremity of the earth's axis. And he reports the strange creatures he has seen in these realms.

Beyond the temperate regions of the south, he reports, one comes to one great ocean that encircles the world. Here, where the storm-blast roars forever and ships perish, live birds as wide from one wing-tip to the other as two men placed end to end. For years they do not come near the land, but rising and descending in circles, their wings held rigid to the blast, they travel ever eastward around the earth, returning again and again upon their courses. And everywhere they go there are small fowl and middle-sized fowl spread over the waves in their myriads, wandering this way and that, moving carpets of bird-life, such an abundance as has never been known in the waters of the familiar world.

In this ocean there are also sea beasts larger than the largest ships. They cruise with mouths open through pastures of minute red creatures like shrimps, or they sound to submarine depths in which darkness is perpetual and fish fantastic of shape bear lanterns with them as they move.

Finally, voyaging ever southward, as the atmosphere and the sea become colder islands of ice appear, some twice as large as Rhodes, and on or about them may be seen swarms of seabirds, far greater in their numbers, again, than any birds in the familiar world.

Still farther on, the sea is covered with plates of ice on which beast that seem half dog and half fish, but many times the size of a man, repose; upon which, also, stand upright creatures with the heads of birds and bodies like those of men.

Beyond this ice is open sea again, and then one comes to a

mountainous land all white, and along its coasts seamed cliffs rise ten times higher than the Acropolis. Now for half the year the sun turns constantly in a circle overhead, never dipping to the horizon, and the bright daylight is perpetual. After half a year the sun goes down, the gloom of night descends on the world, and the day returns no more though many months go by. In this season of night the cold becomes so intense that the very peak of Parnassus in winter would seem warm by comparison. Out from the land the salt sea freezes over distances that it would take many days to traverse on foot. Then the world is given over completely to the storm-blast that fills the darkness with driven snow, so that one would say no life could survive. Yet it is in this dead world of darkness, upon the frozen sea itself, and in the very teeth of the storm-blast, that the creatures with the heads of birds on human bodies lay eggs, hatch them, and rear their young; while under the same ice at the same time the great creatures which seem half dog and half fish forage in the darkness, rising from time to time to ice-holes of their own making, where they breathe with only their nostrils exposed, and having breathed descend again.

In the interior of the land the world is permanently frozen, during the summer-long day no less than during the winter-long night, and here one would be sure that there could be no life, no more in summer than in winter. But there are some valleys without snow or ice that in the season of daylight are jewelled with colored stones; and through them rivers flow like the River Meander, sometimes broadening into lakes; and in their waters grows the green weed called "alga." Still deeper in the interior are ranges of mountains, and here or there in cracks of the rock near their summits, kept free of snow by the scouring wind, a scrap of the paper-thin lichen is reported to adhere. And even in the very middle of the ice plain, at the southern extremity of the earth, far beyond the last frontier of life, here where nothing living can survive in nature — even here a winged pirate of the seas, perhaps the greatest traveller of all, has been known to pass in his wanderings.

•

Beyond the narrow frontiers of their geographical knowledge the ancient Greeks applied logic to the understanding of the world, and beyond the frontiers of logic they applied imagination. But what can imagination create that reality will not match? At last in our own day, two thousand years later, we men know the reality that the men of Greece could only try to imagine.

As I review the account I have now completed I remember all this. Remembering, I offer the account, to all who will accept it in that spirit, as a report to the Greeks of what is true.

The End

Appendixes

Publications Cited

Index

Appendix A.
The Coriolis Effect

➤ I said on page 16 that the westerly winds which prevail in the temperate zones of the northern and southern hemispheres do so in consequence of the earth's rotation, as do the easterlies of high southern latitudes. Because the connection between cause and effect is not self-evident, I offer the following explanation.

Imagine a missile fired from the North Pole that starts south at the longitude of Greenwich (i.e., longitude 0°). If the earth were not revolving beneath it, it would continue along longitude 0° across the Equator and to the South Pole. However, because the earth is, in fact, revolving eastward under it as it moves south, longitude 0° will move off to the east from under it, and the lines of longitude west of 0° will pass under it successively as it moves south. At a certain moment it will be over longitude 5°W., then over 10°W., and so forth. Its course, plotted on the earth's surface beneath it, will be south as a matter of its own motion and west as a matter of the earth's revolution, the two motions combining to give it a southwestward course relative to the earth's surface.

From the North Pole to the Equator, the eastward velocity of the earth's surface around its axis increases. Thus, while a point 10 nautical miles south of the Pole would have an orbit of only 63 miles, which it completed in twenty-four hours, a point on the Equator, having to travel 21,600 miles in the same time, would have to travel 343 times as fast. Therefore, as the missile moved south, although the southward component of its velocity would not change, the westward component relative to the earth's surface (actually the eastward velocity of the earth's surface) would constantly increase. This is to say that the westward component of its relative southwestward course would constantly increase, so that it would appear to curve more and more to the west. While approaching a course due west, however, it would never reach such a course, because the fixed southward component would remain. It would continue to move south at the same rate as ever.

When the missile crossed the Equator and moved on toward the South Pole, the eastward velocity of the earth's surface would decrease until, at the South Pole, it was zero. Therefore, as the missile crossed the southern hemisphere, the relative westward component of its southwestward course would diminish progressively, and so, having previously curved around to the right, it would now curve around to the left (i.e., more and more southward) relative to the earth's surface.

This apparent deflection, rightward in the northern hemi-

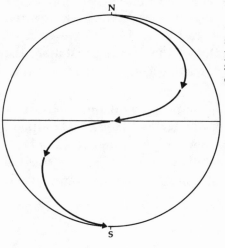

Coriolis effect. Diagram represents the course of a missile in polar orbit as plotted by an observer attached to the revolving earth beneath it.

sphere, leftward in the southern, is known as the "Coriolis effect" (after the nineteenth-century French mathematician Gaspard G. de Coriolis).

The relative rightward deflection in the northern hemisphere, leftward in the southern, is the same no matter what direction the object, of its own motion, is moving in — whether north, south, east, or west. Thus a missile fired from the South Pole would curve left (the earth moving eastward under it), taking an ever more westerly direction relative to the earth's surface, until it crossed the Equator, when it would curve right toward an ever more northerly course. (With respect to the Coriolis effect, the northern and southern hemispheres are mirror images of each other, in which left and right are reversed.)

How about a missile fired due east or due west?

We are assuming that these missiles fly freely, that they are not being steered or pushed off course. Flying freely, their course is always along a geodesic (i.e., the line that represents the shortest distance between two points), which on the surface of a sphere like the earth is a great-circle course that, in its entirety, makes a complete circle equal to the sphere's circumference. (Stretch a string between any two points on a globe and it will form a great circle rather than the straight line that it would form on a flat surface, a geodesic on a sphere being necessarily curved rather than, as on a flat surface, straight.) The Equator is one such geodesic. The continuous circle crossing the two poles, formed by longitude 0° and its continuation, longitude 180°, is another. This latter forms a right angle with the Equator. Other geodesics or great circles can be drawn, always half in the northern and half in the southern hemisphere, that make various angles with the Equator as they cross it.

Imagine, now, a missile fired due west from latitude 60°N., longitude 0°. It will follow a geodesic that has, as its farthest north, the 60th parallel of north latitude (from which it starts), as its farthest south, the 60th parallel of south latitude. If the earth were not revolving, it would leave the 60th parallel of north latitude at longitude 0° flying west, but would move ever farther south along the geodesic to cross the Equator at 90°W. and reach the 60th parallel of south latitude at 180° of longitude — after which it would start moving north again. However, since the earth is, in fact, revolving eastward under it, instead of crossing the Equator at 90°W., it will cross it at some point still farther west (as much farther west as the earth's surface has moved eastward in the time since its departure from longitude 0°), and so would have undergone a relative rightward deflection.

I have mentioned the fact that the eastward velocity of the earth's surface increases from zero at the North Pole to a maximum (actually 900 knots or nautical miles per hour) at the Equator. However, since its velocity is relative to distance from the earth's axis, it doesn't increase at a uniform rate per unit of distance over the curved surface between the Pole and the Equator, but only at the rate that it is changing its distance from the axis. At first, the direction away from the Pole is almost perpendicular to the earth's axis, so that the first ten miles away from the Pole would represent virtually ten miles away from the axis (exactly ten miles from the axis if there were no downward curvature at all). However, as the surface curves more and more toward the Equator it comes constantly closer to being parallel with the axis, so that the last ten miles before the Equator would involve virtually no increase in distance from the axis. It follows that the eastward velocity of the earth's surface, as one goes south from the North Pole, increases most rapidly at first, continuing to increase at a less and less rapid rate until, at the Equator, the rate of increase has fallen to zero — after which, now in the southern hemisphere and curving back toward the earth's axis, the velocity of the earth's surface begins to decrease, slowly at first, but at an ever more rapid rate as the curving surface of the earth comes constantly nearer to being perpendicular to the axis, until the maximum rate of decrease is attained as one reaches the South Pole. Since the tightness of the rightward curve (relative to the earth's surface) of a missile travelling at constant speed in the northern hemisphere, and of its relative leftward curve in the southern hemisphere, is a function, not of the velocity of the earth's surface underneath it, but of the rate at which that velocity is changing (whether increasing or decreasing), it is tighter the nearer the missile is to either Pole, and flatter the nearer it is to the Equator. Because there would be no change at all in the velocity of the earth under a missile travelling along the geodesic that we call the Equator, such a missile would undergo no relative deflection at all, which is to say that there is no Coriolis effect on the Equator. (Purists, see last paragraph of this Appendix for an exception to this statement.)

·

In the case of a missile in orbit, the only Coriolis displacement would be along the east-west axis, the north-south component in its course remaining unaffected — so that the arc through which it was displaced, eastward or westward, would never extend so far (90 degrees or more) as to eliminate or reverse the north-south component. But the missile in orbit is a special case, and in other cases the Coriolis effect will cause an object moving freely over the earth's surface to complete, in its course, the full 360 degrees of a circle.

Imagine, now, an idealized earth that is a perfect sphere with a frictionless surface over which objects slide freely. On a fine midday, when the sun is due south of it, an object at rest on this surface in the northern hemisphere is given a push toward the sun. According to the basic laws of motion, the object tends to maintain the direction — with respect to the surrounding space, but not with respect to the earth's surface — in which it is going at any given moment. To simplify what is really a complicated situation, we shall suppose here that it keeps trying to go toward the sun, regarded as a fixed point in space. It begins sliding southward over the earth's surface. But the earth is turning eastward under it so that, relative to the earth's surface, the object's unchanging direction toward the fixed sun is increasingly westward as the hour of sunset approaches. The time will come, at about sunset, when the object is moving due west over the earth's surface, its course having curved through 90 degrees.

Now the sun is behind the earth and, by midnight, the object, still sliding toward it over the earth's surface, will have veered around with respect to that surface until it is moving due north. As the earth continues to revolve, the direction of the sun relative to its surface will be constantly more to the east — so that, about the time of sunrise, the object will have continued to curve around in its course until it is moving due east. This displacement in its trajectory relative to the earth's surface continues until, at noon, the direction of the sun is again due south, as at noon the previous day, and the object has completed a full circle of 360 degrees.

In fact, the situation would be far more complicated, if only because the freely moving object would be forced constantly to change its direction with respect to the sun as well as with respect to the earth's surface. But this simplified thought experiment will suffice to illustrate the principle involved. The fact is that a bullet fired from a rifle, continuing in flight long enough, would go through 360 degrees of arc — more likely in a spiral than in a closed circle — and all on account of the Coriolis effect. (I am supposing that the bullet does not, like the aforementioned missile, go into orbit.)

The most familiar manifestation of the Coriolis effect, which bears on every object moving over the earth's surface, is in the spiralling courses of the winds as shown on any weather map — although other factors enter into their movement as well. And what applies to the winds applies also to the ocean currents.

The katabatic winds that flow in a generally northward direction from the center of the Antarctic continent curve increasingly to the left, because of the Coriolis effect, until they become the easterlies that encircle it. What prevents them from continuing to curve leftward until they flow back again toward the center of the continent is simply the pressure of the air that, newly arrived from the north at high altitudes, descends over the center of the continent to flow outward against them in all directions, at last curving about under the influence of the Coriolis effect to join them in their encircling course.

·

There is a final simplification in this account to which I call attention in conclusion. I have indicated that the tendency of a body moving over the earth's surface to be apparently displaced from a direct course is entirely due to the rotation of the earth on its axis. In fact, it is also due in part to the movement of the earth in its orbit around the sun, and even to the movement of the entire solar system with respect to the Milky Way. A precise plotting of the Coriolis effect in any given situation would have to take these movements, as well as the rotation of the earth on its axis, into account.

Appendix B. The Royal
Albatrosses of Taiaroa

◆─ ADULTS OF THE TWO SPECIES of great albatross appear alike except for fine details, not noticeable when the birds are seen on the wing, so that it was not until nearly the end of the last century that what had been regarded as one species, the Wandering Albatross, was recognized as, in fact, two. Closely related as they are, the two differ from each other in a couple of significant points. One is that the Royal assumes the adult plumage upon fledging, while the Wanderer assumes it gradually, taking up to thirty years or more to complete the process. The other is that the yearling Wanderers remain on their nests until the adults have returned to inaugurate a new nesting season, while the yearling Royals leave before the adults return. W. L. N. Tickell speculates that the acquisition of a distinctive immature plumage by the young Wanderers has the function of enabling the adults, when they arrive for a new nesting season, to distinguish readily between them and the adults who are their rivals or possible mating partners.*

Like the Wandering Albatross, the Royal has two races geographically separated by the latitudinal separation of their respective breeding grounds. As is to be expected, the larger of the two (*epomophora*) is the one that breeds the farther south, at Campbell Island and the Aucklands. I say "as is to be expected"

* Tickell, 1968.

because it is a rule (Bergmann's Rule) that geographical forms inhabiting colder regions tend to be larger than their counterparts in warmer regions — presumably because the larger a body is, the smaller the proportion of its surface, through which it loses heat, to its volume. The white area on the southern form is also slightly more extensive. At first thought this seems to conform to the rule that the plumage of birds, like the pelage of mammals, evolves to suit their respective backgrounds, so that the forms of the higher latitudes tend to acquire the whiteness of snow and ice (or, alternatively, to choose the environment that matches their plumage).* But the southern race of the Royal Albatross is not a bird of the snow and the ice, and the fact that it nests in a cooler climate than the northern might argue in favor of more of the black, which absorbs the heat of the sun, and less of the white, which reflects it. In men, the dark skin of tropical races filters out the excessive ultraviolet radiation from the sun, but the skin of birds is not exposed. Doubtless there is a reason for everything, but we don't always know what it is.

The smaller race (*sanfordi*) nests at the Chatham Islands and in recent decades has started a colony, after what may well have been a long interval of absence, in New Zealand proper. It would be odd if these albatrosses had not nested there before the first men came, between one and four thousand years ago, in the form of the Polynesian race, Maori branch, which was larger and darker than the race of Europeans that was to come later. For primitive man, given the conditions in which he lived, the chief importance of birds was as food, and he had no textbooks to tell him of the critical relationship between rates of mortality and rates of reproduction. Consequently, man in New Zealand is presumably responsible for the extermination of the moas,

* Murphy, p. 588.

ostrichlike birds of which the largest species stood some ten to fourteen feet tall (depending on how it carried itself). He would presumably have extirpated any albatrosses as well, since their eggs, their young, and perhaps the adults themselves might well have served for the appeasement of hunger, and they would have had no defence at all against the big, new, predatory mammal. The moas are gone forever, but now the Royal Albatross may be returning with the active encouragement and help of modern man as represented by the New Zealand Government and the citizens of New Zealand's fourth largest city, Dunedin.

I quote here from a leaflet issued by the Wildlife Service of the Government's Department of Internal Affairs. (The Otago Peninsula to which it refers is a few miles from Dunedin, on the east coast of South Island near its southern extremity.)

> Between 1914 and 1919 royal albatrosses were known to land at Taiaroa Head, Otago Peninsula, and in 1919 the first egg was found there. The Otago Branch of the Royal Society of New Zealand and Dr. L. E. Richdale, an ornithologist of Dunedin, strove to protect the colony from interference and their efforts were rewarded in 1938 when the first Taiaroa-reared chick flew. The Otago Harbour Board and its officers and the Department of Internal Affairs added their support to this work. Later the citizens of Dunedin, led by members of the Dunedin Rotary Club, raised £1,250 . . . which helped to provide for the appointment in 1951 of a full-time field officer to act as caretaker of the albatross colony and as wildlife ranger for Otago Peninsula.

The colony has known its vicissitudes. At one point it rose to eleven or twelve nesting pairs annually. Since the Royals, like the Wanderers, take a season off from nesting after each successful nesting season, eleven or twelve pairs annually means a total nesting population of over twenty pairs. In the season of 1970–1971 the nesting population was down to eight pairs, but every precaution was being taken to protect them.

The public is necessarily excluded from the nesting area. However, at the initiative and with the kind help of Mr. G. A. Tunnicliffe of the Canterbury Museum in Christchurch, and of that distinguished ornithologist, Mr. F. C. Kinsky of the Dominion Museum in Wellington, the Department of Internal Affairs made exceptional provision for me to visit the site in the company of Mr. Alan Wright, the local representative of the Wildlife Service, who met me at my hotel in Dunedin at 9:00 on the morning of January 16.

So it was that I spent a golden day enjoying the hospitality of Mr. and Mrs. Wright, as well as calling on the albatrosses at Taiaroa Head. The privacy of their colony, on a grassy headland bounded by cliffs and rock-falls (in which Blue Penguins nest), is protected by a high wire-mesh fence with a door to which only Mr. Wright has the key. As at Campbell Island, the nests were widely separated in the grass — and, as at Campbell, there was a "visitor" sitting on the brow of the headland. It got to its feet respectfully when we came up to it, and took a few wobbling steps (albatrosses are not as sure on their feet as on their wings), then remained indifferently looking at us as we squatted beside it and talked to it in kindly terms — talked to it as fellow creatures who, like it, were doing their best to survive in a world that neither albatrosses nor men understand.

I had the impression that the Taiaroa birds (*sanfordi*) were not quite as stalwart of build as those of Campbell Island (*epomophora*). Seen close up on their nests, however, what chiefly distinguishes the two races is the more solid and slightly more extensive black on the wings of the New Zealand race. The black feathers of its wing coverts lack almost entirely the fine white margin that those of the southern race have. Most had, in addition, some black feathers on crown and tail.

One hopes that the Taiaroa colony will survive within the fenced enclosure of its reservation, and that the reservation may even be extended to accommodate its growth, for its sure establishment will surely require an increase in its numbers, which will surely require, in turn, a larger nesting area. Experience has shown that, outside a fenced-in area, it could not possibly survive. Ignorant people, having access to the colony, would be bound to steal the eggs and to harass the birds on their nests simply because they were big, because they were extraordinary in their dignity and beauty, and because they were helpless. To persecute what is both distinguished and helpless gives us little individuals a sense of power, thereby relieving, for the moment, the frustration we all suffer from our ordinary inadequacy in coping with the impositions of the great world we inhabit. Even in the absence of human persecution, however, the colony could not survive outside an enclosure and without human protection, for it would be subject to the depredations of the dogs, the cats, and the ferrets that men have brought into New Zealand, and that remain forever.

In all this, the situation at Taiaroa is representative of the situation over our planet as a whole, now that we men have domesticated it and are remaking it to suit ourselves. The creatures of the wild can survive, for the most part, only to the extent that we men deliberately make whatever provision is necessary for their survival in our midst.

Appendix C. International Agreement on Measures of Conservation in the Antarctic

➤ THE FOLLOWING STATES are parties to the Antarctic Treaty, which entered into force on April 30, 1962: Argentina, Australia, Belgium, Chile, Czechoslovakia, Denmark, France, Japan, the Netherlands, New Zealand, Norway, Poland, the Republic of South Africa, the Union of Soviet Socialist Republics, the United Kingdom of Great Britain and Northern Ireland, and the United States of America. Article IX provides that the parties shall meet together from time to time in order to consult on a variety of matters including "preservation and conservation of living resources in Antarctica." The third meeting held in accordance with this provision produced the following document entitled "Agreed Measures for the Conservation of Antarctic Fauna and Flora":

The Governments participating in the Third Consultative Meeting under Article IX of the Antarctic Treaty,

Desiring to implement the principles and purposes of the Antarctic Treaty;

Recognising the scientific importance of the study of the Antarctic fauna and flora, their adaptation to their rigorous environment, and their inter-relationship with that environment;

Considering the unique nature of these fauna and flora, their circum-polar range, and particularly their defencelessness and susceptibility to extermination;

Desiring by further international collaboration within the framework of the Antarctic Treaty to promote and achieve the objectives of the protection, scientific study, and rational use of these fauna and flora; and

Having particular regard to the conservation principles developed by the Scientific Committee on Antarctic Research (SCAR) of the International Council of Scientific Unions;

Hereby consider the Treaty Area as a Special Conservation Area and have agreed on the following measures:

ARTICLE I

1. These Agreed Measures shall apply to the same area to which the Antarctic Treaty is applicable (hereinafter referred to as the Treaty Area) namely the area south of 60° South Latitude, including all ice shelves.

2. However, nothing in these Agreed Measures shall prejudice or in any way affect the rights, or the exercise of the rights, of any State under international law with regard to the high seas within the Treaty Area, or restrict the implementation of the provisions of the Antarctic Treaty with respect to inspection.

3. The Annexes to these Agreed Measures shall form an integral part thereof, and all references to the Agreed Measures shall be considered to include the Annexes.

ARTICLE II

For the purposes of these Agreed Measures:

a) "Native mammal" means any member, at any stage of its life cycle, of any species belonging to the Class Mammalia indigenous to the Antarctic or occurring there through natural agencies of dispersal, excepting whales.

b) "Native bird" means any member, at any stage of its life cycle (including eggs), of any species of the Class Aves indigenous to the Antarctic or occurring there through natural agencies of dispersal.

c) "Native plant" means any kind of vegetation at any stage of its life cycle (including seeds), indigenous to the Antarctic or occurring there through natural agencies of dispersal.

d) "Appropriate authority" means any person authorised by a Participating Government to issue permits under these Agreed Measures.

e) "Permit" means a formal permission in writing issued by an appropriate authority.

f) "Participating Government" means any Government for which these Agreed Measures have become effective in accordance with Article XIII of these Agreed Measures.

ARTICLE III

Each participating Government shall take appropriate action to carry out these Agreed Measures.

ARTICLE IV

The Participating Governments shall prepare and circulate to members of expeditions and stations information to ensure understanding and observance of the provisions of these Agreed Measures, setting forth in particular prohibited activities, and providing lists of specially protected areas.

ARTICLE V

The provisions of these Agreed Measures shall not apply in cases of extreme emergency involving possible loss of human life or involving the safety of ships or aircraft.

ARTICLE VI

1. Each Participating Government shall prohibit within the Treaty Area the killing, wounding, capturing or molesting of any native mammal or native bird, or any attempt at any such act, except in accordance with a permit.

2. Such permits shall be drawn in terms as specific as possible and issued only for the following purposes:

a) to provide indispensable food for men or dogs in the Treaty Area in limited quantities, and in conformity with the purposes and principles of these Agreed Measures;

b) to provide specimens for scientific study or scientific information;

c) to provide specimens for museums, zoological gardens, or other educational or cultural institutions or uses.

3. Permits for Specially Protected Areas shall be issued only in accordance with the provisions of Article VIII.

4. Participating Governments shall limit the issue of such permits so as to ensure as far as possible that:

a) no more native mammals or birds are killed or taken in any year than can normally be replaced by natural reproduction in the following breeding season;

b) the variety of species and the balance of the natural ecological systems existing within the Treaty Area are maintained.

5. The species of native mammals and birds listed in Annex A of these Measures shall be designated "Specially Protected Species" and shall be accorded special protection by Participating Governments.

6. A Participating Government shall not authorise an appropriate authority to issue a permit with respect to a Specially Protected Species except in accordance with paragraph 7 of this Article.

7. A permit may be issued under this Article with respect to a Specially Protected Species, provided that:

a) it is issued for a compelling scientific purpose, and

b) the actions permitted thereunder will not jeopardise the existing natural ecological system or the survival of that species.

ARTICLE VII

1. Each Participating Government shall take appropriate measures to minimise harmful interference within the Treaty Area with the normal living conditions of any native mammal or bird, or any attempt at such harmful interference, except as permitted under Article VI.

2. The following acts and activities shall be considered as harmful interference:

a) allowing dogs to run free,

b) flying helicopters or other aircraft in a manner which would unnecessarily disturb bird and seal concentrations, or landing close to such concentrations (e.g. within 200 m.),

c) driving vehicles unnecessarily close to concentrations of birds and seals (e.g. within 200 m.),

d) use of explosives close to concentrations of birds and seals,

e) discharge of firearms close to bird and seal concentrations (e.g. within 300 m.),

f) any disturbance of bird and seal colonies during the breeding period by persistent attention from persons on foot.

However the above activities, with the exception of those mentioned in (a) and (e) may be permitted to the minimum extent necessary for the establishment, supply and operation of stations.

Publications Cited

Amundsen, Roald. *The South Pole.* Translated from the Norwegian by A. G. Chater. London, 1912.

Austin, Oliver L., Jr. *Birds of the World.* New York, 1961.

———, ed. *Antarctic Bird Studies.* Antarctic Research Series, vol. 12. Washington, D.C., 1968.

Boswall, Jeffrey, ed. *Look.* London, 1969.

———, ed. *Private Lives.* London, 1970.

Carson, Rachel. *The Sea Around Us.* New York, 1951.

Cherry-Garrard, Apsley. *The Worst Journey in the World.* London, 1965.

Cline, D. R., Siniff, D. B., and Erickson, A. W. *The Auk.* October 1969.

Fisher, James. *Watching Birds.* Hammondsworth, Middlesex, 1951 (cited in Pettingill, p. 400).

———, and Peterson, Roger T. *The World of Birds.* London, 1964.

Goodwin, Derek. *Pigeons and Doves of the World.* London, 1967.

Holdgate, M. W., ed. *Antarctic Ecology.* Vol. 1. London and New York, 1970.

King, H. G. R. *The Antarctic.* London, 1969.

Kooyman, Gerald L. "The Weddell Seal." *Scientific American,* August 1969, pp. 100–106.

Krutch, Joseph Wood. *The Twelve Seasons.* New York, 1949.

Mayr, Ernst. *Populations, Species, and Evolution.* Cambridge (Massachusetts), 1970.

Murphy, Robert C. *Oceanic Birds of South America.* New York, 1936. (I am grateful to Dr. Murphy for permission to quote from this work. L.J.H.)

Publications Cited

————. "The Oceanic Life of the Antarctic." *Scientific American,* September 1962, p. 94 ff.

Penney, Richard L., and Lowry, George H. *Ecology.* Late Summer, 1967.

Pequegnat, Willis E. "Whales, Plankton, and Man." *Scientific American,* January 1958, pp. 84–86 ff.

Pettingill, Olin S., Jr. *Ornithology in Laboratory and Field.* Minneapolis, 1970.

Prévost, Jean, and Mougin, Jean-Louis. *Guide des Oiseaux et Mammifères des Terres Australes et Antarctiques Françaises.* Neuchâtel (Switzerland), 1970.

Priestley, Sir Raymond, Adie, R. J., and Robin, G. de Q. (editors). *Antarctic Research.* London, 1964.

Ross, Sir James Clark. *A Voyage of Discovery and Research to Southern and Antarctic Regions.* London, 1847.

Scott, Robert F. *Scott's Last Expedition.* London, 1923.

Seaver, G. *Edward Wilson of the Antarctic.* London, 1933.

————. *Edward Wilson: Nature Lover.* London, 1937.

Sladen, W. J. L., and Ostenso, N. A. *The Auk.* October 1960.

Sladen, W. J. L., Wood, R. C., and Monaghan, E. P., in Austin, 1968.

Soper, T., in Boswall, 1969.

Thomson, A. Landsborough. *A New Dictionary of Birds.* London, 1964.

Tickell, W. L. N. "The Biology of the Great Albatrossess," in Austin, 1968.

U.S. Naval Oceanographic Office. *Sailing Directions for Antarctica.* Washington, D.C., with changes through 18 July 1970.

Vane, Sutton. *Outward Bound.* London, 1934.

Voous, Karl H. *Atlas of European Birds.* London, 1960.

Waterston, G. *British Birds.* January 1968.

Wildlife Service, Department of Internal Affairs, *The Royals of Taiaroa* (leaflet), Wellington, New Zealand, 1969.

Wilson, Edward A. *Birds of the Antarctic.* London, 1967. (His journal is extensively quoted, as well, in Seaver, 1933 and 1937.) (I am grateful to the publishers, Blandford Press, for permission to quote from *Birds of the Antarctic,* which is copyrighted by the Scott Polar Research Institute in Cambridge, England, and published in the United States by Humanities Press, Inc. L.J.H.)

———. *Diary of the Discovery Expedition to the Antarctic Regions 1901–1904.* London, 1966.

———. *Diary of the Terra Nova Expedition to the Antarctic 1910–1912.* London, 1972.

Young, E. C., in Holdgate, p. 498.

Index

As WELL AS being listed by their scientific names (both genus and species), animal and vegetable species are listed alphabetically according to the vernacular names by which they are most commonly known. These names are followed by the scientific names and by any alternative vernacular names in common use. Where species of the same genus are listed successively, only the initial letter of the genus is given after the first entry.